国家林业和草原局普通高等教育"十三五"规划教材

中国文化英语
Culture Album China

杨亚丽　王　馨　主编

中国林业出版社
·北京·

图书在版编目（CIP）数据

中国文化英语 / 杨亚丽，王馨主编. —北京：中国林业出版社，2020.1
国家林业和草原局普通高等教育"十三五"规划教材
ISBN 978-7-5219-0341-6

Ⅰ. ①中… Ⅱ. ①杨… ②王… Ⅲ. ①中华文化—英语—高等学校—教材 Ⅳ. ①K203

中国版本图书馆 CIP 数据核字（2019）第 248284 号

中国林业出版社·教育分社

责任编辑：曹鑫茹　高红岩　　　　责任校对：苏　梅
电话：（010）83143560　　　　　　传真：（010）83143516

出版发行	中国林业出版社（100009　北京市西城区德内大街刘海胡同 7 号）
	E-mail: jiaocaipublic@163.com　　电话：（010）83143500
	http://www.forestry.gov.cn/lycb.html
经　销	新华书店
印　刷	三河市祥达印刷包装有限公司
版　次	2020 年 1 月第 1 版
印　次	2020 年 1 月第 1 次印刷
开　本	787mm×1092mm　1/16
印　张	14.25
字　数	420 千字
定　价	36.00 元

未经许可，不得以任何方式复制或抄袭本书之部分或全部内容。
版权所有　侵权必究

《中国文化英语》编写人员

主　编　杨亚丽　王　馨
副主编　侯文瑜　姜睿萍　高延宏　杨　帆

前 言
Preface

　　文化是一个丰富、复杂和多元的体系，包含了多种内涵。中国，作为四大文明古国之一，有着悠久的历史和灿烂的文化。传承和发展中华优秀传统文化是党的十八大以来习近平总书记对全国人民的倡导和要求。中国文化在新时代被赋予了新的内涵和意义，并转化成为实现中华民族伟大复兴的强大精神力量。在漫长历史发展中积累起来的人类文明优秀成果中，中国文化逐渐向世界展示出它的深厚底蕴和足够的包容性。中华优秀传统文化蕴含着丰富的爱国思想，如以天下为己任的担当意识，赤胆忠心、舍身为国的爱国情怀等，都在潜移默化地影响着中国人的思维方式和道德标准。中国人的文化基因里深藏着的文化自信成为这个国家和民族发展中更深沉和持久的力量。中国文化走出去的战略成为建设文化强国、增强国家文化软实力的必经之路，在新的时代背景下被赋予了全新的意义。

　　中国文化以人为本，强调自觉自律，树立文化自信心。向学生展示中华民族博大精深的优秀文化，加强学生对自己国家文化的认同感、自豪感，减少对中国文化的模糊认识和片面性。随着我国的国际影响力逐渐提升，新时代要求我们培养学生对本国文化的热爱，展示中华文化的独特魅力，激发爱国主义情怀，增强民族自豪感，推动中华文化走向世界。

　　《中国文化英语》章节内容选取得当，突出中国文化的特点，展示华夏文明的精髓。用代表性的素材和具体的人物事例进行具体和深入的介绍，力求突出思想内涵、彰显价值观念，不断增强中华文化的吸引力和感召力。这些事例尽数彰显出我国人民的智慧、信念、向往和追求。

　　本书分别从传统思想、民俗、名胜古迹、民间艺术等八大部分介绍了中国的哲学和古代思想家、古代书籍、文字、剪纸艺术、国粹京剧等方面的内容。其中，不但包括了中国文化的基础知识，也涵盖了中国的戏曲、书法、绘画等传统文化的瑰宝。

　　从儒家思想中我们可以感受人们对仁、德、礼仪、文明、智慧的追求，对和谐、稳定的社会秩序和生活环境的向往。天人合一，遵循自然规律是老子留给世人的处世原则，道家思想探索了平凡世界的伦常关系，解答了人们对生命中各种问题的困惑。《孙子兵法》谈兵论战，用缜密的军事思想体系和变化无穷的战略战术对中国乃至世界军事领域都产生了深远的影响。

　　长城，是中华民族意志、勇气和力量的象征，代表了百折不挠、众志成城、坚不可摧的民族精神和意志。兵马俑，作为令人感叹的历史文化瑰宝，从形体把握、色彩运用和细部刻画等方面表现出了非凡的艺术成就和艺术价值。京剧，作为中国传统文化的精粹，蕴涵着深厚的文化底蕴和艺术内涵，在服饰、舞姿、身段、唱腔上都彰显十足的魅力。民间艺术，包括戏曲、皮影戏、剪纸，用自己特定的表现语言，传达出传统文化的内涵和本质。

为了帮助学生了解更多关于中国文化的知识以及更好地进行中西方文化的对比，编者在每个单元的正文后都增设了课后习题，其中包括主观题和客观题，题型丰富多样，帮助学生消化吸收教材内容，更系统地掌握知识，形成连贯的知识体系。同时，每一章节都配有注释、生词表和富有针对性和启发性的注解，有助于学生更好地理解和掌握教材里的内容。为了学生更好地理解本书，笔者开发了幕课（http://www.icourse163.org/course/NEAU-1205968810）。

本书图文并茂，信息量大，适用于大专院校的英语专业低年级，大学英语拓展课以及公选课使用，同时也适合对中国文化感兴趣的外国友人。

中华文明包罗万象，博大精深，本书只是沧海一粟，不能道尽文化之精髓，有不当之处敬请读者和专家批评指正。

本书由东北农业大学杨亚丽、王馨、侯文瑜、姜睿萍、高延宏和哈尔滨工业大学杨帆合作完成。本书出版得到了黑龙江省教育科学规划重点课题 GBB138008 和 GJB1319040，以及 2018 年黑龙江省普通本科高等学校青年创新人才项目 UNPYSCT-2018167 的资助。

编 者

2019 年 6 月

Contents

Unit 1 Confucius and Confucian Thought ·········· 1

Unit 2 Lao Tzu and Taoism ·········· 29

Unit 3 Sun Tzu and *The Art of War* ·········· 53

Unit 4 The Great Wall ·········· 80

Unit 5 The Terra-cotta Warriors ·········· 115

Unit 6 Peking Opera ·········· 138

Unit 7 Folk Arts ·········· 163

Unit 8 The Silk Road ·········· 197

Unit 1 Confucius and Confucian Thought

1.1 Introduction of Confucius and His Thought

1.1.1 Confucius

Confucius (Kongzi) (551 BC—479 BC) whose given name is Qiu was a native of Lu in late Spring and Autumn period. He was a great thinker, politician and educationist in the history of ancient China.

In Shandong province of eastern China stands a famous city named Qufu which is Confucius' hometown. It is listed as one of "Excellent Tourist City" in 1998. Confucius' parents came to Niqiu Mountain to worship before his birth. They prayed for a son. Their prayers were answered. There was a custom to name boys in ancient China, successive sons would be called Bo, Zhong, Shu and Ji. Because Confucius was the second son in the family, then he got his name as Kong Zhongni.

Confucius was poor in his childhood. His father died when he was three years old. When Confucius was still a child, he became attached to ceremony and propriety. The game he gained most pleasure from was to arrange plates and bowls, in an effort to imitate the adults who would arrange such items in order to worship the Heavens and their ancestors. "Propriety" and "music", the two passions of his childhood, which came about because of family circumstances, would become two of the most centrally important elements in Confucius' later life.

When he was young, he was at one time an official in charge of accounting and animal husbandry. At the age of fifty, he was appointed attorney general of the State of Lu. Afterwards, he travelled to many states, including Song, Wei, Chen, Cai, Qi, Chu, etc., never attaining a high office in these states. In his late years, he authored and edited many classic texts including *Shi (Book of Songs)*, *Shu (Book of History)*, *Li (Book of Rites)*, *Yue (Book of Music)*, *Yi (Book of Change)* and *Chun Qiu (Spring and Autumn Annuals)*. According to legend, Confucius had three thousand disciples out of those were 72 virtuous persons. His words and life stories were recorded by his followers in a book, known as the *Analects* (*Lunyu*) which has influenced China for more than 2000 years in history. For countless years the thoughts and wisdom of Confucius have been communicated to countless numbers of people through this book as Chinese scholars in ancient times were used to say: "Half of the *Analects* is enough to govern the whole country." This gives us some idea of the extraordinary influence of the book.

山东曲阜孔子铜像

Confucius was highly respected in the long history of the Chinese nation. Nowadays, most Chinese recognize Confucius as the great thinker and educator in Chinese history; as one of the great representative figures of Chinese civilization. Why is he so recognized? The most important reason is that Confucius was the conscious inheritor of the culture of the Xia, the Shang, and the Zhou dynasties which existed before him, and that he passed on this deep-rooted culture to future Chinese generations. Confucianism representing the pre-Qin culture, together with Legalism, Taoism and Mohism, formed the traditional culture of China. This culture ensures that the Chinese nation leads the world for a long time.

1.1.2 Confucian Thought

As the most influential philosopher in ancient China, Confucius set up a system of philosophical thoughts including theory on nature law, theory on human nature, epistemology and methodology.

Propriety and benevolence are at the very core of Confucian thought. Propriety is the exterior manifestation of benevolence, while benevolence is the interior content of propriety. So we can say, propriety embodies benevolence, but not as an instrument or means to control others. In Confucian view, this is the only way in which social harmony can be achieved.

Confucius ever said "at fifty, I knew the decrees of heaven (五十而知天命)". The decree of heaven doesn't mean absolute will and the command of God. It refers to historical inevitability cannot be changed by manpower. However, Confucius did not think that man could not do anything. People should have a positive attitude to fate. He is suspicious of ghosts and gods. That's why he never talks about strange powers and confused spirits.

On human nature, Confucius advocated the establishment of rites and combination of benevolence and ceremony. "Rite" is an important category in Confucian thought system. In Confucius' view, rite is the code of conduct that everyone must abide by. From the point of view of self-cultivation, he thinks that the first thing to do is to learn from etiquette. From the point of view of governing the country, he proposed to serve one's country with courtesy. "Don't do to others what you don't want others to do to you (己所不欲，勿施于人)". "Ren" is the core of Confucian thought. "Ren" means "loving people". Confucian stressed the value and function of "benevolence" in particular. It is considered that "benevolence" is a necessary accomplishment for everyone. It is also a principle that must be followed in governing the country.

On epistemology, Confucius believed wisdom obtained by learning. He ever said "learning without thought means labor lost; thought without learning is perilous (学而不思则罔，思而不学则殆)" which emphasizes the importance of thinking. "Two heads are always better than one (三人行必有我师)" is a good advice to ask and learn from others. He further proposed to evaluate a man by "listening to what he says and watch what he does (听其言而观其行)". This sentence is still the criterion for judging a person to this day.

Confucius absorbed the idea of "neutralization" in the Western Zhou Dynasty and the Spring and Autumn period. He developed it into the "mean" thought. The mean is not only a world view, but also a basic attitude to the nature, society and life. It was regarded as the supreme principle of morality, which refers to the mastery of appropriateness to keep balance and to make the words and behaviors of human beings fit for the established moral standards.

1. the Spring and Autumn period: was a period in Chinese history from approximately 771 to 476 BC (or according to some authorities until 403 BC). Which corresponds roughly to the first half of the Eastern Zhou Dynasty. The period's name derives from the *Spring and Autumn Annals*, a chronicle of the state of Lu between 722 and 479 BC, which tradition associates with Confucius.

2. Six arts: Rites, music, archery, equestrianism, calligraphy and arithmetic.

3. *Liu Jing*: *Books of Songs*, *Book of History*, *Book of Rites*, *Book of Music*, *Book of Change* and *Spring and Autumn*.

Culture Notes

1. 曲阜：春秋战国时期鲁国国都，位于山东省西南部，是中国古代伟大的思想家、教育家、儒家学派创始人孔子的故乡。被列为我国首批历史文化名城之一。曲阜有著名的"三孔"：孔府、孔庙、孔林。曲阜历史悠久、文物众多、具有"东方圣城"之说。

2. 《论语》：是儒家学派的经典著作之一。是孔子弟子将孔子的言行及与弟子的对话记录整理的语录集。全书共20篇492章，集中体现了孔子的政治主张、伦理思想、道德观念及教育原则等。与《大学》《中庸》《孟子》并称"四书"，再加上《诗经》《尚书》《礼记》《周易》《春秋》，总称"四书五经"。《论语》作为一部涉及人类生活诸多方面的儒家经典著作，许多篇章谈到做人的问题，都对当代人具有借鉴意义。

3. 《中庸》：是《礼记》的篇目之一，在南宋前从未单独刊印，相传为战国时孔子之孙子思所作。宋代朱熹将其与《大学》《论语》《孟子》并称"四书"。其内容肯定"中庸"是道德行为的最高标准，把"诚"看成是世界的本体，认为"至诚"则达到人生的最高境界。"中庸"主张处理事情不偏不倚，认为过犹不及，是儒家核心观念之一。

New Words

husbandry	n.	the practice of cultivating the land or raising stock	饲养、管理
attorney	n.	a professional person authorized to practice law; conducts lawsuits or gives legal advice	律师
author	v.	be the author of	编著，出版
edit	v.	prepare for publication or presentation by correcting, revising, or adapting	校订、编辑
disciple	n.	someone who believes and helps to spread the doctrine of another	门徒、弟子、信徒
analects	n.	a collection of excerpts from a literary work	文选、论集
Confucianism	n.	the teachings of Confucius emphasizing love for humanity; high value given to learning and to devotion to family (including ancestors); peace; justice; influenced the traditional culture of China	儒学
rite	n.	an established ceremony prescribed by a religion	礼仪
philosopher	n.	a specialist in philosophy	哲学家
epistemology	n.	the philosophical theory of knowledge	认识论

decree	n.	a legally binding command or decision entered on the court record	命令
suspicious	adj.	openly distrustful and unwilling to confide	怀疑的
etiquette	n.	rules governing socially acceptable behavior	礼仪，礼节

Exercises

I. Filling the Blank

1. In the Chinese traditional culture, the culture of _____ is the rational accumulation and internal manifestation of the wisdom of Chinese nation.

2. Confucius is a great thinker, educator and founder of _____ and also an ancient sage to the Chinese people.

3. Much of Confucian thought on Heaven and people represents universal human _____.

4. Confucius held the view that humans are born with a sense of _____ which is the meaning of human life.

5. The ancient Chinese people developed a sense of awe and belief in _____.

6. _____ is one of the core concepts of Confucianism, which is the highest principle of morality.

7. Confucius defined "ren" as _____ and it is the core meaning of "ren".

8. A student of Confucius, _____ , summarized "ren" as "loving one's parents, loving the people, loving everything in the world".

9. The thought of Li can coordinate the relationship between individuals and society to construct the _____ of society.

10. Zhong means the proper degree in speaking and doing, which is the primary method to realize _____.

II. Multiple Choice

1. Which of the following is not the subject of "Six arts"?
   A. music   B. calligraphy   C. great virtue   D. carriage driving

2. Confucius words and life story were recorded in the _____.
   A. *Book of Change*   B. *Doctrine of the Mean*
   C. *Book of Songs*   D. *Analects*

3. Confucius lived in the _____.
   A. First Emperor of Qin period   B. Shang Dynasty
   C. Spring and Autumn period   D. Zhou Dynasty

4. Confucianism representing the pre-Qin culture, together with_____, Taoism and Mohism, formed the traditional culture of China.
   A. Legalism   B. Buddhism

C. Christ　　　　　　　　D. Master Sun's art of War

5. Confucius set up a system of philosophical thoughts including theory on nature law, theory on human nature, _____ and methodology.

　　A. heaven　　　B. epistemology　　C. consciousness　　D. virtue

III. True or False

1. (　　) The doctrine of mean is regarded as the supreme principle of morality, which refers to the mastery of appropriateness to keep balance and to make the words and behaviors of human beings fit for the established moral standards.

2. (　　) *Book of Change, Book of Music, Book of Songs* are all written by Confucius.

3. (　　) Confucius ever said "at sixty, I knew the decrees of heaven".

4. (　　) "Ren" is the core of Confucius thought. "Ren" means "loving people".

5. (　　) Confucius absorbed the idea of "neutralization" in the Western Zhou Dynasty and the Spring and Autumn period.

IV. Answer the Questions

1. What do you know about Confucius?
2. Say something about *Analects*.
3. Why does Confucius speak highly of "ren"?
4. Say your understanding about "at fifty, I knew the decrees of heaven".
5. What are the Six arts?

V. Translate the Following Sentences into English

1. 五十而知天命。
2. 己所不欲，勿施于人。
3. 学而不思则罔，思而不学则殆。
4. 三人行，必有我师。
5. 听其言而观其行。

VI. Reading Comprehension

Confucius

Confucius (551 BC—479 BC), born at Zouyi (south-east of the present Qufu, Shandong Province), whose given name was Qiu and courtesy name Zhongni, was the founder of Confucianism.

As one of the greatest thinkers and educators in the history of China, Confucius' legacy lies in the following three aspects.

Firstly, he compiled and preserved literary works of three generations. The six documents (Six Classics) under his compilation, including *Shi* (*Book of Songs*), *Shu* (*Book of History*), *Li* (*Book of Rites*), *Yue* (*Book of Music*), *Yi* (*Book of Change*), and *Chun Qiu* (*Spring and Autumn Annals*), are considered as the classics of Confucianism. This accomplishment makes an enormous impact on the succession and development of the traditional Chinese culture.

Secondly, Confucius established a system of philosophical thoughts with "ren" (benevolence) as its fundamental virtue. This virtue is the central theme of his *Analects*.

As a moral and ethical system, ren focuses on human love that is hierarchical and differentiated. Thus Confucius created his version of humanism.

Based on "ren", Confucius objected to the fantastic powers that confused the human spirit. He took a skeptical and indifferent attitude toward religion and further developed his humanistic ideas. Confucian' concept of "li" refers to a set of ritual and musical systems, with the hierarchical system as its core.

Ren and "li" are complementary. Li is the exterior principle of "ren" while "ren" is "li's" intrinsic guiding power. To accomplish "ren", one must abide by "li", while "ren" will be naturally generated in the process of practicing "li".

Fundamentally, the purpose of Confucius' Li is to restore the traditional rifles of the Zhou Dynasty.

Thirdly, Confucius established private schools and founded a systematic educational framework.

He maintained the idea that everyone has the right to be educated despite class differences. In teaching practice, Confucius adopted flexible teaching methods which involve the combinations of learning and thinking, learning and reviewing as well as teaching and learning. He strived for educating students in accordance with their aptitude and adopted a heuristic style of teaching.

These philosophical thoughts are still valuable in application today.

1. What are the literary works compiled and preserved by Confucius?
2. What is the connection between "ren" and "li" ?

Confucian Thought on "Ren"

1.2.1 Confucianism

Confucianism was founded by Confucius. It was originally referred to a priest in the funeral profession. Gradually, it became a complete system of Confucian philosophy. It was regarded as the mainstream of Chinese traditional culture and has profound influence on Chinese people. It is the most influential philosophy and the main consciousness in the ancient China. "Benevolence, righteousness, propriety, wisdom and faith" became the most core factors of the value system of China. The reason why later China worshipped Confucius and his Confucianism for a long time was not only in Confucius' personal charm, but also in his important contribution to ideology and culture.

1.2.2 The Doctrine of "ren"

As the core concept of Confucianism, "ren" has been mentioned many times in the *Analects*. It takes great place in the Confucianism and has influenced Chinese society in the profound way. The most fundamental meaning of "ren" is to love. It refers to caring, loving,

respecting others and be broad-minded toward others. Confucius himself regarded it as a holy character. He added that to be a man infused with "ren", you should love people; love others. Such a concept of benevolence Confucius believed to be inherent in one's inner self and he regarded the most fundamental manifestation of such benevolence to love and respect for your relatives. "Young people should be filial to their parents at home and respectful to their brothers when they are with them. (入则孝，出则悌)" Filial piety is the basic point of "ren" and everyone should love their parents. Confucius believed that "ren" should begin with the love to one's parents and no one could love people in general without love for their parents. It was insufficient only to love your relatives and show filial piety to your parents. He believed that one should expand this love to the extent of loving all the people under Heaven, and only by doing this could one be entitled to be described as showing the qualities of "ren".

On the political level, Confucian thought of "ren" gradually developed into running the country by virtue. Thus, the moral theory system with "ren" as the core is established. Confucius said "A gentleman's loyalty to his relatives makes the people happy with benevolence. (君子笃于亲，则民兴于仁)" "ren", filial piety and the leader should be treated as joint part. For leaders, to love the parents is to love the country. Those who do benevolent government gain the world; those who lose it lose the world. Confucius' benevolence played an important and positive role in the clarity of politics. With the spirit of benevolence, the Chinese nation has gradually cultivated many fine traditions.

Confucius' benevolence not only influenced ancient Chinese ethics, but also affected family relations today. For Chinese people, loving and respecting their parents has become the standard of a virtuous person.

Notes

1. Confucianism: is described as tradition, a philosophy, a religion, a humanistic or rationalistic religion, a way of governing, or simply a way of life. Confucianism developed from what was later called "the Hundred Schools of Thought" from the teachings of the Chinese philosopher Confucius (551 BC—479 BC), who considered himself a recodifier and retransmitter of the theology and values inherited from the Shang (1600 BC—1046 BC) and Zhou Dynasties.

2. Ren: It is one of the core concepts of Confucianism, which is the highest principle of morality. The original meaning of "ren" refers to the friendly relationship between people, while Confucius further emphasized "ren" to be the highest category and standard of personality.

Culture Notes

儒家思想的仁：中国古代一种含义极广的道德范畴。本指人与人之间相互亲爱。孔子把"仁"作为最高的道德原则、道德标准和道德境界。他第一个把整体的道德规范集于一体，形成了以"仁"为核心的伦理思想结构，它包括孝、弟（悌）、忠、恕、礼、知、勇、恭、宽、信、敏、惠等内容。

New Words

priest	n.	a spiritual leader in a non-Christian religion	牧师
mainstream	n.	the prevailing current of thought	主流
consciousness	n.	an alert cognitive state in which you are aware of yourself and your situation	意识，观念
propriety	n.	correct or appropriate behavior	适当
worship	v.	love unquestioningly and uncritically or to excess; venerate as an idol	爱慕，崇拜
fundamental	adj.	serving as an essential component	基本的，重要的
filial	adj.	relating to or characteristic of or befitting an offspring	子女的
virtue	n.	the quality of doing what is right and avoiding what is wrong	美德
moral	adj.	relating to principles of right and wrong; i.e. to	道德的

		morals or ethics	
benevolence	n.	disposition to do good	仁慈
clarity	n.	free from obscurity and easy to understand; the comprehensibility of clear expression	清楚，明晰
ethics	n.	motivation based on ideas of right and wrong	道德规范

Exercises

I. Filling the Blank

1. Confucianism was founded by_____.

2. "Benevolence, righteousness, propriety, wisdom and _____" become the most core factors in the value system of China.

3. As the core concept of Confucianism, _____has been mentioned many times in the *Analects*.

4. _____is the basic point of "ren" and everyone should love their parents.

5. On the political level, Confucian thought of "ren" gradually developed into running the country by_____.

II. Multiple Choice

1. Confucianism was founded by Confucius. It was originally referred to a _____ in the funeral profession.
   A. priest   B. master of ceremonies
   C. husbandry   D. teacher

2. _____ is the most influential philosophy and the main consciousness in the ancient China.
   A. Taoism   B. Legalism   C. Confucianism   D. Mohism

3. The most fundamental meaning of "ren" is to_____.
   A. love   B. care   C. respect   D. admire

4. Ren should begin with the love to one's _____.
   A. brother   B. leader   C. children   D. parents

5. Confucian' benevolence not only influenced ancient Chinese ethics, but also affected _____ relations today.
   A. neighbor   B. relative   C. family   D. colleague

III. True or False

1. (   ) Confucianism is the most influential philosophy and the main consciousness in the ancient China.

2. (   ) The reason why later China worshipped Confucius and his Confucianism for a long time was only in Confucius' personal charm.

3. (　　) The most fundamental meaning of "ren" is to love. It refers to caring, loving, respecting oneself and be broad-minded toward oneself.

4. (　　) Ren was only referred to the standard of personal morality. It had nothing to do with governing the country.

5. (　　) For Chinese people, loving and respecting their parents has become the standard of a virtuous person.

IV. Answer the Questions

1. What is Confucianism?
2. The understanding of the doctrine of "ren".
3. How to realize "ren" in daily life?

V. Translate the Following Sentences into English

1. 入则孝，出则悌。
2. 泛爱众而亲仁。
3. 君子笃于亲，则民兴于仁。

VI. Reading Comprehension

Confucianism

Since Confucius initiated Confucianism, though it has gone through changes of past dynasties, it has been the mainstream of Chinese ideology, politics and culture all through the ages. "The traditional culture of China has a long history and Confucianism basically occupies a backbone position."

The three phases of its development are additionally introduced here: The first phase is pre-Qin Confucianism, which is also called primitive Confucianism. The society that it appeared in is at the key period of great revolution. Under the social climate of collapsed rites and music, Confucius and Mencius took the enlightenment of King Wen of the Zhou Dynasty and transformed the norm of rites and music into the foundation of the practice of human relations.

Confucius is a great thinker and educator in the period of Spring and Autumn and Warring States and the founder of the Confucian School. The main literature representative of his thoughts is the *Analects*. The basic thoughts of Confucius can be embodied in the following six aspects:

The first one is "humanity". As the core of the political thoughts of Confucius, it put forward the problems of how to conduct oneself and deal with relationship between people. There should be respect, lenience, honesty, modesty and mutual favor between people. Moreover, people should be "humane" and "humane people have a loving heart for others". In order to practice "humanity", people must also place an emphasis on "filial piety", follow the "doctrine of faithfulness and forgiveness" and advocate that "do as you would be done by others" and "be forced to work by no one else but myself". He regards "humanity" as the highest principle, standard and mode of conducting oneself, the object of which is to optimize human relationships.

The second one is "rite", which has an interaction relationship with "humanity". "Rite" is the form of "humanity" and also the norm and intention of practicing "humanity". That "devote wholeheartedly to rites for humanity" and "do not look, listen, speak and act contrary to propriety" are the rules for practicing "rites". Therefore, Confucius advocates "rectifying names". "If names be not correct, language is not in accordance with the truth of things. If language be not in accordance with the truth of things, affairs cannot be carried on to success." The specific stipulation of rectifying names is "monarch, official, father and son" with "faithfulness" and "filial piety" as the root. These stipulations constitute relations of the patriarchal clan system that hammer at social stability, forbidding ranking and distinguishing status.

The third one is "neutrality", namely, "mediocrity". It is the standard for practicing "humanity". It requires people to follow "the doctrine of mediocrity". Whatever happens, people should "take hold of their two extremes, determine the Mean, and employed it in his government of the people" (Book of Rites, Mediocrity). "Going too far is as bad as not going far enough." Therefore, people should be within reason when doing all kinds of things and dealing with all kinds of problems. There should be no excessiveness and falling short.

This is a thought way of Confucianism and also their social philosophy.

The fourth one is "virtue". It mainly refers to "humanitarian rule" and "virtuous governing" in the strategies of managing state affairs and criticizes that "tyranny is fiercer than a tiger". Confucius proposes that rulers themselves should "cultivate virtue", "command oneself" and "rule by virtue". If the people be led by virtue, and uniformity sought to be given them by the rules of propriety, they will have the sense of shame, and moreover will become good. He argues against collecting heavy taxes from people, advocates using the resources of people moderately, proposes thoughts such as "saving penalty", "reducing tax collection", "economizing in the use of resources and loving the people", "employing people when it is timely" and "benevolence saves people", and devises a political route from cultivating one's morality to managing state affairs and conquering the world. However, the "humanitarian rule" and "virtuous governing" don't mean immense leniency but alternating "leniency" with "fierceness". Those who "go against superiors" must be corrected forcefully. This is the "kingly way" of Confucius and Conficianism.

The fifth one is "education". He not only puts forward the educational thoughts of establishing private institution, educating without distinction and teaching students in accordance of their aptitude, but also spread them. He advocates providing education for people and contends that "people" can be educated so that they might easily accept the administration of "the kingly way".

The sixth one is "cultivation". He contends that people should strengthen the cultivation of individual mind, "self-command", and "the cultivation of one's morality" to enhance the consciousness of implementing humanity and virtue, and cultivate and perfect the ideal interpersonal relationship. Therefore, it is also called "human science". Since it places an extreme emphasis on rites, it is also called "heart science". Because it attaches extreme importance to politics, it is also called the science of "governing a country and conquering the world". In fact, Confucianism can be divided into the two aspects of "inner sageliness" and "outer kingliness": one is cultivation. Everyone can become a sage in virtue through individual cultivation. The other is learning from the world. Everyone should realize individual and national ideal through such effort. The former is basically within the extent of cultivating one's moral and togethering one's family and is internalized as the doctrine of self-cultivation; the latter is basically within the province of governing a country and conquering the world and externalized as the politics of governing the people. Therefore, Confucianism has been classified as the learning of cultivating one's morality, togethering one's family, governing a country and conquering the world and "the doctrine of inner sageliness and outer kingliness".

1. What are the basic thoughts of Confucius?
2. How to understand "neutrality"?

1.3 Confucian Thought on Li

Confucian thought of "ren" and "li" has a profound influence on ancient Chinese culture. "li" was the inheritance and innovation of the three dynasties of the Xia, the Shang and the Zhou, especially the ritual and music system of the Zhou Dynasty. The formation of ritual music in the Zhou Dynasty is mainly the contribution of Zhou Gong. Confucius lived in a time of the mess of the Spring and Autumn period. Confucius spoke highly of "li" to regulate all the behaviors of human being. He thought that the system of "li" established by Zhou Gong made the Zhou Dynasty presented a long-term stable situation. He maintained that in practicing the rules of propriety, a natural ease should be cultivated. The purpose of propriety or in the other words, the whole ritual system, was to effect a harmonious situation among people. Thus if a governor of a state could demonstrate to the common people how best to conduct themselves so as to treat others well, the society could not fail to be a smooth running entity.

The original "li" was a ceremony that the ancient noble person offered sacrifices to the gods and prayed for happiness. Later, it gradually evolved into a norm covering all aspects of social life. In Confucius' view, ritual is an indispensable social and ethical order. Form is very important to ceremony, especially to the great sacrificial activities and political activities. Confucius respected the "rites" of the canonical system, because it was a means of national governance and social harmony. However, Confucius emphasized the traditional habits and moral standards of behavior formed into the rules of "li". First of all, Confucius believed that "li" is the basic requirement of life. "If you do not know your life, you will not think of a gentleman; if you do not know the propriety, you will not be able to get on in the world.(不知命，无以为君子也；不知礼，无以立也)" "li" was conducted into the daily life and regulate people's clothing, food, shelter and activity. One of the students of Confucius Yan Hui died. His father asked Confucius to sell the carriage to bury him. Although Yan Hui was his favorite student, Confucius refused it. It was not because Confucius preferred carriage than Yan Hui, he just seriously abided by "li". According to Zhou Li, he had to take the carriage instead of walking on foot. He did this just to show the respect to "li".

Confucius expanded the scope and social function of "li". He extended the ceremony from the upper levels of society to the general public which became the general model of family, society and country. Confucius said "How to be courteous to a man without kindness? (人而不仁，如何礼？)" For him, "li" should be conducted and abided by everyone, from the ruler of the country to the common people.

As for the governance of country, Confucius put forward the concept of "serving the country with courtesy." The master of a country must set an example for his people and carry forward the spirit of "li". This is the only way to make the country stable for a long time.

Ren and "li" are both core concept of Confucianism. To restrain oneself and to behave in conformity with "li", that will be benevolence (克己复礼为仁). The best way to achieve it is to "see no evil, hear no evil, speak no evil and do no evil (非礼勿视，非礼勿听，非礼勿言，非礼勿动)". Confucius ever emphasized the importance of "ren" as the basis of "li". "Ren" is an inherent rule while "li" is external standard. In Confucius' eyes, a man could achieve the highest outer formal state only through esteemed rituals; while the highest inner substantial state the might reach was his very ideal state of "ren" that he had all along pursued.

Notes

1. The rites and music in the Zhou Dynasty: In the Zhou Dynasty, the culture of rites and music reached its peak. The Zhou Dynasty succeeded the rules of etiquette of the Shang Dynasty. The ceremony to offer sacrifices occupied an important position in this culture. Its development shows a stylized trend, and has established a certain order which gradually become a symbol.

2. Li: is the other core concept of Confucianism and refers to rituals, moralities and norms of the social life in our society.

Culture Notes

1. 祭祀仪式：在周人的信仰系统中，"天"是至高神。"天"有其喜恶，也会因其喜恶而庇佑或惩罚人间的君主。人间君主自称"天子"，假借与天的虚构的血缘关系来维护其统治的合法性。也因此，郊天之祭，成了两周时期最为隆重的祭祀。凡在天之神，都属于天神祭祀，包括祭至高神（天）、各类天体（日月星辰）、各类天象（大雪寒暑）等。

2. 孔子与颜回：颜回为孔子弟子，40岁时就死了。孔子为此悲痛。颜回的父亲颜路，早年跟随孔子学习，也是孔子的弟子。颜路家里贫穷，颜回死了，他没钱为儿子办理丧葬之事，于是请求孔子卖掉马车来安葬颜回。孔子回应说："不管有没有才能，就说我的儿子和你的儿子吧。我儿孔鲤死了，他只有内棺而没有外椁，我不能为他置办棺材而卖掉马车，从此只能步行。这是因为自从我当了官，就不可以在地上步行。"

New Words

inheritance	n.	hereditary succession to a title or an office or property	继承，遗传
innovation	n.	a creation (a new device or process) resulting from study and experimentation	改革，创新
mess	n.	a state of confusion and disorderliness	混乱，肮脏
ceremony	n.	a formal event performed on a special occasion	典礼，仪式
noble	adj.	having high moral qualities	高尚的，贵族的
sacrifice	n.	the act of losing or surrendering something as a penalty for a mistake or fault or failure to perform etc.	牺牲，奉献
dispensable	adj.	capable of being dispensed with or done without	不必要的
canonical	adj.	an established ceremony prescribed by a religion	权威的
emphasize	v.	to stress, single out as important	强调

shelter	n.	a structure that provides privacy and protection from danger	居所，避难所
abide by	v.	act in accordance with someone's rules, commands, or wishes	遵守，信守
extend	v.	extend in scope or range or area	延伸，扩大
restrain	v.	keep under control; keep in check	抑制，压抑

I. Filling the Blank

1. Confucian thought of_____ has a profound influence on ancient Chinese culture.

2. Li was the inheritance and innovation of the three dynasties of Xia, Shang and_____ Dynasties.

3. Confucius spoke highly of "li" to _____ all the behaviors of human being.

4. Confucius respected the "rites" of the canonical system, because it was a means of national governance and_____.

5. _____ is an inherent rule while "li" is external standard. Li should serve the "ren".

II. Multiple Choice

1. The formation of ritual music in the Zhou Dynasty is mainly the contribution of_____.
   A. Confucius   B. Lao Tzu   C. Zhou Gong   D. Mencius

2. The original "li" was a ceremony that the ancient noble person offered sacrifices to the gods and prayed for_____.
   A. wealth   B. happiness   C. peace   D. title

3. For him, "li" should be conducted and abided by_____, from the king of the country to the common people.
   A. everyone   B. ordinary people   C. upper level   D. leader

4. As for the governance of the country, Confucius put forward the concept of "serving the country with_____."
   A. violence   B. courtesy   C. love   D. respect

5. _____are both core concept of Confucianism.
   A. "Ren" and neutralization   B. Li and neutralization
   C. "Ren" and "li"   D. Li and wisdom

III. True or False

1. (   ) Confucius thought that the system of "ren" established by Zhou Gong made the Zhou Dynasty present a long-term stable situation.

2. (   ) The original "li" was a ceremony that the ancient ordinary person offered

sacrifices to the gods and prayed for happiness.

3. (　　) Confucius believed that "li" is the basic requirement of life.

4. (　　) The master of a country must set an example for its people and carry forward the spirit of "li". This is the only way to make the country stable for a long time.

5. (　　) "Ren" is an inherent rule while "li" is external standard. "Ren" should serve "li".

IV. Answer the Questions

1. Why does Confucius give a high appraisal to "li" ?
2. What does "li" actually mean?
3. What is the relationship between "ren" and "li" ?

V. Translate the Following Sentences into English

1. 不知命，无以为君子也；不知礼，无以立也。
2. 人而不仁，如何礼？
3. 克己复礼为仁。
4. 非礼勿视，非礼勿听，非礼勿言，非礼勿动。
5. 礼之用，和为贵。

1.4　Confucian Thought on Filial Piety

Filial piety is a basic concept of Confucianism and it is also an ethic of human value advocated by Confucius. It is essential and indispensable for social stability, historical continuity, people's happiness and family harmony in ancient China. For thousands of years, the Chinese, rich and poor, have been deeply influenced by the culture of filial piety.

Filial piety is the most basic principle for each of us. It is the original emotion based on the natural blood relationship. Filial piety as the basis for social ethics, the family is its most fundamental stage. Home should be a place full of affection, there is no affection of the family can not be regarded as the true sense of home. And filial piety is the basis for preservation of the family affection. The parents' age should be always kept in mind by the children. On the one hand, children are happy with their longevity; on the other hand, they fear that their parents will die soon. This conflicted feeling just shows that filial piety is the natural expression of human emotion.

Confucius explained the filial piety from five aspects.

First, support the parents when they are old to repay them. This is the basic request for Confucian filial piety. Children should always respect their parents and make it a rule of conduct to inherit and carry forward the will of the ancestors.

Second, respect and honor the parents in spirit. This is the high requirement of filial piety. Only supporting parents is not enough. Everyone should keep filial respect in mind all the time. Confucius thought that he who is a son of parents should not impose a mental burden on his parents. Parents are always worried about the health of children. Those who are children should be aware of the heart of their parents and take care of the body. That is a kind of filial piety. "While the parents are alive, the son may not go far away. If he does it, he must have a fixed place to which he goes. (父母在，不远游，游必有方)" Communication and transportation is not convenient in ancient times. The one that will go out must tell the parents the place or the direction. If the parents are in need, one can go back to them as soon as possible. Otherwise, offsprings will regret all their life.

Love the parents and also respect the elder brother is a basic ethic to maintain family harmony. Brothers should love and help each other. The fraternal duty will make parents happy and joy.

Third, if parents have made a mistake, the children should not blindly follow. Persuade the parents gently and softly. Do not hurt their feeling if they don't accept the advice. Make a chance to persuade them again after a while. That would be manifestation of filial piety.

Forth, filial piety also refers to inherit father's will. When the father is alive, the son is not in charge of family matters. His ambition is important here. When the father passed away, the action and behavior of the son would get close attention by others. (父在，观其志。父没，观其行) Follow the will and keep the habit of father, make the father's career flourish. "There are three forms of unfilial conduct, of which the worst is to have no descendants. (不孝有三，无后为大)" Creating the new life to carry on the parents' will and make it alive forever.

Fifth, Confucianism regards burial ceremony as one of the main symbols of filial piety. The funeral is for the dead, but it is the inner expression of the filial piety of the living. As a consolation to death, the funeral ceremony is also a realization of filial piety.

Confucius' filial piety is the compilation of the thought in the *Book of History*. He developed and improved the filial piety of Zhou Dynasty. Filial piety is the natural feeling from the depth of one's heart. It has been handed down from father to son for countless generations and remains very much alive today.

Notes

1. Filial piety: In Confucian, filial piety (Chinese: 孝, xiào) is a virtue of respect for one's parents, elders, and ancestors. The Confucian Classic of Filial Piety, thought to be written around the Qin-Han period, has historically been the authoritative source on the Confucian tenet of filial piety.

2. *The Book of History*: It also named Shang Shu which is one of the Six arts of ancient Chinese literature. It is a collection of rhetorical prose attributed to figures of ancient China, and served as the foundation of Chinese political philosophy for over 2000 years. It was the subject of one of China's oldest literary controversies, between proponents of different versions of the text.

Culture Notes

孝道：孝是子女对父母的一种善行和美德，是家庭中晚辈在处理与长辈的关系时应该具有的道德品质。我国孝道文化包括敬养父母、生育后代、推恩及人、忠孝两全、缅怀先祖等。最传统的孝道是始于西周时期最原始的含义，即尊祖敬宗、传宗接代。

1. 尊祖敬宗。孝道主要的表现形式是祭祀，在宗庙通过奉献贡品祭祀祖先来表达对祖先的敬意和缅怀。

2. 传宗接代。古语说"不孝有三，无后为大"。祖先是我辈的生命之所生，因此，崇拜祖先就是把祖先的生命延续下去，生生不息。

孝道精神源远流长，是中华民族的传统美德。帝王以孝治天下，做人则以孝为根本，一个"孝"可以说贯穿整个中华民族的历史。

New Words

stability	n.	the quality or attribute of being firm and steadfast	稳定，稳固
principle	n.	a basic generalization that is accepted as true and that can be used as a basis for reasoning or conduct	原则
emotion	n.	any strong feeling	情感
longevity	n.	the property of being long-lived	长寿
repay	v.	pay back	偿还，报答
inherit	v.	obtain from someone after their death	继承
mental	adj.	involving the mind or an intellectual process	内心的，精神的

fraternal	adj.	of or relating to a fraternity or society of usually men	兄弟的
offspring	n.	the immediate descendants of a person	后代，子孙
flourish	v.	grow stronger	繁荣，蓬勃
burial	n.	the ritual placing of a corpse in a grave suspicious	葬礼
consolation	n.	the comfort you feel when consoled in times of disappointment	安慰

I. Filling the Blank

1. Filial piety is a basic concept of Confucianism and it is also an _____ of human value advocated by Confucius.

2. The birth of filial piety is the original _____ based on the natural blood relationship.

3. This conflicting feeling just shows that filial piety is the _____ expression of human emotion.

4. Children should always respect their parents and make it a rule of conduct to _____ and carries forward the will of the ancestors.

5. Love the parents and also respect _____ is a basic ethic to maintain family harmony.

II. Multiple Choice

1. Filial piety is a basic concept of Confucianism and it is also an ethic of human value advocated by _____.

  A. Mencius B. Confucius C. Lao Tzu D. Chuang-Tzu

2. Supporting the parents when they are old to repay them. This is the _____ request of Confucian filial piety.

  A. higher B. only C. basic D. lowest

3. Confucianism regards _____ ceremony as one of the main symbols of filial piety.

  A. wedding B. teacher worship C. sacrificial D. burial

4. Confucian teachings about filial piety can be found in numerous texts, including the following books except_____.

  A. Four Books   B. The Great Learning
  C. Mencius   D. Sun Tzu's Art of War

5. Filial piety is the _____ feeling from the depth of one's heart.

  A. natural B. strong C. inward D. basic

III. True or False

1. ( ) For thousands of years, the Chinese, rich and poor, have been deeply influenced

by the culture of filial piety.

2. (   ) Confucius thought that he who was a son of parents should not impose a mental burden on his parents.

3. (   ) If parents have made a mistake, the children should blindly follow.

4. (   ) Love the parents and also respect the elder brother is a basic ethic to maintain social harmony.

5. (   ) Confucius' filial piety is the compilation of the thought in the *Book of History*. He developed and improved the filial piety of Zhou Dynasty.

IV. Answer the Questions

1. Why Chinese people treat filial piety as the most important virtue for a person?
2. What is the exact meaning of filial piety?
3. What are the five aspects to explain filial piety?

V. Translate the Following Sentences into English

1. 父母在，不远游，游必有方。
2. 父在，观其志。父没，观其行。
3. 不孝有三，无后为大。
4. 事孰为大，事亲为大。
5. 老吾老以及人之老，幼吾幼以及人之幼。

VI. Further Reading

Sell Oneself for Burial of Father

According to the legend, Dong Yong was a man of Qiancheng (today's north of Gaoqing County, Shandong) in the East Han Dynasty. His mother died when he was young and the family moved to Anlu (in today's Hubei) to avoid the war.

Later, his father died and Dong Yong sold himself to a rich family as a slave so as to bury his father.

When he was on his way to work, Dong Yong met with a woman under a pagoda tree and she said that she was homeless. So they got married.

The woman wove 300 bolts of cloth in one month and bought back Dong Yong's freedom.

When they passed the pagoda tree on their way home, the woman told Dong Yong she was the daughter to the Emperor of Heaven and was ordered to help him repay the debt.

With that said, she flew away. Henceforth the pagoda tree was renamed "compassion for piety".

Lying Down on the Ice to Fetch Carp for His Stepmother: Wang Xiang

During the Jin Dynasty, a young boy named Wang Xiang lost his mother to illness.

His father took another wife so that the boy would have maternal care. His stepmother, however, was a bad-tempered, evil-natured woman, who took a dislike to her stepson, and often berated him in front of his father.

This went on incessantly, and eventually, she managed to turn Lucky Wang's father against the boy. Despite this hardship, Lucky Wang remained devoted in his filial regard for them both.

One winter it was unusually cold, and snow fell for many days. The snow piled up on all sides of the house, and the small creek nearby froze solid with ice.

The severe weather forced the family indoors, and all the animals found shelter wherever they could. The world outdoors was a broad blanket of white. Wang Xiang's stepmother took sick. She craved medicine, and her thoughts fixed on the image of fresh fish.

She demanded fresh carp as medicine to cure her illness. As it was still snowing, and everywhere the rivers had long since frozen solid, where could fresh fish be found? Lucky Wang was a dutiful son, however, and could not bear seeing his parents unhappy.

He forced his way out into the cold and walked to the creek side to see what he could do. The snow was piled deep, and the boy shivered in the cold.

He looked and looked, but found no access to running water. Tired and disappointed, he sat down on the ice and lamented his failure to find fish to cure his mother.

Having no way to solve the problem, he simply let his tears flow. An idea came to him as he cried, and having no recourse, in his desperation, he removed his coat and shirt, and lay down on the ice amid his hot tears.

The more he cried, the more upset he got. The more upset he got, the more his tears flowed. Before long, his body heat and the apidly expanding puddle of tears melted a hole in the ice. Two carp that had been frozen into the river-water suddenly leaped up out of the crack in the ice and flopped onto the bank. Amazed and delighted, Wang Xiang scooped them up and carried them home to his mother.

Seeing the two live fish, Wang Xiang's stepmother felt thoroughly ashamed of her selfishness. Afterwards, she changed her attitude towards her stepson, and became a kind and caring person.

Many people said that Wang Xiang's response came from his sincere filial devotion. His noble attitude moved nature into giving him a reward.

1.5 Confucian Thought on Education

As a great educator, Confucian thought about education is flexible and changeable. He advocated to educate student according to his natural ability. These educational thoughts, which still shine brilliantly up to now, have a profound impact on modern education.

Confucius proposed that in education there should be no distinction between classes of men (rich or poor, high-born or low).In other words, everyone in society should enjoy the right to an education. His belief of teaching students in line with their ability implies adopting different methods of teaching in light of the various dispositions of the students. Teaching without discrimination explains that regardless of if the student is rich or poor, a sage or a simpleton, the individuals should be treated equally, irrespective of backgrounds. Besides this, Confucius set up the private school to widely accept the students.

In his long-term educational practice, Confucius saw the fact that everyone has different character and personality. Educating them according to their natural ability was first proposed bravely by Confucius. "By nature, men are nearly alike; by practice, they get to be wide apart. (性相近，习相远)"It became the educational principle and concept for Confucius. Confucius paid much attention to observing and studying the students. "Judge people by their deeds, not just by their words. (听其言观其行)" Confucius was very familiar with the characteristics and individuality of his students. It is based on the full understanding of the students that Confucius' education and teaching can be carried out according to the students' actual level and personality.

Confucius advocated a way of teaching to inspire and encourage students to speak out their own thought. In the *Analects*, it can be seen that confucius thought that governing the country, politics, military affairs, and law were all indispensable, but the most fundamental thing was education, which he placed in a very high position. Education can spread the social political thought, ethics and morality to the public, thus exerting a great influence on politics. Confucius believed that education was one of the three elements of national rule. The development of education should be based on economic development. "People should be rich first, then could get education." Only when the economy is developed, can education be better improved. Education was restricted by the economy. Confucius held the positive attitude that education played a key role in the process of human development. He disagreed the idea that slave owners' nature was superior to the common people. Recommending excellent talents and his whole educational thought was based on this natural and equal theory of human nature. He tried his best to make common people have chance to get education.

Training the "superior man" was the goal of Confucius' education. As a "superior man", he should cultivate himself and maintain a respectful and humble attitude. Virtue is the first and basic character of "superior man". Then, he should make friends and relatives, as well as the common people, happy. A gentleman was with both morality and ability in which morality came first.

"He who excels in learning can be an official. (学而优则仕)" is another main target of Confucius' education. Learning is a good way for becoming an official. The cultivation of officials is the main political aim at education. Good academic achievement is an important condition to be an official. Learning for official reflected the social needs of the rise of the feudal system, and it became a huge driving force for intellectuals to actively learn at that time.

Confucius stressed that the school moral education should be put in the first place. Studying of cultural knowledge must serve for moral education. Rites, music, archery, equestrianism, calligraphy and arithmetic, which are called "Six arts", are main course of Confucius class. "*Books of Songs*", "*Book of History*", "*Book of Rites*", "*Book of Music*", "*Book of Change*" and "*Spring and Autumn*" were the books he used.

We can conclude that Confucius' idea about education gives the great contribution to the ancient teaching in the history and also has the huge influence on the present education today.

Confucius was a great thinker and educator in ancient China. His thoughts were supplemented and developed by later generations and formed into Confucianism which occupied a dominant position in ancient China for a long time. Ancient rulers spoke highly of Confucius and his thought. By the time of Emperor Wu of the Han Dynasty, the ruler rejected the other schools of thought and respected only Confucianism. Temples were built and ceremony was held to memorize Confucius. "Da Cheng Temple", located in Qu Fu of Shan Dong province, became one of three main temples in China. Until now, in order to make the world understand Chinese culture, there are already more than 500 Confucian Institutes set up around the world. As a representative of Chinese culture, Confucian thought has transformed into the values of Chinese traditional culture. Confucian culture, the preeminent culture in the lands of China for 2000 years, has been a prime force in shaping a nation's character. About 2500 years have past since Confucius was alive, but the light shone on the world by this man seems remarkably undimmed.

Notes

1. Private school: Confucius was the first person to set up the private school in China. He taught and educated many students of whom were 72 virtuous persons. He and his students discussed philosophical idea. His followers collected the sayings and compiled the book named *Analects*.

2. Confucius Institute (孔子学院): is a non-profit public educational organization affiliated with the Ministry of Education of the People's Republic of China, whose stated aim is to promote Chinese language and culture, support local Chinese teaching internationally, and facilitate cultural exchanges.The organization also promotes the interests of the Chinese Communist Party in the countries in which it operates.

Culture Notes

1. 有教无类：有教无类，字面上的意思就是，所有人都可以接受教育，在教育面前人人平等，人人都有接受教育的机会和权利。孔子对所有学生都是一视同仁。在孔子以前，教育所服务的对象是贵族子弟，平民百姓是没有权利接受教育的。孔子私人设立学校，开门招生，打破了这一格局，开辟了我国教育事业的新篇章。"有教无类"的思想在中国教育史上，具有划时代的伟大意义。孔子的有教无类思想，还认为学习不应受年龄限制，不论老少都应该有受教育的权利，所以孔子的学生年龄参差不齐，什么年龄的都有。

2. 因材施教：出自于《论语·先进篇》。有一次，孔子讲完课，回到自己的书房，学生公西华给他端上一杯水。这时，子路匆匆走进来，大声向老师讨教："先生，如果我听到一种正确的主张，可以立刻去做吗？"孔子看了子路一眼，慢条斯理地说："总要问一下父亲和兄长吧，怎么能听到就去做呢？"子路刚出去，另一个学生冉有悄悄走到孔子面前，恭敬地问："先生，我要是听到正确的主张应该立刻去做吗？"孔子马上回答："对，应该立刻实行。"冉有走后，公西华奇怪地问："先生，一样的问题你的回答怎么相反呢？"孔子笑了笑说："冉有性格谦逊，办事犹豫不决，所以我鼓励他临事果断。但子路逞强好胜，办事不周全，所以我就劝他遇事多听取别人意见，三思而行。"

3. 罢黜百家，独尊儒术：汉代初期，儒、道两家在政治、思想上的斗争相当激烈。儒家的春秋大一统思想，仁义思想和君臣伦理观念与汉武帝时所面临的形势和任务相适应，董仲舒提出了这种方略，以统一思想，并且为政策寻找合理解释。他改革了儒家的传统思想，宣扬统一。汉武帝对董仲舒的这种大一统思想非常赏识。独尊儒术以后，官吏主要出自儒生，儒家逐步发展，成为此后两千年间统治人民的正统思想。

汉武帝时儒生董仲舒为适应君主专制中央集权政治的需要，提出了"大一统"的思想和"罢黜百家、独尊儒术"的建议。儒家思想逐渐成为封建社会正统思想。

董仲舒

New Words

flexible	adj.	cable of change	灵活的
adopt	v.	choose and follow; as of theories, ideas, policies, strategies or plans	采纳，采用
sage	n.	a mentor in spiritual and philosophical topics who is renowned for profound wisdom	圣人
irrespective	adj.	in spite of everything; without regard to drawbacks	不考虑的，不顾的
indispensable	adj.	not to be dispensed with; essential	不可缺少的
exert	v.	make a great effort at a mental or physical task	使受影响
restrict	v.	place restrictions on	限制，约束
cultivate	v.	train to be discriminative in taste or judgment	教养，栽培
humble	adj.	marked by meekness or modesty; not arrogant or prideful	谦逊的
feudal	adj.	of or relating to or characteristic of feudalism	封建的
backbone	n.	a central cohesive source of support and stability	脊梁骨，支柱

Exercises

I. Filling the Blank

1. As a great educator, Confucian thought about education is_____ and changeable.
2. Confucius proposed that education should not be_____ according to people.
3. Teaching without _____explains that regardless of if the student is rich or poor, a sage or a simpleton, the individuals should be treated equally, irrespective of backgrounds.
4. Educating them according to their _____ability was first proposed bravely by Confucius.
5. A gentleman was with both morality and ability in which_____ comes first.

II. Multiple Choice

1. Confucius was the first person to set up the _____ school.
   A. private   B. public   C. philosophy   D. ceremony
2. Confucius advocated a way of teaching to _____and encourage students to speak out their own thought.
   A. teach   B. force   C. inspire   D. tell
3. In the Analects, it can be seen that Confucius thought that governing the country, politics, military affairs, and law were all indispensable, but the most fundamental thing was_____.
   A. virtue   B. politic   C. filial piety   D. education
4. He disagreed the idea that slave owners' nature was _____to the common people.
   A. similar   B. superior   C. inferior   D. equal
5. By the time of Emperor _____of the Han Dynasty, the ruler rejected the other schools of thought and respected only Confucianism.
   A. Jing   B. Wu   C. Wen   D. Hui

III. True or False

1. (   ) In his long-term educational practice, Confucius saw the fact that everyone has same character and personality.
2. (   ) Confucius paid no attention to observing and studying the students.
3. (   ) In the *Analects*, it can be seen that Confucius thought that governing the country, politics, military affairs, and law were all dispensable.
4. (   ) The development of education should be based on political development.
5. (   ) Confucius stressed that the school moral education should be put in the first place.

IV. Answer the Questions

1. Why does Confucius speak highly of education?
2. What is your understanding of "make no social distinctions in teaching?"
3. Confucius used to teach students in accordance of their aptitude, what is the

significance of that?

V. Translate the Following Sentences into English
1. 性相近，习相远。
2. 听其言观其行。
3. 学而不思则罔，思而不学则殆。
4. 三人行，必有我师焉。
5. 敏而好学，不耻下问。

Unit 2 *Lao Tzu and Taoism*

2.1 Lao Tzu and *Tao Te Ching*

2.1.1 Lao Tzu

Lao Tzu, is generally believed to be Li Er, with the cognomen Dan, who lived in Ku County of the State of Chu during the Spring and Autumn period. He was an ideologist, philosopher, literateur and historian. He was also the founder and main representative of Taoism. Together with Chuang-Tzu, both of them were called Lao Zhuang. He ever served as the leading official of Zhou's state document collection museum. Lao Tzu was knowledgeable and eager to learn. In the class of his teacher Shang Rong, Lao Tzu liked to ask questions and seek the truth. In order to resolve his confusion, he often gazed at the brilliant moon perched in the heavens and thought about what the heaven is. That made him sleepless all the time.

The Spring and Autumn period he lived was mess with war caused by each feudal prince fighting for hegemony. Lao Tzu witnessed the sufferings of the people and put forward a series of ideas of governing the country. He stayed in Zhou for a long time. Later, when he saw the decline in the Zhou Dynasty which was hard to rise again, he left Zhou and went out to Hangu Pass. Yin Xi, who guarded the pass, asked him to write a book. Lao Tzu wrote a book and left it to Yin Xi, then went away. After that, no one knew where he was. In the Tang Dynasty, Lao Tzu was conferred a posthumous title as "emperor taishangxuanyuan" (太上玄元皇帝) that because the royal family of the Tang Dynasty surnamed Li, and thus respected Lao Tzu as his ancestors. In the birthplace of Lao Tzu, a temple offering sacrifices to Lao Tzu was designated as a key cultural relic conservation unit in Henan Province in 1986.

2.1.2 Taoism

Taoism, which originated in the Spring and Autumn period and the Warring States period, is a primordial form of polytheism that worships many gods. The main goal of Taoism is to live forever, become immortal and relieve the common people. It occupies an important position in ancient Chinese traditional culture and strongly and deeply influences modern world. Taoism regards Tao as the highest belief and believes that Tao is the origin of all living things. Taoism, together with Confucianism and Buddhism, occupies a dominant position in the history of ancient China.

2.1.3 *Tao Te Ching*

Lao Tzu was regarded as the founder of Taoism and later respected as the ancestor of Taoism. The book he left in Hangu Pass was regarded as a classic which consists of two parts. One is called *Tao* with 37 chapters. The other is called *De* with 44 chapters. Joining the two parts together were called *Tao Te Ching*, also known as *Lao Tzu*. Analects, Changing Books and *Tao Te Ching* are considered to be the three most influential ideological masterpieces in China. As one of the most influential book, *Tao Te Ching* has a profound influence on Chinese philosophy, science, politics and religion. According to UNESCO, *Tao Te Ching* is second only to the *Bible* in terms of circulation of translated copies. It has broken the boundaries of nations and countries and attracted global attention and recognition.

The main parts of *Tao Te Ching* were "Tao" and "De". Tao is not only the way of the universe, but also the way of nature, the method of individual practice. De is not a moral thought, but a special worldview, methodology, and ways of dealing with the world.

Tao and De was closely linked. Lao Tzu intended to teach people the way of Tao based on De. Without De, it was likely to fail in governing the country and the people. People who pursue Tao need peace of mind and tranquil mood which both come from De.

Notes

1. Lao Zhuang: Lao Tzu and Chuang-Tzu, both of them are representatives of Taoism.

2. Yin Xi: general, philosopher and educator of Zhou Dynasty. Reading the classic books from the early age. He is good at astronomy and is able to predict the things that will happen in the future. He was regarded as one of the ancestor of Taoism and has the same fame with Lao Tzu.

3. UNESCO: The United Nations Educational, Scientific and Cultural Organization. UNESCO has 193 member states and 11 associate members. Most of its field offices are "cluster" offices covering three or more countries; national and regional offices also exist. UNESCO pursues its objectives through five major programs: education, natural sciences, social/human sciences, culture and communication/information.

Culture Notes

函谷关：函谷关关口位于现在河南省灵宝市境内。东北方位是太行山脉的南端起点，整个南面就是秦岭，北边是黄河，在黄河与秦岭中间有一个狭长的地带就是函谷关谷道。是中国历史上建置最早的雄关要塞之一。

New Words

cognomen	n.	a familiar name for a person (often a shortened version of a person's given name)	姓氏
ideologist	n.	an advocate of some ideology	思想家
historian	n.	a person who is an authority on history and who studies it and writes about it	历史学家
hegemony	n.	the domination of one state over its allies	霸权
suffering	n.	a state of acute pain	身体或心灵的痛苦
confer	v.	present	授予，颁与
posthumous	adj.	occurring or coming into existence after a person's death	死后的
moral	adj.	concerned with principles of right and wrong or conforming to standards of behavior and character based on those principles	道德的
relieve	v.	provide physical relief, as from pain	解除
ideological	adj.	concerned with or suggestive of ideas	思想的
masterpieces	n.	the most outstanding work of a creative artist or craftsman	杰作

methodology	n.	the system of methods followed in a particular discipline	方法论
tranquil	adj.	characterized by absence of emotional agitation	安静的

I. Filling the Blank

1. Lao Tzu, is generally believed to be Li Er, with the cognomen Dan, who lived in Ku County of the State of_____ during the Spring and Autumn period.

2. Lao Tzu was an ideologist, philosopher, _____and historian.

3. Lao Tzu was also the founder and main representative of_____.

4. Lao Tzu witnessed the sufferings of the people and put forward a series of ideas for_____.

5. Taoism, which originated in the Spring and Autumn period and the Warring States period, is a primordial form of polytheism that worships_____.

II. Multiple Choice

1. The Spring and Autumn period Lao Tzu lived was mess with war caused by each feudal prince fighting for_____.
   A. fortune   B. title   C. honor   D. hegemony

2. The main goal of Taoism is to live forever, _____and relieve the common people.
   A. relieve from suffering   B. become immortal
   C. eliminate desire   D. Nirvana

3. Taoism regards _____as the highest belief and believes that Tao is the origin of all living things.
   A. Tao   B. the way of life   C. De   D.virtue

4. Taoism, together with Confucianism and_____, occupies a dominant position in the history of ancient China.
   A. Legalists   B. Buddhism   C. Mohist School   D. Sun Tzu

5. *Analects*, _____and *Tao Te Jing* are considered to be the three most influential ideological masterpieces in China.
   A. *Book of History*   B. *Book of Change*
   C. Book of Rites   D. Spring and Autumn

III. True or False

1. (   ) Lao Tzu ever served as the leading official of Zhou's state document collection museum. He was knowledgeable and eager to learn.

2. (   ) Lao Tzu was an ideologist, philosopher, litterateur, educator and historian.

3. (   ) Lao Tzu stayed in Zhou for a long time. Later, he was framed up, he left Zhou and went out to Hangu Pass.

4. (   ) As one of the most influential book, *Tao Te Ching* has a profound influence on Chinese philosophy, science, politics and religion.

5. (   ) The main parts of *Tao Te Ching* were "Tao" and "De". Tao is not only the way of the universe, but also the way of nature, the method of individual practice.

IV. Translate the Following Sentences into English

1. 道，可道，非恒道；名，可名，非恒名。
2. 人法地，地法天，天法道，道法自然。
3. 知人者智，自知者明；胜人者力，自胜者强。

V. Answer the Questions

1. What do you know about Lao Tzu?
2. Why do Chinese put *Tao Te Ching* in a very important place in the traditional culture of China?
3. How does Taoism influence Chinese people?

VI. Reading Comprehension

Tao Te Ching

Lao Tzu is traditionally regarded as the author of *Tao Te Ching*, though the identity of its authors or compilers have been debated throughout history. It is one of the most significant treatises in Chinese cosmogony. As with most other ancient Chinese philosophers, Lao Tzu often explains his ideas by way of paradox, analogy, appropriation of ancient sayings, repetition, symmetry, rhyme, and rhythm. In fact, the whole book can be read as an analogy – the ruler is the awareness, or self, in meditation and the myriad creatures or empire is the experience of the body, senses and desires.

Tao Te Ching, often called simply Tao Tzu after its reputed author, describes *Tao* as the source and ideal of all existence: it is unseen, but not transcendent, immensely powerful yet supremely humble, being the root of all things. People have desires and free will (and thus are able to alter their own nature). Many act "unnaturally", upsetting the natural balance of Tao. *Tao Te Ching* intends to lead students to a "return" to their natural state, in harmony with Tao. Language and conventional wisdom are critically assessed. Taoism views them as inherently biased and artificial, widely using paradoxes to sharpen the point.

Livia Kohn provides an example of how Lao Tzu encouraged a change in approach, or return to "nature", rather than action. Technology may bring about a false sense of progress. The answer provided by Lao Tzu is not the rejection of technology, but instead seeking the calm state of wu wei, free from desires. This relates to many statements by Lao Tzu encouraging rulers to keep their people in "ignorance", or "simple-minded". Some scholars insist this explanation ignores the religious context, and others question it as an apologetic of the philosophical coherence of the text. It would not be unusual political advice if Lao Tzu literally intended to tell rulers to keep their people ignorant.

Wu wei, literally "non-action" or "not acting", is a central concept of *Tao Te Ching*. The concept of wu wei is multifaceted, and reflected in the words' multiple meanings, even in English translation; it can mean "not doing anything", "not forcing", "not acting" in the theatrical sense, "creating nothingness", "acting spontaneously", and "flowing with the moment."

It is a concept used to explain *ziran* (自然), or harmony with *Tao*. It includes the concepts that value distinctions are ideological and seeing ambition of all sorts as originating from the same source. Lao Tzu used the term broadly with simplicity and humility as key virtues, often in contrast to selfish action. On a political level, it means avoiding such circumstances as war, harsh laws and heavy taxes. Some Taoists see a connection between *wu wei* and esoteric practices, such as *zuowang* "sitting in oblivion" (emptying the mind of bodily awareness and thought) found in Chuang-Tzu.

1. What is Lao Tzu's main idea of philosophy?
2. How could we interpret the meaning of "wu wei"?

 Lao Tzu's philosophy: naturalness

2.2.1 Lao Tzu's Philosophy

As a representative of Taoism, although it was only five thousand words, *Tao Te Ching* had a great influence on the history of Chinese ideology and culture. It has rich thought involving the universe, the politics and the life.

Lao Tzu was good at thinking dialectically. He mentioned many times that the high and low, long and short, beautiful and ugly, good and evil all exist in opposition to each other. Based on this, he put forward the idea of "doing nothing will lead to accomplishing everything". He discovered that things have the possibility of transforming into their opposites. Then he got the idea of "Misfortunes come from good fortune and fortune from bad fortune." That is to say, under certain conditions, the blessing becomes a disaster, and the calamity can also become a blessing.

In terms of the concept of moving and changing, Lao Tzu believes that everything in the world circulating under the domination of Tao is always in motion at all time. But Tao itself is independent and permanent. All things in the earth under control of Tao, proceed from the emergence, the development, the growth to the blossom, then from blossom to the weak, the destruction and the extinction. In consideration of this, Lao Tzu proposed to keep gentle and week. Don't get to the top so as to avoid weakness and destruction which will probably terminate the cycle.

On political issue, he was dissatisfied with the society his living in, and thought that the rules of society were extremely unfair. He strongly criticized the leaders that ignore the plight of the people, but only want to enjoy. In the face of such a dark reality, Lao Tzu put forward his vision of an ideal society. The country with small population although has no advanced technology and culture, there is no war and fighting. The people live and work in peace and contentment.

About life, Lao Tzu advocated the thought of being modest, simple, tolerant and so on. With the virtue of modesty, those in high positions will be more prosperous. And the humble man with modesty will not be transcended by others. A gentleman should be humble all his life. Simplicity is the very important principle of life. For only by being frugal can make a man difference. In addition, he called upon the society to pursue a principle that would allow the people to eat well and dress warmly and do not pursue the luxury life. Lao Tzu also requested the people should tolerate each other and warm others.

2.2.2 Tao

The main category of Lao Tzu's thought is Tao, which appears 73 times in *Tao Te Ching*. Tao is an initial state in which the mixture is not separated. It is the beginning of heaven and earth, the origin of all living things. Tao is just like water which benefits all things but not to compete with all things. Tao is unspeakable, and the human senses are not directly aware of it. Tao is the ontology of the universe, the rule of all living things and also the principle of human life. The Confucianism regards heaven, earth and man as the "San Cai (三才)". Lao Tzu took Tao, Heaven, Earth and Man as the "Si Da (四大)". Tao has opened up an extremely high and imaginative ideological space for the framework of Chinese cultural thought 2500 years ago, Tao of Lao Tzu was a great invention based on the fundamental transformation of primitive Taoism.

2.2.3 Naturalness

Naturalness is the essence of Lao Tzu's thought. Tao is the way of nature. "Tao begets the One; the One consists of the Two in opposition (the Yin and Yang);the Two begets the Three; the Three begets all things of the world. [道生一，一生二（阴阳两极），二生三，三生万物]" Tao begets all living things gradually and independently without following any human being's will.

The supreme way of nature is naturalness, following the natural way as it goes. "Man takes Earth as his model; Earth takes Heaven as its model; Heaven takes the Tao as its model; the Tao takes what is natural as its model". Lao Tzu summed up the way of life, the way of Heaven, the way of Earth, and the way of whole universe. Naturalness reveals the character of the whole universe, including the rules of all the living things. People live on the earth and they should have the courage to undertake the responsibility. They should be humble, conscious of their behavior.

1. 三才：就是天地人。人效法天地之道，体现了中华民族乐于与天地合一，与自然

和谐的精神,对天地和自然充满了和谐的精神。

2. 四大:出自《道德经》。《道德经》第二十五章中有:"故道大,天大,地大,人亦大。域内有四大,而人居其一焉。人法地,地法天,天法道,道法自然。"印度指地、水、火、风、空为五种构成物质的基本元素。佛教加以改造,谓地、水、火、风四种物质均能保持各自的形态,不相紊乱。亦名四大种。种,有能生的作用,如种子。本文指道、天、地、人。

New Words

ideology	n.	an orientation that characterizes the thinking of a group or nation	思想体系
universe	n.	everything that exists anywhere	宇宙,天地万物
dialectically	adv.	in a dialectic manner	辩证地
blessing	n.	a desirable state	祝福,好事
circulate	v.	move in circles	循环
extinction	n.	no longer in existence	灭绝
terminate	v.	bring to an end or halt	结束
plight	n.	a situation from which extrication is difficult especially an unpleasant or trying one	困境
contentment	n.	happiness with one's situation in life	满足
transcend	v.	go beyond	超越
frugal	adj.	avoiding waste	节省的,节俭点
category	n.	a collection of things sharing a common attribute	类型,种类
ontology	n.	the metaphysical study of the nature of being and existence	本体论
essence	n.	the choicest or most essential or most vital part of some idea or experience	本质,精华

I. Filling the Blank

1. As a representative of Taoism, although it was only five thousand words, *Tao Te Ching* had a great influence on the history of Chinese _____ and culture.

2. It has rich thought involving the_____, the politics, the life and so many other

aspects.

3. Lao Tzu was good at thinking_____.

4. Lao Tzu mentioned many times that the high and low, long and short, beautiful and ugly, good and evil all exist in _____ to each other.

5. Lao Tzu discovered that things have the possibility of _____ into their opposites.

II. Multiple Choice

1. In terms of the concept of moving and changing, Lao Tzu believes that everything in the world circulating under the domination of Tao is always _____ at all time.

    A. in motion   B. developing   C. declining   D. growing

2. All things in the earth under the control of_____, proceed from the emergence, the development, the growth to the blossom, then from blossom to the weak.

    A. heaven   B. Tao   C. human   D. nature

3. With the virtue of_____, those in high positions will be more prosperous.

    A. confident   B. humble   C. modesty   D. tolerant

4. _____reveals the character of the whole universe, including the rules of all the living things.

    A. Naturalness   B. Tao   C. Heaven   D. Virtue

5. People live on the earth and they should have the courage to undertake the _____.

    A. courage   B. modesty   C. filial piety   D. responsibility

III. True or False

1. (　　) Under certain conditions, the blessing becomes a disaster, and the calamity can also become a blessing.

2. (　　) Taoism encourages people to try to get to the top and be confident to change the way of nature.

3. (　　) The ideal society for Lao Tzu is the country with small population although has no advanced technology and culture, there is no war and fighting.

4. (　　) Tao is an initial state in which the mixture is separated.

5. (　　) Tao begets all living things gradually and independently without following any human being's will.

IV. Translate the Following Sentences into English

1. 道生一，一生二（阴阳两极），二生三，三生万物。

2. 祸兮福之所倚，福兮祸之所伏。

3. 人法地，地法天，天法道，道法自然。

V. Answer the Questions

1. What is Tao?

2. What is main thought of Lao Tzu's philosophy?

3. How to understand Naturalness?

VI. Reading Comprehension

In the mid-twentieth century, a consensus emerged among scholars that the historicity of the person known as Lao Tzu is doubtful and that the *Tao Te Ching* was "a compilation of Taoist sayings by many hands".

The earliest certain reference to the present figure of Lao Tzu is found in the 1st-century BC. Records of the Grand Historian collected by the historian Sima Qian from earlier accounts. In one account, Lao Tzu was said to be a contemporary of Confucius during the 6th or 5th century BC. His surname was Li and his personal name was Er or Dan. He was an official in the imperial archives and wrote a book in two parts before departing to the west. In another, Lao Tzu was a different contemporary of Confucius titled Lao Laizi (老莱子) and wrote a book in 15 parts. In a third, he was the court astrologer Lao Dan who lived during the 4th century BC reign of Duke Xian of the Qin Dynasty. The oldest text of the *Tao Te Ching* so far recovered was written on bamboo slips and dates to the late 4th century BC.

According to traditional accounts, Lao Tzu was a scholar who worked as the keeper of the archives for the royal court of Zhou. This reportedly allowed him broad access to the works of the Yellow Emperor and other classics of the time. The stories assert that Lao Tzu never opened a formal school but nonetheless attracted a large number of students and loyal disciples. There are many variations of a story retelling his encounter with Confucius, most famously in the Zhuang Tzu.

He was sometimes held to have come from the village of Chu Jen in Chu. In accounts where Lao Tzu married, he was said to have had a son named Zong who became a celebrated soldier. The story tells of Zong the warrior who defeats the enemy and triumphs, and then abandons the corpses of the enemy soldiers to be eaten by vultures. By coincidence Lao Tzu, traveling and teaching the way of the Tao, comes on the scene and is revealed to be the father of Zong, from whom he was separated in childhood. Lao Tzu tells his son that it is better to treat respectfully a beaten enemy, and that the disrespect to their dead would cause his foes to seek revenge. Convinced, Zong orders his soldiers to bury the enemy dead. Funeral mourning is held for the dead of both parties and a lasting peace is made.

Many clans of the Li family trace their descent to Lao Tzu, including the emperors of the Tang Dynasty. This family was known as the Longxi Li lineage. According to the Simpkinses, while many (if not all) of these lineages are questionable, they provide a testament to Lao Tzu's impact on Chinese culture.

1. What is the legend of Lao Tzu?
2. Which surname of the family traces Lao Tzu as its ancestor?

Non-action

Non-action is the most important thought in Lao Tzu's philosophical system. It was essentially a laissez-faire philosophy of non-enforcement for the management of state affairs. Lao Tzu advocated self-cultivation and self-rectification, which means that the rulers of a country should have faith in the people. Human nature he saw as essentially honest and true. If this nature was allowed to unfold, the state would be naturally a well administered state. This is the essence of Lao Tzu's non-action theory of government: "Non-enforcement and non-contention."

Non-action is mainly directed against action on politics. For him, doing randomly in politics will bring massive disaster. The more the ban is, the more people are in poverty. There are more burglars under the more laws and orders. The ruler collected a large amount of taxes which causing people starved and poor. As a result, people were reluctant to obey orders.

Lao Tzu is strongly opposed to "promising" politics. The government was corrupt and left all the farmland desolate. The ruler lived a luxurious life while exploited the people. In response to this phenomenon, Lao Tzu suggested that the ruler should govern the country by the rule of non-action. In *Tao Te Ching,* Lao Tzu said: "Exalt not the wise, so that the people shall not scheme and contend; Prize not rare objects, so that the people shall not steal. Shut out from sit the things of desire, so that the people's hearts shall not be disturbed. Therefore in the government of the Sage, he keeps empty their heart and makes full their bellies. Discourages their ambitions, strengthens their frames. So that the people may be innocent of knowledge and desires. And the cunning ones shall not presume to interfere. By action without deeds may all live in peace." The ruler should have less desire, less action to let the people take its course. To conform to public opinion without taking any action is Lao Tzu's political proposition. The monarchs and emperors in history unifying the country made the world peaceful and made the people live and work in peace and contentment. They truly benefited the people. But they relied on their great efforts to be the ruler and lived the most luxurious life. Do the things and try to get power and title is called "promising" in politics. Meanwhile, retiring after winning merits is real non-action.

Non-action is not idleness and laziness. It doesn't mean doing nothing or doing things passively, either. Its real meaning is to govern and control the world by non-action. For non-action, something can not be done and should not be done is primary. Stupid and unwise things should be avoided and also the immoral thing should never be done. Everything has its way of growing and developing. Respecting it is the embodiment of non-action.

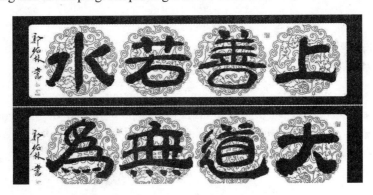

"The highest level of ethics is like water" is the good example of non-action. The best of men is like water. Water benefits all things and does not compete with them. It dwells in (the lowly) places that all disdain where in it comes near to the Tao. Water nourishes everything but never contends with them. That means water is "promising" to everything. However, water goes to the lowest place. Men always go up, but water flows down. It benefits everything but not gain the merit after that. According to Lao Tzu, water is the softest element but simultaneously also the most powerful.

Lao Tzu believed that the non-action of Saint is to serve for the people but not be above all the people. Saint makes the world peaceful and retires from political life after winning tremendous successes. So the people have no idea of who was the ruler. They thought that it was peaceful and quiet primitively. That was non-action of Saint. However, non-action doesn't mean to accomplish nothing or do nothing. It is not passive to escape from the real world. It told us a generally acknowledged truth which can not be ignorant when we tried to discuss the society of great harmony. Lao Tzu's doctrine will be of great use for the future and that is also why we learn Lao Tzu for modern people.

Non-action, as a principle to govern the country, left a profound influence in history. The first monarch who deliberately adopted the policy of "ruling by non-action" was Liu Heng, the fourth son of Liu Bang, and the third emperor who came to power in 180 BC. Before acceding to the throne, a major outbreak of civil strife had just been quelled. The first thing Liu Heng did after his succession was to abolish the widespread practice of torture and to thoroughly reform the rural taxation system. The reign of Liu Heng was immortalized as the very "pinnacle of Wen and Jing." During his reign, taxes upon peasants were only 3 percent and would be often exempted when bad harvests occurred. Liu Heng's policies created a strong country and a prosperous nation.

The second emperor Li Shimin of Tang Dynasty adopted a set of non-action policy popular with the common people. A famous Silver Age in history was created. Li once said: "Managing the country is like planting a tree. Branches and leaves will grow freely only when the root is secure. When the emperor is free, the common people will also live and work in peace and contentment." Actively standing by the idea of educating people with virtue, emperor Wen and Jing of Tang Dynasty also benefited from non-action in politics. Both of them make people frugal and modest. Economy was developed and people all led the simple and happy life.

Non-action: wu wei, literally "non-action" or "not acting", is a central concept of the *Tao Te Ching*. The concept of wu wei is multifaceted, and reflected in the words' multiple meanings, even in english translation; it can mean "not doing anything", "not forcing", "not acting" in the theatrical sense, "creating nothingness", "acting spontaneously", and "flowing with the moment".

Culture Notes:

1. 上善若水：出自《道德经》第八章。水善利万物而不争，处众人之所恶，故几于道。身居高位的人最好的行为像自然界的水一样呵护大家。水善于滋润万物而不与万物相争，停留在众人都不喜欢的地方，所以最接近于"道"。在道家学说里，水为至善至柔；水性绵绵密密，微则无声，巨则汹涌。水有滋养万物的德行，它使万物得到它的利益，而不与万物发生矛盾、冲突，人生之道，莫过于此。

2. 文景之治：是指西汉汉文帝、汉景帝统治时期出现的治世。文景时期，重视"以德化民"，当时社会比较安定，使百姓富裕起来。汉朝的物质基础亦大大增强，是中华文明迈入帝国时代后的第一个盛世。文景之治不仅是中国历史上经济文化飞速发展的一个伟大时代，同时也是为后来汉武帝征伐匈奴奠定了坚实物质基础的养精蓄锐时期。

New Words

randomly	adv.	in a random manner	随便地
massive	adj.	imposing in scale or scope or degree or power	大量的
burglar	n.	a thief who enters a building with intent to steal	盗贼
reluctant	adj.	unwillingness to do something contrary to your custom	不情愿的，勉强的
corrupt	v.	make illegal payments to in exchange for favors or influence	贪污，腐败
desolate	adj.	pitiable in circumstances especially through abandonment	荒凉的
luxurious	adj.	furnishing gratification of the senses	奢侈的，豪华的
exalt	v.	raise in rank, character, or status	提高，提升
disturb	v.	destroy the peace or tranquility of	打扰，妨碍
cunning	adj.	marked by skill in deception	狡猾的，欺诈的
interfere	v.	come between so as to be hindrance or obstacle	干预，干涉
conform	v.	adapt or conform oneself to new or different conditions	适应
monarch	n.	a nation's ruler or head of state usually by hereditary right	君主，帝王
unify	v.	become one	统一
idleness	n.	the trait of being idle out of a reluctance to work	懒惰，闲散
tyranny	n.	dominance through threat of punishment and violence	暴虐，专横

Exercises

I. Filling the Blank

1. Do the things and try to get power and title is called_____ in politics.
2. Meanwhile, retiring after winning merits is real_____.
3. The highest level of ethics is like_____.
4. _____ is a generally acknowledged truth which can not be ignorant when we tried to discuss the society of great harmony.
5. Lao Tzu is strongly_____ "promising" politics.

II. Multiple Choice

1. Non-action is mainly directed against action on_____.
   A. economy   B. politics   C. education   D. law
2. Water_____ all things and does not compete with them.
   A. cleans   B. uses   C. benefits   D. washes
3. Lao Tzu believed that the non-action of Saint is to _____ the people but not be above all the people.
   A. serve to   B. control   C. govern   D. force
4. Non-action, as a_____ to govern the country, has a great influence in history.
   A. idea   B. proposition   C. order   D. principle
5. _____ reduced the taxes and abolished tyranny of Qin dynasty. He was deeply influenced by non-action of Lao Tzu.
   A. Emperor Tai Zong of Tang   B. Emperor Xian of Han
   C. Emperor Gao Zu of Han   D. Emperor Gao Zong of Tang

III. True or False

1. (   ) Non-action is not idleness and laziness. It doesn't mean doing nothing or doing things passively.
2. (   ) Non-action means to accomplish nothing or do nothing.
3. (   ) The government was corrupt and left all the farmland desolate because the leader did nothing.
4. (   ) The monarchs and emperors in history unifying the country made the world peaceful and made the people live and work in peace and contentment. They truly benefited the people.
5. (   ) Actively standing by the idea of educating people with virtue, emperor Wen and Jing of Tang also benefited from non-action in politics.

IV. Translate the Following Sentences into English

1. 金玉满堂，莫之能守。富贵而骄，自遗其咎。
2. 大道废，有仁义；智慧出，有大伪。
3. 六亲不和，有孝慈；国家混乱，有忠臣。

V. Answer the Questions

1. Could you say your understanding of non-action in politics?
2. Why did Lao Tzu speak highly of non-action?
3. How to understand "The highest level of ethics is like water"?

VI. Reading Comprehension

The story of Lao Tzu has taken on strong religious overtones since the Han Dynasty. As Taoism took root, Lao Tzu was worshipped as a god. Belief in the revelation of the Tao from the divine Lao Tzu resulted in the formation of the Way of the Celestial Masters, the first organized religious Taoist sect. In later mature Taoist tradition, Lao Tzu came to be seen as a personification of the Tao. He is said to have undergone numerous "transformations" and taken on various guises in various incarnations throughout history to initiate the faithful in the "way". Religious Taoism often holds that the "Old Master" did not disappear after writing the *Tao Te Ching* but rather spent his life traveling and revealing the Tao.

Taoist myths state that Lao Tzu was conceived when his mother gazed upon a falling star. He supposedly remained in her womb for 62 years before being born while his mother was leaning against a plum tree. (The Chinese surname Li shares its character with "plum".) Lao Tzu was said to have emerged as a grown man with a full grey beard and long earlobes, both symbols of wisdom and long life. Other myths state that he was reborn 13 times after his first life during the days of Fuxi. In his last incarnation as Lao Tzu, he lived nine hundred and ninety years and spent his life traveling to reveal the Tao.

1. What does religious Taoism often hold?
2. What is the legend of Lao Tzu's birth?

2.4 Dialectical Thought of Lao Tzu

In *Tao Te Ching*, there are many sentences full of dialectical thought. They proved one thing that is "the contradiction of things and the transformation of opposites are immutable." The rule of changing and moving is cyclic. Contradictory things are always transformed into their own opposites.

2.4.1 Contradictory Dialectics

Things have the opposite nature in themselves. Lao Tzu believes that there are contradictions in everything in the world which are mutually transformed and interdependent. "When the people of the earty all know beauty as beauty, there arises (the recognition of) ugliness. When the people of the earth all know the good as good, there arises (the recognition of) evil. " When people in the world know what the beauty is, the beauty begins to turn to ugliness. When they know what the good is, the good thing begins to turn in the wrong direction. Being or non-being, difficult or easy, long or short, high or low, these contradictions are interdependent and mutually transformed. One side does not exist, the other side is difficult to exist. There is a lot of antinomy between beauty and ugliness, good and evil in Lao Tzu's philosophy. They are interdependent and unified. However, Lao Tzu opposed the contradiction among people. Lao Tzu lived in an unsettled society which had successive years of war. Lao Tzu deeply realized the pain brought to people by the turbulent times. He was worried about the society and people. So he rejected the contradictions among people because that will cause conflict and argument.

2.4.2 Moving in Circles

The thing is a qualitative change caused by the accumulation of quantitative change. All the things are from quantitative change to qualitative change, then to new quantitative change. Then these processes roll on in cycles and continue circularly. It is the basic rule of development proposed by Lao Tzu. He said: "Attain the utmost in passivity. Hold firm to the basis of Quietude. The myriad things take shape and rise to activity. But I watch them fall back to their repose. Like vegetation that luxuriantly grows. But returns to the root from which it springs."

Lao Tzu observed the cycle of things with non-action attitude. All the things are complex, but they finally will return to their own start point. That starting point maybe the death or the end. But after death they will regain a new life. This process will be never changed. Knowing this would make people wise. Otherwise, people will make themselves in trouble. People will be tolerant of everything by understanding this truth and treat things fairly. That will be helpful to get the inspiration for governing a country and comprehend the natural rule. As a result, people will live in longevity and peace without danger.

"A tree with a full span's girth begins from a tiny sprout; a nine-storied terrace begins with a clod of earth. A journey of a thousand li beings at one's feet." Things start from easy, then become hard step by step. No matter how hard things are, as long as persisting in, it will success. The success of things is gradually accumulated from small to large. Failing to abide by the above principles and act according to one's own will lead to the failure. The more you want to have, the easier to loss.

"The difficult problems of the world must be dealt with while they are yet easy; the great problems of the world must be dealt with while they are yet small. Therefore the Sage by never dealing with great problems accomplishes greatness." Difficult and easy, great and small are two pairs of contradictory words. They are unified by transforming from one to the other.

2.4.3 Things will Develop in the Opposite Direction When They Become Extreme

The development of things is from small to large. When it goes to a certain extent and a certain stage, it will be transformed into the opposite direction. "Things age after reaching their prime. That violence would be against Tao. And he who is against Tao perishes young."

When things go to flourish, it is bound to decline and perish. Seeking strength blindly is not in conformity with Tao which would cause extinction. "Therefore when an army is headstrong, it will lose in a battle. When a tree is hard, it will be cut down. The big and strong belong underneath. The gentle and weak belong at the top." The army will be easily destroyed when it goes strong. The tree will break off when it grows big. It can be seen that Lao Tzu thinks that things must be transformed into the opposite direction to a certain extent, which is a universal and inevitable rule.

"Disaster is the avenue of fortune, and fortune is the concealment for disaster." Disaster and fortune is an opposed contradiction. "Disaster" has the potential to lead to a "fortune" by learning from a lesson. Too great pleasure will bring about sadness. No matter what, when it reaches the pole, it will certainly develop into the opposite direction. This is the basic law of natural development. If you don't move, you won't develop. Tao needs to move and moving is the main part of Tao. Everything is constantly changing and such changing is natural.

Lao Tzu's dialectics are the intuition of human beings to understand the outside world. At the same time, it makes full use of man's subjective initiative. In the understanding of the outside world, it realized the transcendence of society and nature.

Culture Notes

矛盾辩证法：事物自身蕴含着相反的性质。老子认为世间万事万物都存在矛盾，这些矛盾是相互转化，相互依存的。"天下皆知美之为美，斯恶已；皆知善之为善，斯不善。"有无，难易，长短，高下，这些矛盾都是相互依存，相互转化的，一方不存在，另一方也难以存在。

New Words

immutable	adj.	that cannot be changed; that will never change	永恒不变的
cyclic	adj.	repeated many times and always happening in the same order	循环的，周期的
dialectic	n.	a method of discovering the truth of ideas by discussion and logical argument and by considering ideas that are opposed to each other	辩证法
interdependent	adj.	that depend on each other; consisting of parts that depend on each other	相互依赖的
transform	v.	to completely change the appearance or character of sth, especially so that it is better	使改观
antinomy	n.	a contradiction between two statements that seem equally reasonable	矛盾

unified	adj.	formed or united into a whole	统一的
unsettled	adj.	that may change; making people uncertain about what might happen	不平稳的,动荡不安的
qualitative	adj.	connected with how good sth is, rather than with how much of it there is	定性的,质量的
quantitative	adj.	connected with the amount or number of sth rather than with how good it is	定量的
myriad	n.	an extremely large number of sth	无数,大量
inspiration	n.	the process that takes place when sb sees or hears sth that causes them to have exciting new ideas or makes them want to create sth especially in art, music or literature	灵感
girth	n.	the measurmement around sth, especially a person's waist	周长,腰围
sprout	v.	to produce new leaves or buds; to start to grow	萌芽
terrace	n.	one of a series of flat areas of ground that are cut into the side of a hill like steps so that crops can be grown there	梯田

1. Filling the Blank

1. Contradictory things are always transformed into their own_____.

2. Lao Tzu believes that there are_____in everything in the world which are mutually transformed and interdependent.

3. So he rejected the_____among people because that will cause conflict and argument.

4. The success of things is gradually accumulated from_____.

5. Things will develop in the_____ direction when they become extreme.

II. Multiple Choice

1. According to Lao Tzu, When things go flourish, it is bound to_____.
   A. decline   B. blossom   C. boom   D. die

2. "Disaster" has the potential to lead to a_____by learning from a lesson.
   A. extinction   B. fortune   C. death   D. hatred

3. No matter what, when it reaches the_____, it will certainly develop into the opposite direction. This is the basic law of natural development.

A. end B. start C. pole D. middle

4. Everything is constantly changing and the such changing is_____.

A. special B. unusual C. specific D. natural

5. How to resolve conflicts between humans and the world according to Lao Tzu?

A. Overcome the strong by being weak B. Appear to be stupidity

C. Follow the way of nature D. Manipulate the nature

III. True or False

1. (   ) The contradiction of things and the transformation of opposites are changable.

2. (   ) when people in the world know what the beauty is, the beauty begins to turn to ugliness.

3. (   ) There is a lot of antinomy between beauty and ugliness, good and evil in Lao Tzu's philosophy. They are interdependent and unified. Lao Tzu also advocates the contradiction between people.

4. (   ) Lao Tzu lived in the time when the country is prosperous and the people are at peace.

5. (   ) "A journey of a thousand li beings at one's feet." Means things start from easy, then become hard step by step.

IV. Translate the Following Sentences into English.

道教是一种哲学、伦理或宗教的传统，起源于中国，强调与道和谐相处。"道"一词的意思是"道路"或"原则"，除了道教，也可以在中国的哲学和宗教中找到这个词。道家的礼教和伦理非常依赖于某一特殊学派，但从整体上看，他们倾向于强调无为、自然、简单。

V. Answer the Questions

1. What are the dialectical thoughts of Lao Tzu?

2. How do you understand the sentence of "A journey of a thousand li beings at one's feet."?

3. Why do people say "Disaster is the avenue of fortune, and fortune is the concealment for disaster."?

Influence of Lao Tzu

Lao Tzu, as most influential philosopher in China, his principle of "naturalness", "non-action" and "the greatest virtue is like water" has strongly and deeply influenced the historical view, political view and educational view to the later generations.

2.5.1 Influence on Chuang Tzu

Lao Tzu advocated "naturalness" and put forward his own political proposition of "a small Utopian society". Chuang Tzu inherited and developed Lao Tzu's thought. In Chuang

Tzui's philosophy, "Heaven" and "Man" is two opposite concepts. "Heaven" stands for nature, and "man" refers to everything "man-made" which derives from nature. Chuang Tzu requested everyone should be obedient to Tao of Heaven and abandoned anything of man-made. Obeying "Tao of Heaven" is to connect with heaven and earth which reaches the principle of De. The ideal society of Chuang Tzu is to "live with animals and exist with everything". (同于禽兽居，族与万物并) In such society, people don't admire the virtuous people and don't make full use of talents. That is the inherit of Lao Tzu.

Lao Tzu opposed that people were alienated by civilization. He pursued non-action and rejected "promising". The highest ideal of Chuang Tzu was that man is an integral part of nature. Yearning for the natural nature, he proposed to cast away emotion and desire. Man and nature should exist harmoniously. That can be called the real development between man and nature. Such harmonious environment was the ideal society for Chuang Tzu.

The ideal society for Chuang Tzui was that everything is equal. People were ignorant of power and there is no distinction between rich and poor, human and animals. Man is not greedy by nature and is able to live in harmony with nature and others. There is no need for social system to exist. Neither need ethics nor scientific and technological civilization.

2.5.2 Influence on Hsun Tzu

Hsun Tzu, one of the most famous thinkers, writers, historians, and representatives of Confucianism in the Warring States period, wrote the book of *Hsun Tzu*. Hsun Tzu witnessed the chaos surrounding the fall of the Zhou Dynasty and rise of the Qin State – which upheld "doctrines focusing on state control, by means of law and penalties". Hsun Tzu believed that humanity's inborn tendencies were evil and that ethical norms had been invented to rectify people. Compare with Lao Tzu's concept of everything is in motion. Hsun Tzu believes that everything composed of Qi is constantly changing. Such natural motion follows the inherent law. Nature is the true law and it will not be changed by anyone and anything. Whether the harmonious society under the rule of Yao or trouble times caused by Jie, the laws of nature are the same. They will not be changed by social disorder, nor by preferences of people.

In order to eliminate social chaos, Hsun Tzu called for establishing etiquette norms and social systems. He gave the positive affirmation of the role of man in the social and historical development. This also has something in common with Lao Tzu thought of "Tao of Heaven". They both believed that the peace or the mess of society is not related to Heaven which is a complete rejection of "Kismet theory" in Western Zhou Dynasty. It is no doubt that this attitude towards Heaven is progressive at that time. Both of them paid attention to people's subjective initiative. They both have a faith that people could know and improve the nature which will benefit all human being.

2.5.3 Influence on Han Fei Tzu

Han Fei Tzu, the ideologist, philosopher and representative of legalist, his ideas are collected mainly in the book of *Han Fei Tzu*. His writings were very influential on the future first emperor of Qin, Qin Shi Huang. After the early demise of the Qin Dynasty Han's philosophy was officially vilified by the following Han Dynasty. Despite its outcast status throughout the history of imperial China, his political theory continued to heavily influence every dynasty thereafter.

Han borrowed Shang Yang's emphasis on laws, Lao Tzu's emphasis on administrative technique. Han Fei Tzu held different view of Tao from Lao Tzu's. It emphasized autocracy and Shu (technique). Han Fei admitted the progress of the history and believed that the history is moving forward constantly. That is total different from "stateless world" of Confucius, "little population of Utopia country" of Lao Tzu. Han Fei Tzu's attitude to the progress of history is positive and conscious. He thought the history can't be reversed.

Lao Tzu laid great emphasis not on supernatural beings in the heavens but rather on the laws of nature and dedicated his whole life to seek after links in the cosmic chain that bound the Heavens and Earth. He left a profound influence on many aspects of Chinese culture. In philosophy, Lao Tzu founded the Taoism lasting for more than two thousand years. Together with Confucianism and Buddhism, they are regarded as mainstream of Chinese philosophy. In religion, his influence is equally great. In the Eastern Han Dynasty, Lao Tzu has been regarded as a deity by the royal family. Actually, Lao Tzu's influence goes far beyond that. The rays reflected by his thoughts have already shined upon the inner world of the modern people of the entire planet. "The net of the Heavens has large meshes, but it lets nothing through", "Great minds mature slowly" are not only absolutely familiar to Chinese people but indeed to all the people of the world will be handed down from one generation to the next.

1. Chuang Tzu: commonly known as Zhuangzhou, was an influential Chinese philosopher who lived around the 4th century BC during the Warring States period, a period corresponding to the summit of Chinese philosophy, the Hundred Schools of Thought. He is credited with writing—in part or in whole—a work known by his name, *Zhuang Tzu*, which is one of the foundational texts of Taoism.

2. Hsun Tzu: was a Chinese Confucian philosopher who lived during the Warring States period and contributed to the Hundred Schools of Thought. A book known as the *Hsun Tzu* is traditionally attributed to him. His works survived in an excellent condition, and became a major influence in forming the official state doctrines of the Han Dynasty, but his influence during the Tang Dynasty were relative to that of Mencius.

3. Han Fei Tzu: was a Chinese philosopher of the Warring States period. He is often considered to be the greatest representative of Chinese Legalism for his eponymous work *Han Fei Tzu*, synthesizing the methods of his predecessors.

Culture Notes

1. 秦始皇：中国历史上著名的政治家、战略家、改革家，完成华夏大一统的铁腕政治人物，也是中国第一个称皇帝的君主。对中国和世界历史产生深远影响，把中国推向大一统时代，奠定中国两千余年政治制度基本格局，被誉为"千古一帝"。

2. 商鞅：商鞅（约公元前 395 年—前 338 年），战国时期政治家、改革家、思想家，法家代表人物，卫国人，卫国国君的后裔。商鞅通过变法使秦国成为富裕强大的国家，史称"商鞅变法"。政治上，商鞅改革了秦国户籍、军功爵位、土地制度、行政区划、税收、度量衡以及民风民俗，并制定了严酷的法律；经济上商鞅主张重农抑商、奖励耕织，军事上商鞅作为统帅率领秦军收复了河西。

New Words

Utopian	adj.	characterized by or aspiring to impracticable perfection	乌托邦的
obedient	adj.	dutifully complying with the commands or instructions of those in authority	顺从的
alienated	adj.	socially disoriented	不合群的
integral	adj.	constituting the undiminished entirety; lacking nothing essential especially not damaged	完整的
yearn	v.	desire strongly or persistently	渴望，向往
chaos	n.	a state of extreme confusion and disorder	混乱，紊乱
uphold	v.	stand up for; stick up for; of causes, principles, or ideals	支持，赞成
penalty	n.	the act of punishing	惩罚，刑法
rectify	v.	bring, lead, or force to abandon a wrong or evil course of life, conduct, and adopt a right one	改正，校正
inborn	adj.	normally existing at birth	天生的，固有的
vilify	v.	spread negative information about	中伤，诽谤

outcast	*adj.*	excluded from a society	被抛弃的
autocracy	*v.*	a political system governed by a single individual	独裁，统治
arguably	*adv.*	as can be shown by argument	可论证地

Exercises

I. Filling the Blank

1. Lao Tzu advocated _____ and put forward his own political proposition of "a small Utopian society".

2. "Heaven" stands for_____, and "Man" refers to everything "man-made" which derives from nature.

3. Yearning for the natural nature, Chuang Tzu proposed to cast away emotion and_____.

4. The ideal society for Chuang Tzu was that man is not _____ by nature and is able to live in harmony with nature and others..

5. Han borrowed _____ emphasis on laws, Lao Tzu's emphasis on administrative technique.

II. Multiple Choice

1. Chuang Tzu inherited and developed_____ thought.
   A. Han Fei Tzu   B. Mencius'   C. Confucius'   D. Lao Tzu

2. Lao Tzu opposed that people were alienated by_____.
   A. war   B. civilization   C. title   D. desire

3. The highest ideal of Chuang Tzu was that man is an integral part of_____.
   A. nature   B. society   C. world   D. group

4. Hsun Tzu, one of the most famous thinkers, writers,_____ and representatives of Confucianism in the Warring States period.
   A. educator   B. historians   C. politician   D. psychologist

5. Hsun Tzu gave the positive affirmation of the role of _____in the social and historical development.
   A. nature   B. ruler   C. heaven   D. man

III. True or False

1. (   ) Chuang Tzu requested everyone should be obedient to Tao of Heaven and anything of man-made.

2. (   ) The ideal society for Chuang Tzu was that everything is equal. People were ignorant of power and there is no distinction between rich and poor, human and animals.

3. (   ) Hsun Tzu and Lao Tzu both believed that the peace or the mess of society is related to heaven in the Zhou Dynasty.

4. (   ) Han Fei Tzu admitted the progress of the history and believed that the history is

moving forward constantly. That is total different from "stateless world" of Lao Tzu, "little population of Utopia country" of Confucius.

5. (　　) Lao Tzu's influence goes far beyond that. The thought of naturalness deeply influenced the area of literature, calligraphy and painting, music and architecture.

IV. Translate the Following Sentences into English

大多数西方人都是从《道德经》中知道老子的。欧洲的第一版《道德经》是斯坦尼斯拉斯·朱利安（Stanislas Julien）翻译的法文版，1842年在巴黎出版。不久之后，德语和英语版本开始出现。朱利安的法语翻译引起了巨大的分歧。另一个法国人声称已经翻译了这本书，认为朱利安抄袭了他的作品。这是一场激烈的争论，持续了15年。

V. Answer the Questions

1. What influence does Lao Tzu have on Chuang Tzu?
2. What influence does Lao Tzu have on Hsun Tzu?
3. What influence does Lao Tzu have on Han Fei Tzu?

VI. Further Comprehension

Hsun Tzu

Hsun Tzu, 325 BC to 238 BC, was Confucian philosopher and scholar. Some texts recorded his surname as Sun instead of Xun, either because the two surnames were homophones in antiquity or because Xun was a naming taboo during the reign of Emperor Xuan of Han (73 BC–48 BC), whose given name was Xun.

Nothing is known of his lineage, and the early years of Hsun Tzu's life are enshrouded in mystery. Accounts of when he lived conflict; he is said to have met a King Kuai of Yan during the time of Mencius, while Liu Xiang states that he lived more than a hundred years after Mencius. The Sima Qian records that he was born in Zhao, and County has erected a large memorial hall at his supposed birthplace. He is recounted at the age of fifty as going to the state of Qi to study and teach at the Jixia Academy. The Shi Ji states that he became a member of the academy during the time of King Xiang of Qi, discounting the story of his being a teacher of Han Fei Tzu, but it's chronology would give him a lifetime of 137 years.

After Qi Hsun Tzu is said to have visited the state of Qin, possibly from 260 to 265 BC, and praised its governance, and debated military affairs with Lord Linwu in the court of King Xiaocheng of Zhao. Later, Hsun Tzu was slandered in the Qi court, and he retreated south to the state of Chu. In 240 Lord Chunshen, the prime minister, invited him to take a position as Magistrate of Lanling , which he initially refused, but Lord Chunshen was assassinated. In 238 BC by a court rival and Hsun Tzu subsequently lost his position. He retired, remained in Lanling, a region in what is today's southern Shandong Province, for the rest of his life and was buried there. The year of his death is unknown, though if he lived to see the ministership of supposed student Li Si, as recounted, he would have lived into his nineties, dying shortly after 219 BC.

Unit 3 Sun Tzu and The Art of War

3.1 A brief Introduction to Sun Tzu

Sun Tzu (about 545 BC—470 BC) was a legendary general, philosopher, writer, and most importantly, a military strategist, who lived in the Eastern Zhou period of ancient China. He is best remembered as the author of the book *The Art of War*, which includes his wisdom and experiences in warfare. *The Art of War* is believed to be the best single book ever written on the military subject. Although, written more than 2500 years ago, many of the strategies and wisdom illustrated in the book are timeless and they still work in today's environment.

As a heroic man, he got many names—Sun Wu, Changqing, Sun Tzu. His birth name was Sun Wu. Wu is his first name, Sun is surname. He was known outside of his family by his courtesy name Changqing. The name Sun Tzu by which he is best known in the Western World is an honorific, which means "Master Sun". Tzu is a respectable suffix in ancient Chinese culture.

It is said that some time around 500 BC, Sun Wu was born in a minor nobility family in what is now Shandong Province, a part of China north of Shanghai that became famous for Confucius. Both his great grandfather and his grandfather have great military achievements, so his interests and ambition in military grew naturally in such a family. He was given a good education, and in order to get noticed and hired by royalty, he wrote a military treatise *The Art of War*. He went to meet King Ho-lu (or Helu or Holu) of the state of Wu and presented his work *The Art of War*. King Ho-lu was a man with great political ambition and he was in want of military talents. *The Art of War* was highly valued by King Ho-lu and this book won Sun Tzu the title of general.

He was active as a strategist serving Holu. Sun Tzu is said to have led the Wu forces at the decisive battle of Boju, by which Wu conquered the state of Chu. Although his troops were once outnumbered one to ten, he was always victorious. Many successes followed and continued after his death. Some considered his death to be another of his deceptions. Legend has it that Sun Tzu vanished after his victory, believing that the Wu political leadership was growing mad with power.

According to Sima Qian, the following story well illustrates Sun Tzu's temperament: In order to test his ability as a commander, before hiring him, the King of Wu ordered Sun Tzu to train the court concubines into soldiers. Sun Tzu divided those women into two parts and named two women to be the leaders of their own part respectively. These two were actually the most beloved concubines of Holu. Sun Tzu repeatedly explained the command for marching but when the drums sounded the women burst out laughing. After his command failed several times, he had to punish the leaders of the two parts. He believed that if the orders were given but not followed then it was the fault of the officers. So he had the king's two favorite concubines beheaded. After the two were executed and replaced, all the women stopped giggling and obeyed the orders flawlessly. The king, though sickened by the deaths, saw Sun's firmness and talents and gave Sun Tzu command of the army.

Notes

1. Zhou Dynasty (1027 BC—221 BC): The Zhou Dynasty was the first dynasty to unite most of China under a single government. It was composed of Western Zhou (1045 BC—771 BC) and Eastern Zhou (770 BC—256 BC). The early Western Kings did not attempt to exert direct control over the entire territory they had conquered. They secured their position by selecting loyal supporters and relatives to rule walled towns and the surrounding territories.

2. Eastern Zhou kings' power: Eastern Zhou kings no longer exercised much political or military authority over the states they had once ruled. The political structure of the Eastern Zhou was more like a confederation with the Zhou kings remaining nominal overlords. There were two major subdivisions in the Eastern Zhou period: the Spring and Autumn period, and the Warring States period. Sun Tzu lived in the Spring and Autumn period.

Culture Notes

1. 孙武：字长卿。《孙子兵法》的作者。中国春秋时期著名的军事家、政治家，尊称兵圣或孙子。经吴国重臣伍员(伍子胥)举荐，向吴王阖闾进呈所著兵法十三篇，受到重用为将。他曾率领吴国军队大败楚国军队，占领楚国都城郢城，几近灭亡楚国。著有巨作《孙子兵法》十三篇，为后世兵法家所推崇，被誉为"兵学圣典"，置于《武经七书》之首。《孙子兵法》在中国乃至世界军事史、军事学术史和哲学思想史上都占有极为重要的地位，并在政治、经济、军事、文化、哲学等领域被广泛运用。被译为英文、法文、德文、日文，该书成为国际间最著名的兵学典范之书。

2．吴王阖闾（hé lú）：春秋末期吴国君主，军事统帅。公元前 514 年—前 496 年在位。孙武助其于柏举之战大败楚国，阖闾因此称霸南方。

3．柏举之战：公元前 506 年（周敬王十四年），由吴王阖闾率领的 3 万吴国军队深入楚国，在柏举（今湖北省麻城市境内，一说湖北汉川北）击败楚军 20 万主力，继而占领楚都的远程进攻战。在战争中，吴军灵活机动，因敌用兵，以迂回奔袭、后退疲敌、寻机决战、深远追击的战法而取胜。此战是中国古代军事史上以少胜多、快速取胜的成功战例。

New Words

legendary	adj.	very famous and be told about in many stories	传奇般的
strategist	n.	someone who is skilled in planning the best way to gain an advantage or to achieve success, especially in war	战略家
illustrate	v.	clarify by giving an example of	阐明说明
courtesy	n.	polite behaviour	有礼的举止
honorific	adj.	in a way showing respect or honour to someone	尊敬的，表示敬意的，敬称的
suffix	n.	a suffix is a letter or group of letters, for example '-ly' or '-ness', which is added to the end of a word in order to form a different word	后缀，词尾
nobility	n.	the nobility of a society are all the people who have titles and belong to a high social class	贵族（阶层）
treatise	n.	a treatise is a long, formal piece of writing about a particular subject	论文；论述；专著；
anecdote	n.	an anecdote is a short, amusing account of something that has happened	轶事
court	n.	the court of a king or queen is the place where he or she lives and carries out ceremonial or administrative duties	王宫；宫殿；宫廷
concubine	n.	in former times, a concubine was a woman who lived with and had a sexual relationship with a man of higher social rank without being married to him	妾
behead	v.	if someone is beheaded, their head is cut off, usually because they have been found guilty of a crime	砍…的头；将…斩首

Exercises

I. Simple Selection

1. Sun Tzu's birth name was _____.
   A. Sun Wu   B. Sun Changqing   C. Sun Tzu   D. Sun Bin
2. Sun Wu was born in a _____ family.
   A. poor family   B. royal family   C. minor nobility   D. businessman's
3. Sun Wu was born in what is now _____.
   A. Shanghai   B. Shandong   C. Hunan   D. Hubei
4. He was active as a strategist serving the King _____.
   A. Helu   B. Goujian   C. Qinshihuang   D. Xiaqi
5. As a test, King of Wu ordered Sun Tzu to train the _____.
   A. soldiers   B. generals   C. the servants   D. concubines
6. To answer Helu's test, Sun Tzu trained people from the court, and he had the king's two _____ beheaded.
   A. close friends   B. favorite concubines
   C. talented soldiers   D. loyal servants

II. Multiple Choice

1. The author of *The Art of War* can be called _____.
   A. Sun Wu   B. Changqing   C. Sun Tzu   D. Sun Bin
2. Sun Tzu was a _____.
   A. general   B. philosopher   C. writer   D. strategist
3. Sun Tzu's achievement is _____.
   A. becoming the king of the state of Wu   B. winning the war of Boju
   C. becoming a general   D. writing the thirty-six stratagems
4. Which of the following is true about Sun Tzu _____.
   A. He was a talented general
   B. He served the king of Chu
   C. He developed from a soldier to a general
   D. He helped in winning the war of Boju
5. Sun Tzu lived in _____ of Chinese history
   A. the Eastern Zhou period   B. the Western Zhou period
   C. the Spring & Autumn period   D. the Warring States period

III. Fill in the Blanks

1. He was active as a _____ serving Helu.
2. Both his great grandfather and his grandfather has great _____ achievements.
3. It is said that some time around 500 BC, Sun Wu was born in a _____ family.
4. Sun Wu had the king's two favorite _____ beheaded.

5. He went to meet King _____ of the state of _____ and presented his work "The Art of War".

IV. True or False

1. Sun Wu was born in a soldiers' family in what is now Shandong Province.

2. The Art of War wins Sun Tzu the title of general.

3. He was active as a strategist serving Helu.

4. In order to test's ability as a commander, before hiring him, the King of Wu ordered Sun Tzu to train the court bodyguards into soldiers.

5. Sun Tzu is said to have led the Wu forces at the decisive battle of Julu.

V. Matching

1. 兵者，国之大事，死生之地，存亡之道，不可不察也。
2. 兵者，诡道也。
3. 攻其无备，出其不意。
4. 故不尽知用兵之害者，则不能尽知用兵之利也。
5. 故兵贵胜，不贵久。
6. 故知兵之将，生民之司命，国家安危之主也。
7. 故能而示之不能，用而示之不用。
8. 近而示之远，远而示之近。
9. 利而诱之，乱而取之。
10. 实而备之，强而避之。

A. Let your great object be victory, not lengthy campaigns.

B. If he is secure at all points, be prepared for him. If he is in superior strength, evade him.

C. The art of war is of vital importance to the State. It is a matter of life and death, a road either to safety or to ruin. Hence it is a subject of inquiry which can on no account be neglected.

D. Thus it may be known that the leader of armies is the arbiter of the people's fate, the man on whom it depends whether the nation shall be in peace or in peril.

E. All warfare is based on deception.

F. When able to attack, we must seem unable; when using our forces, we must seem inactive.

G. Attack him where he is unprepared, appear where you are not expected.

H. When we are near, we must make the enemy believe we are far away; when far away, we must make him believe we are near.

I. It is only one who is thoroughly acquainted with the evils of war that can thoroughly understand the profitable way of carrying it on.

J. Hold out baits to entice the enemy. Feign disorder, and crush him.

3.2 Chapter Summaries of *The Art of War*

The Art of War is composed of 13 chapters. Each one is devoted to an aspect of warfare and how it applies to military strategy and tactics. There are approximately 6000 Chinese characters in the book.

Chapter summaries

1. Detail assessment and planning: It teaches how to calculate chances of victory. Five factors are decisive, including the moral law, seasons, terrain, leadership, and management. By prudent comparing and assessing the above points, a commander can calculate the outcomes of his military engagements. Habitual deviation from these calculations will bring about improper actions and failures. The text warns that war is a very grave matter for the state and must not be commenced without due consideration.

2. Waging a war: A very important part of successful military campaigns is limiting the cost. Raging a war means a state has to pay price for armor, chariot, transportation, accommodation and so on. The expenditure for even one day is enormous. If the war is protracted, and the financial burden grows, the state and the people will be trapped in tiring condition. Success requires winning decisive engagements quickly. A qualified commander should be economy-conscious.

3. Strategic attack: The best result of all is to take the enemy's country whole and intact without fighting and destroying. In the highest form of generalship, a leader should know himself and know the enemy, design his strategy and win a battle with the least military cost.

4. Disposition of the army: It is important to defend existing positions, do not advance unless the commander is sure of safety. It teaches commanders the importance of recognizing strategic opportunities, and teaches not to create opportunities for the enemy.

5. Forces: It teaches how to give efficient direction by strict and detail management. It also suggests the use of creativity and timing in building an army's momentum.

6. Weaknesses and strengths: This chapter teaches commanders to attack the weak part of the enemy and explains how an army's opportunities come from the openings in the environment caused by the relative weakness of the enemy and how to respond to changes in the fluid battlefield over a given area.

7. Military maneuvers: This chapter is about balancing the advantages and the dangers. It explains the dangers of direct conflict and how to win those confrontations when they are forced upon the commander.

8. Variations and adaptability: It is about the "dos and don'ts" in changing situation. Flexibility is vital in real practice. It explains how to respond to shifting circumstances successfully.

9. Movement and development of troops: It describes the different situations in which an army finds itself as it moves through new enemy territories, and how to respond to these situations. Much of this section focuses on evaluating the intentions of others.

10. Terrain: The natural formation of the country is soldiers' best ally. A great general knows shrewdly calculating and estimating the adversary, difficulties, dangers and distance.

Basically there are three general areas of resistance (distance, dangers and barriers) and the six types of ground positions that arise from them. Each of these six field positions offers certain advantages and disadvantages.

11. The nine battlegrounds: It describes the nine common situations (or stages) in a campaign. Each has its own advantages and disadvantages, leaders should respond respectively.

12. Attacking with fire: It discusses five targets for fire attack and explains the general use of weapons and the specific use of the environment as a weapon. Commanders should predict the outcomes of the fire attack and made appropriate preparation.

13. Intelligence and espionage: It focuses on the importance of developing good information sources and five types of spies.

Today, we can see different English versions of the Art of War by different translators. The character "Tao" (道) was translated as "way" or "moral law". We choose the later, since Sun Tzu says when the ruler rages a war with Tao, his people will completely follow him even risking their lives, so we can tell that in this context Tao means the nature of the war is in accord with morality or justice.

Culture Notes

《孙子兵法》又称《孙武兵法》《吴孙子兵法》《孙子兵书》《孙武兵书》等，是中国现存最早的兵书，也是世界上最早的军事著作。

《孙子兵法》全部内容可主要归纳：

第一，战略运筹（第一篇至第三篇）。第一篇《始计篇》讲的是庙算，即出兵前在庙堂上比较敌我的各种条件，估算战事胜负的可能性。第二篇《作战篇》讲的是庙算后的战争动员及取用于敌，胜敌益强。"作"是"制造""兴起"之意。"作战"这里不是指战争，而是指战争前的准备和筹划。第三篇《谋攻篇》讲的是以智谋攻城，即不专用武力，而是采用各种手段使守敌投降。

第二，作战指挥（第四篇至第六篇）。第四篇《军形篇》讲的是具有客观、稳定、易见等性质的因素，如战斗力的强弱、战争的物质准备。第五篇《兵势篇》讲的是主观、易变、带有偶然性的因素，如兵力的配置、士气的勇怯。第六篇《虚实篇》讲的是如何通过分散集结、包围迂回，造成预定会战地点上的我强敌劣，以多胜少。

第三，战场机变（第七篇至第九篇）。第七篇《军争篇》讲的是如何"以迂为直""以患为利"，夺取会战的先机之利。第八篇《九变篇》讲的是将军根据不同情况采取不同的战略战术。第九篇《行军篇》讲的是如何在行军中宿营和观察敌情。

第四，军事地理（第十篇至第十一篇）。第十篇《地形篇》讲的是六种不同的作战地形及相应的战术要求。第十一篇《九地篇》讲的是依"主客"形势和深入敌方的程度等划分的九种作战环境及相应的战术要求。

第五，特殊战法（第十二篇至第十三篇）。第十二篇《火攻篇》讲的是以火助攻与"慎战"思想。第十三篇《用间篇》讲的是五种间谍的配合使用。

New Words

tactic	n.	the practice of cultivating the land or raising stock	战术；战略
terrain	n.	terrain is used to refer to an area of land or a type of land when you are considering its physical features	地形；地势
prudent	adj.	careful and sensible; marked by sound judgment	细心的；明辨的
habitual	adj.	a habitual action, state, or way of behaving is one that someone usually does or has, especially one that is considered to be typical or characteristic of them	习惯的；惯常的；习以为常的
deviation	n.	doing something that is different from what people consider to be normal or acceptable	背离，偏离
commence	vt.& vi.	when something commences or you commence it, it begins	开始；着手
wage	vt.& vi.	if a person, group, or country wages a campaign or a war, they start it and continue it over a period of time	实行，进行
armor	n.	protective covering made of metal and used in combat	装甲；盔甲
chariot	n.	a two-wheeled horse-drawn battle vehicle	战车
protract	vt.	lengthen in time; cause to be or last longer	〈贬〉延长，拖延（某事物）
intact	adj.	constituting the undiminished entirety; lacking nothing essential especially not damaged	完整无缺的，未经触动的
timing	n.	he skill or action of judging the right moment in a situation or activity at which to do something	时机掌握

momentum	*n.*	if a process or movement gains momentum, it keeps developing or happening more quickly and keeps becoming less likely to stop	势头
maneuver	*v.& n.*	act in order to achieve a certain goal	操纵
flexibility	*n.*	the quality of being adaptable or variable	机动性，灵活性
shrewd	*adj.*	a shrewd person is able to understand and judge a situation quickly and to use this understanding to their own advantage	机灵的，精明的
adversary	*n.*	someone you are competing with, or arguing or fighting against	对手，敌手
espionage	*n.*	the activity of finding out the political, military, or industrial secrets of your enemies or rivals by using spies	侦察；间谍活动

Exercises

I. Simple Selection

1. *The Art of War* is composed of _____ chapters.
   A. 11   B. 12   C. 13   D. 14
2. There are approximately _____ Chinese characters in the book.
   A. 6000   B. 8000   C. 10000   D. 12000
3. _____ teaches how to calculate chances of victory.
   A. Detail assessment and planning   B. Strategic attack
   C. Weaknesses and strengths   D. Variations and adaptability
4. _____ is about limiting the cost and winning decisive engagements quickly.
   A. Forces   B. Military maneuvers
   C. Waging war   D. Movement and development of troops
5. _____ focuses on the importance of developing good information sources
   A. Intelligence and espionage   B. The nine battlegrounds
   C. Attacking with fire   D. Movement and development of troops
6. In calculating chances of victory, five factors are decisive, including _____ _____ and management.
   A. the moral law, weather, terrain, leadership
   B. the moral law, seasons, cost, leadership
   C. the moral law, seasons, terrain, leadership
   D. the moral law, seasons, terrain, cost

II. Multiple Choice

1. Attacking with fire discusses _____.
   A. five targets for fire attack
   B. the general use of weapons
   C. the moral nature of setting fire
   D. the specific use of the environment as a weapon
2. Movement and development of troops describes _____.
   A. evaluating the intentions of others
   B. the different situations the army is to move through
   C. six types of ground positions
   D. the "dos and don'ts" in changing situation.
3. Disposition of the army teaches _____.
   A. not to create opportunities for the enemy
   B. not to advance unless the commander is sure of safety
   C. the importance of recognizing strategic opportunities
   D. it is important to defend existing positions
4. Raging a war means a state has to pay price for _____ and so on.
   A. armor   B. chariot   C. transportation   D. accommodation
5. Military maneuvers is about _____.
   A. battlefield
   B. moving through new enemy territories
   C. the "dos and don'ts" in changing situation
   D. balancing the advantages and the dangers

III. True or False

1. War is a very grave matter for the state and must not be commenced without due consideration.
2. The best result if all is to ruin enemy's country.
3. A very important part of successful military campaigns is limiting the cost.
4. The use of creativity and timing in building an army's momentum is not suggested.
5. Success requires winning decisive engagements quickly.

IV. Fill in the Blanks

1. _____ is vital in real practice. It explains how to respond to shifting circumstances successfully.
2. In movement and development of troops, much of this section focuses on evaluating the _____ of others.
3. _____ of the country is soldier's best ally.
4. Commanders should predict the outcomes of the fire attack and made _____.
5. Forces teaches how to give efficient direction by strict and detail _____.

V. Matching: Here we have another English version of the names of the 13 chapters, try to match them with their Chinese translation

1. Laying Plans
2. Waging War
3. Attack by Stratagem
4. Tactical Dispositions
5. Energy
6. Weak Points and Strong
7. Maneuvering
8. Variation in Tactics
9. The Army on the March
10. Terrain
11. The Nine Situations
12. The Attack by Fire
13. The Use of Spies

A. 始计　B. 军形　C. 作战　D. 谋攻　E. 虚实
F. 九变　G. 九地　H. 兵势　I. 军争　J. 用间
K. 地形　L. 火攻　M. 行军

VI. Translate the Following Sentences into English

1. 知己知彼百战不殆。
2. 不战而屈人之兵。
3. 故上兵伐谋，其次伐交，其次伐兵，其下攻城。
4. 故善战者，立于不败之地，而不失敌之败也。
5. 是故胜兵先胜而后求战，败兵先战而后求胜。

3.3 The Strategic Thoughts of Sun Tzu

As history's finest military tacticians and analysts, Sun Tzu's teachings and strategies formed the basis of advanced military training for centuries to come. These strategies are now echoing loudly in our era (in sports, in politics, in military, and in business). Sun Tzu's teachings and philosophies were used in the Korean War, the Vietnam War, World War Two, Japan (during the civil war), the first Gulf War, and were used by Napoleon and Qin Shi Huang. People summarized that the following three points are typical of Sun Tzu's thoughts.

First, Sun Tzu stressed that raging a war is a very grave matter. A ruler should never start a war unless he has carefully calculated the circumstance and is sure of the positive outcomes.

Second, a ruler should hold dear of soldiers' lives and try his utmost to maintain the power of his state. His cautious attitude towards war and his love for people is widely appreciated. However, he never supposes that combat can be eliminated. Rather, he is mindful of the tremendous risks attendant on any resort to force, especially bankruptcy and the social disintegration of the politically weak Chinese states of his time. So he urges that force not be squandered, but conserved carefully and used only when it may have decisive impact.

Third, he sees war, therefore, not so much as a matter of destroying the enemy materially or physically (although that may play a role), but of unsettling the enemy psychologically; his goal is to force the enemy's leadership and society from a condition of harmony, in which they can resist effectively, toward one of chaos (luàn), which is tantamount to defeat. The best result of a conflict is breaking the enemy's resistance without fighting.

The three points above are the distinguishing features of his military thinking.

Different from Western authors, Sun Tzu's approach to warfare never puts force at the center: His works focus more on alternatives to battle, such as stratagem, delay, the use of spies, the making and keeping of alliances, the uses of deceit and a willingness to submit, at least temporarily, to more powerful foes. Indeed, the concept of force ("li" in Chinese) appears only nine times in thirteen chapters of the test. It is a reflection of the limited conditions of warfare in China at the time (force was then in fact of limited utility). This also reflects Sun Tzu's conviction that victory and defeat are fundamentally psychological states.

Operationally, Sun Tzu lays special stress on the use of psychological method. His exploitation in psychological domain is based on superior knowledge of the enemy, so in his book he encourages the use of spies. He mentioned the concept of kueitao (means "deception" or "unconventional means"). Thus Sun Tzu commends operations that will rob the enemy of their morale, such as splitting alliances, evading battle, attacking by surprise; he warns that it is not advisable to undermine one's own society by getting engaged in protracted wars, such as besieging a walled city, which usually leads to attrition. He gives examples of operations with purely psychological purpose, such as setting fires, which Sun Tzu discusses in effect as a terror weapon. Excellent leaders knows the art of turning opposing plans to his own advantages by "attacking the enemy's strategy" which at its best yields victory without fighting. This concept is well mastered by modern war commanders and was used in World War Two.

Of course, we should notice that Sun Tzu writes about warfare within a single culture, wherein secret agents are difficult to detect and enemy thought processes differ little from one's own. In his time and within his horizon, all states rise from the same Chinese culture and people bear similar facial features. One might question therefore the relevance of Sun Tzu in modern conditions, in which states are robust and force abundantly available, and in wars between nations, in which ethnic differences make spying difficult and enemy thought processes difficult to assess.

Kueitao (诡道): In Sun Tzu's book, this is an important concept that he creatively mentioned in the opening chapter. It is translated as deception. It appears in Sun Tzu's famous sentence "All warfare is based on deception", which is frequently quoted by people afterward. Sun Tzu further explains the sentence: "Hence, when able to attack, we must seem unable, when using our forces, we must seem inactive, when we are near, we must make the enemy believe we are far away, when far away, we must make the enemy believe we are near."

Culture Notes

1. 孙子生活的时期，是中国历史上战争最为频繁的时期。孙子目睹了战争对国家和人民的伤害，因此强调君主发动战争一定要谨慎，即"慎战"思想。难能可贵的是，作为军事家，孙子并不把战争作为解决问题的首要手段，他主张通过谋略或者外交手段达到"不战而屈人之兵"的目的。这些手段行不通的时候，最后的迫不得已的手段才是战争。这反映出他的保国爱民的思想，因为战争消耗的是国力，是民力，是百姓的生命。

2. 唐太宗李世民曾经评论"不战而屈人之兵"思想为"至精至微，聪明睿智，神武不杀"。后人将"不战而屈人之兵"这句话总结为孙子的"全胜"思想。所谓全胜，不是指彻底获胜，而是指在不破坏敌军城池与百姓以及财产的情况下，通过非战争手段，让敌军顺服。这是一种具有高度智慧的理性思想，它符合利益最大化原则。

New Words

tactician	n.	people skilful at choosing the best methods in order to achieve what they want	战术家
attendant	adj.	you use attendant to describe something that results from a thing already mentioned or that is connected with it	随之而产生的
bankruptcy	n.	the state of being bankrupt	破产，倒闭
disintegration	n.	a decomposed state	瓦解；崩溃
squander	v.	waste	挥霍，浪费
chaos	n.	a state of complete disorder and confusion	混乱，紊乱
alternative	n.	if one thing is an alternative to another, the first can be found, used, or done instead of the second	可供选择的事物
alliance	n.	a group of countries or political parties that are formally united and working together because they have similar aims	结盟，同盟
submit	v.	yield to the control of another	顺从，服从
conviction	n.	an unshakable belief in something without need for proof or evidence	信念
domain	n.	a particular environment or walk of life	领域
besiege	vt.	surround so as to force to give up	包围

| attrition | n. | erosion by friction | 消耗；消磨 |
| robust | adj. | physically strong | 强健的；结实的 |

I. Simple Selection

1. According to Sun Tzu, a ruler should never start a war unless he has carefully calculated the circumstance and _____.
   A. has enough soldiers B. is sure of the positive outcomes
   C. has enough weapons D. known the enemy

2. According to Sun Tzu, a ruler should hold dear of soldiers' lives and try his utmost to maintain _____ of his state.
   A. the reputation B. the number of soldiers
   C. the power D. number of chariots

3. Sun Tzu urges that force _____.
   A. be used whenever it is needed
   B. not be squandered
   C. be the best way to solve problem
   D. never be used

4. Sun Tzu sees war as a matter of _____.
   A. destroying the enemy materially
   B. destroying the enemy physically
   C. unsettling the enemy psychologically
   D. unsettling the enemy physically

5. The best result of a conflict is breaking the enemy's resistance _____.
   A. with fighting B. with spy
   C. with advanced weapons D. without fighting

II. Multiple Choice

1. Sun Tzu's teachings and philosophies were used in _____.
   A. the Korean War B. the Vietnam War
   C. World War Two D. the first Gulf War

2. _____ are the distinguishing features of Sun Tzu's military thinking.
   A. Raging a war is a very grave matter
   B. Force is the first way to solve conflict
   C. A ruler should hold dear of soldiers' lives and the power of his state
   D. Breaking the enemy's resistance without fighting

3. Sun Tzu's works focus more on alternatives to battle, such as _____, and so on.
   A. stratagem   B. delay
   C. the use of spies   D. making and keeping of alliances

4. Sun Tzu commends operations that will rob the enemy of their morale, such as_____.
   A. splitting alliances   B. evading battle
   C. attacking by surprise   D. submitting to the enemy

III. True or False

1. Sun Tzu's teachings and strategies are used in military domain only.
2. Sun Tzu supposes that combat can always be eliminated.
3. Sun Tzu urges force not be squandered, but conserved carefully and used only when it may have decisive impact.
4. A willingness to submit, at least temporarily, to more powerful foes is one of alternatives to battle.
5. Operationally, Sun Tzu lays special stress on the use of psychological method.

IV. Fill in the Blanks

1. It is Sun Tzu's conviction that victory and defeat are fundamentally_____states.
2. Sun Tzu's exploitation in psychological domain is based on superior knowledge of the_____.
3. Sun Tzu warns that it is not advisable to undermine one's own society by getting engaged in _____, such as besieging a walled city.
4. He gives examples of operations with purely psychological purpose, such as setting fires, which Sun Tzu discusses in effect as _____.
5. Excellent leaders knows the art of turning opposing plans to his own advantages by "_____" which at its best yields victory without _____.

V. Matching

1. 孙子曰：凡治众如治寡，分数是也。
2. 斗众如斗寡，形名是也。
3. 军争之难者，以迂为直，以患为利。
4. 三军可夺气，将军可夺心。
5. 是故朝气锐，昼气惰，暮气归。
6. 善用兵者，避其锐气，击其惰归，此治气者也。
7. 以治待乱，以静待哗，此治心者也。
8. 以近待远，以佚待劳，以饱待饥，此治力者也。

A. Now a soldier's spirit is keenest in the morning; by noonday it has begun to flag; and in the evening, his mind is bent only on returning to camp.

B. A clever general, therefore, avoids an army when its spirit is keen, but attacks it when it is sluggish and inclined to return. This is the art of studying moods.

C. Fighting with a large army under your command is nowise different from fighting with a small one: it is merely a question of instituting signs and signals.

D. A whole army may be robbed of its spirit; a commander-in-chief may be robbed of his presence of mind.

E. The difficulty of tactical maneuvering consists in turning the devious into the direct, and misfortune into gain.

F. Disciplined and calm, to await the appearance of disorder and hubbub amongst the enemy-this is the art of retaining self-possession.

G. Sun Tzu said: The control of a large force is the same principle as the control of a few men: it is merely a question of dividing up their numbers.

H. To be near the goal while the enemy is still far from it, to wait at ease while the enemy is toiling and struggling, to be well-fed while the enemy is famished-this is the art of husbanding one's strength.

Misattribution between *The Art of War* and *The Thirty-Six Stratagems*

The Art of War presents a philosophy of war for managing conflicts and winning battles. It is accepted as a masterpiece on strategy and has been frequently cited and referred to by generals and theorists since it was first published, translated, and distributed internationally. But some famous quotes about military are misattributed to it, while they are actually from *The Thirty-Six Stratagems*. What's worse is that some even think *The Art of War* is another name for *The Thirty-Six Stratagems*, because both of them are results of ancient Chinese wisdom.

The Thirty-Six Stratagems are the intelligence passed on through generations from the ancestors of China. *The Thirty-Six Stratagems* have variably been attributed to Sun Tzu from the Spring and Autumn period of China, or Zhuge Liang of the Three Kingdoms period, but neither are regarded as the true author by historians. Instead, the prevailing view is that *The Thirty-Six Stratagems* may have originated in both written and oral history, with many different versions compiled by different authors throughout Chinese history. Some stratagems reference occurrences in the time of Sun Bin, approx. 150 years after Sun Wu's death.

The Thirty-Six Stratagems are divided into a preface, six chapters containing six stratagems each, and an afterword that was incomplete with missing text. The first three chapters generally describe tactics for use in advantageous situations, whereas the last three chapters contain stratagems that are more suitable for disadvantageous situations. The original text of *The Thirty-Six Stratagems* has a laconic style that is common to Classical Chinese.

Let's take the most frequently misattributed ones as examples:

Besiege Wèi to rescue Zhào: Wèi and Zhào were states' names. When the enemy is too strong to be attacked directly, then attack something he holds dear. Know that he cannot be superior in all things. Somewhere there is a gap in the armor, a weakness that can be attacked instead. The idea here is to avoid a head-on battle with a strong enemy, and instead strike at his weakness elsewhere. This will force the strong enemy to retreat in order to support his weakness. Battling against the now tired and low-morale enemy will give a much higher chance of success.

Make a sound in the east, then strike in the west: In any battle the element of surprise can provide an overwhelming advantage. Even when face to face with an enemy, surprise can still be employed by attacking where he least expects it. To do this you must create an expectation in the enemy's mind through the use of a feint. The idea here is to get the enemy to focus his forces in a location, and then attack elsewhere which would be weakly defended.

Sacrifice the plum tree to preserve the peach tree: There are circumstances in which you must sacrifice short-term objectives in order to gain the long-term goal. This is the scapegoat strategy whereby someone else suffers the consequences so that the rest do not.

Stomp the grass to scare the snake: Do something unaimed, but spectacular ("hitting the grass") to provoke a response of the enemy ("startle the snake"), thereby giving away his plans or position, or just taunt him. Do something unusual, strange, and unexpected as this will arouse the enemy's suspicion and disrupt his thinking. More widely used as "Do not startle the snake by hitting the grass". An imprudent act will give your position or intentions away to the enemy.

In order to capture, one must let loose: Cornered prey will often mount a final desperate attack. To prevent this you let the enemy believe he still has a chance for freedom. His will to fight is thus dampened by his desire to escape. When in the end the freedom is proven a falsehood, the enemy's morale will be defeated and he will surrender without a fight.

Let the enemy's own spy sow discord in the enemy camp: Undermine your enemy's ability to fight by secretly causing discord between him and his friends, allies, advisors, family, commanders, soldiers, and population. While he is preoccupied settling internal disputes, his ability to attack or defend is compromised.

If all else fails, retreat: If it becomes obvious that your current course of action will lead to defeat, then retreat and regroup. When your side is losing, there are only three choices remaining: surrender, compromise, or escape. Surrender is complete defeat, compromise is half defeat, but escape is not defeat. As long as you are not defeated, you still have a chance. This is the most famous of the stratagems, immortalized in the form of a Chinese idiom: "Of the Thirty-Six Stratagems, fleeing is best".

All the six stratagems mentioned above are from the famous *The Thirty-Six Stratagems*. Some of them echo Sun Tzu's concept of deception, some of them share the same language style with *The Art of War*, hence, misattribution occurred.

(*Thirty-Six Stratagems*)
1. crossing the sea under camouflage

2. besieging Wèi to rescue Zhào
3. killing someone with a borrowed knife
4. waiting at one's ease for the exhausted enemy
5. plundering a burning house
6. make a sound in the east, then strike in the west
7. creating something out of nothing
8. advancing secretly by an unknown path
9. watching a fire from the other side of the river
10. covering the dagger with a smile
11. palming off substitute for the real thing
12. picking up something in passing
13. beating the grass to frighten the snake
14. resurrecting a dead soul by borrowing a corpse
15. luring the tiger out of his den
16. in order to capture, one must let loose
17. giving the enemy something to induce him to lose more valuable things
18. capturing the ringleader first in order to capture all the followers
19. extracting the firewood from under the cauldron
20. muddling the water to catch the fish; fishing in troubled waters
21. slipping away by casting off a cloak; getting away like the cicada sloughing its skin
22. catching the thief by closing / blocking his escape route
23. befriending the distant enemy while attacking a nearby enemy
24. attacking the enemy by passing through a common neighbor
25. stealing the beams and pillars and replacing them with rotten timbers
26. reviling/ abusing the locust tree while pointing to the mulberry
27. feigning madness without becoming insane
28. removing the ladder after the enemy has climbed up the roof
29. putting artificial flowers on trees
30. turning from the guest into the host
31. using seductive women to corrupt the enemy
32. presenting a bold front to conceal unpreparedness
33. letting the enemy's own spy sow discord in the enemy camp
34. deceiving the enemy by torturing one's own man
35. coordinating one stratagem with another
36. if all else fails, retreat; decamping being the best; running away as the best choice

Culture Notes

《三十六计》或称三十六策，是指中国古代三十六个兵法策略，语源于南北朝，成书于明清。它是根据中国古代军事思想和丰富的斗争经验总结而成的兵书，是中华民族悠久非物质文化遗产之一。原书按计名排列，共分六套，即胜战计、敌战计、攻战计、混战计、并战计、败战计。前三套是处于优势所用之计，后三套是处于劣势所用之计。每套各包含六计，总共三十六计。其中每计名称后的解说，均系依据《易经》中的阴阳变化之理及古代兵家刚柔、奇正、攻防、彼己、虚实、主客等对立关系相互转化的思想推演而成，含有朴素的军事辩证法的因素。解说后的按语，多引证宋代以前的战例和孙武、吴起、尉缭子等兵家的精辟语句。全书还有总说和跋。

第一套胜战计，包括瞒天过海，围魏救赵，借刀杀人，声东击西，趁火打劫，以逸待劳。第二套敌战计，包括无中生有，暗度陈仓，隔岸观火，笑里藏刀，顺手牵羊，李代桃僵。第三套攻战计，包括打草惊蛇，借尸还魂，调虎离山，欲擒故纵，擒贼擒王，抛砖引玉。第四套混战计，包括釜底抽薪，浑水摸鱼，金蝉脱壳，关门捉贼，远交近攻，假道伐虢。第五套并战计，包括偷梁换柱，指桑骂槐，假痴不癫，上屋抽梯，树上开花，反客为主。第六套败战计，包括美人计，空城计，反间计，苦肉计，连环计，走为上。

New Words

misattribution	n.	assigning some quality or character to a person or thing wrongly	错误归属
stratagem	n.	an elaborate or deceitful scheme contrived to deceive or evade	诡计，计谋
prevailing	adj.	most frequent or common	普遍的；盛行的
overwhelming	adj.	so strong as to be irresistible	势不可挡的，压倒一切的
scapegoat	n.	someone punished for the errors of others	替罪羊
stomp	v.	walk heavily	踩脚，践踏
taunt	vt.	harass with persistent criticism or carping	嘲笑，奚落
imprudent	adj.	Not wise or cautious	不明智的，不谨慎的
preoccupied	adj.	deeply absorbed in thought	全神贯注的，入神的
discord	n.	lack of agreement or harmony	不和
compromise	v.	settle by concession	折中解决；妥协，退让
surrender	vi.	a verbal act of admitting defeat	投降；屈服
immortalize	vt.	make famous for ever	使永恒；使不灭

Exercises

I. Simple Selection

1. The Thirty-Six Stratagems are divided into a preface, _____ chapters containing _____ stratagems each.

    A. 6, 6   B. 4,9   C. 3,12c   D. 9,4

2. The first three chapters generally describe tactics for use in _____ situations, whereas the last three chapters contain stratagems that are more suitable for _____ situations.

    A. disadvantageous, advantageous   B. advantageous, disadvantageous

    C. dilemma, advantageous   D. disadvantageous, dilemma

3. In "Besiege Wèi to rescue Zhào", Wèi and Zhào were _____ names.

    A. states'   B. generals'   C. cities'   D. rulers'

4. In _____, the idea is to avoid a head-on battle with a strong enemy, and instead strike at his weakness elsewhere.

    A. "make a sound in the east, then strike in the west"

    B. "in order to capture, one must let loose"

    C. "if all else fails, retreat"

    D. Besiege Wèi to rescue Zhào

5. In _____ the idea, is to get the enemy to focus his forces in a location, and then attack elsewhere which would be weakly defended.

    A. "sacrifice the plum tree to preserve the peach tree"

    B. "killing someone with a borrowed knife"

    C. "make a sound in the east, then strike in the west"

    D. "In order to capture, one must let loose"

6. _____ warns people that an imprudent act will give your position or intentions away to the enemy.

    A. Covering the dagger with a smile

    B. Let the enemy's own spy sow discord in the enemy camp

    C. Stomp the grass to scare the snake

    D. Advancing secretly by an unknown path

7. _____ means that cornered prey will often mount a final desperate attack, and to prevent this you let the enemy believe he still has a chance for freedom.

    A. Besiege Wèi to rescue Zhào   B. In order to capture, one must let loose

    C. Picking up something in passing   D. Feigning madness without becoming insane

8. _____ tells that if it becomes obvious that your current course of action will lead to defeat, then retreat and regroup.

    A. If all else fails, retreat

    B. In order to capture, one must let loose

    C. Extracting the firewood from under the cauldron

D. Putting artificial flowers on trees

II. True or False

1. Some famous quotes about military are misattributed to *The Art of War*, while they are actually from *The Thirty-Six Stratagems*.

2. *The Art of War* is another name for *The Thirty-Six Stratagems*.

3. *The Thirty-Six Stratagems* may have many different versions compiled by different authors throughout Chinese history.

4. Some stratagems reference occurrences in the time of Sun Bin, approximately 150 years after Sun Wu's death.

5. The original text of *the Thirty-Six Stratagems* has a tedious style that is common to Classical Chinese.

III. Fill in the Blanks

1. "Sacrifice the plum tree to preserve the peach tree" means there are circumstances in which you must sacrifice _____ in order to gain the long-term goal.

2. "In order to capture, one must let loose " argues that when in the end the freedom is proven a falsehood, the enemy's morale will be defeated and he will_____.

3. When your side is losing, there are only three choices remaining: _____, _____, or _____.

4. When your side is losing, _____ is complete defeat, _____ is half defeat, but _____ is not defeat.

IV. Matching

1. killing someone with a borrowed knife
2. make a sound in the east, then strike in the west
3. creating something out of nothing
4. covering the dagger with a smile
5. picking up something in passing
6. in order to capture, one must let loose
7. muddling the water to catch the fish
8. catching the thief by closing
9. using seductive women to corrupt the enemy
10. deceiving the enemy by torturing one's own man

 A. 无中生有 B. 声东击西 C. 笑里藏刀 D. 美人计 E. 借刀杀人
 F. 浑水摸鱼 G. 顺手牵羊 H. 苦肉计 I. 欲擒故纵 J. 关门捉贼

3.5 Historicity

Some topics about *The Art of War* and Sun Wu have long been controversial among historians.

First, the state where Sun Wu was born. The oldest available sources disagree as to where Sun Tzu was born. The Spring and Autumn Annals states that Sun Tzu was born in Qi, while Sima Qian's later *Records of the Grand Historian* (*Shiji*《史记》) states that Sun Tzu was a native of Wu. Both sources agree that Sun Tzu was born in the late Spring and Autumn period and that he was active as a general and strategist, serving King Holu of Wu in the late sixth century BC, beginning around 512 BC. Sun Tzu's victories then inspired him to write *The Art of War*. *The Art of War* was one of the most widely read military treatises in the subsequent Warring States period, a time of constant war among seven ancient Chinese states – Zhao, Qi, Qin, Chu, Han, Wei, and Yan – who fought to control the vast expanse of fertile territory in Eastern China.

Second, the existence of Sun Wu. Beginning around the 12th century, some scholars began to doubt the historical existence of Sun Tzu, primarily on the grounds that he is not mentioned in the historical classic *The Commentary of Zuo* (*Zuo Zhuan*《左传》), which mentions most of the notable figures from the Spring and Autumn period. The only historical battle attributed to Sun Tzu, the Battle of Boju, has no record of him fighting in that battle.

The name "Sun Wu" (孙武) does not appear in any text prior to the *Records of the Grand Historian* (*Shiji*), and has been suspected to be a made-up descriptive cognomen. The name "Sun Wu" does appear in later sources such as the *Wu Yue Chunqiu*, but they were written centuries after Sun Tzu's era.

Third, the authorship. Skeptics cite possible historical inaccuracies and anachronisms in the text, and that the book was actually a compilation from different authors and military strategists. Attribution of the authorship of *The Art of War* varies among scholars and has included people including Sun Tzu; Chu scholar Wu Zixu; an anonymous author; a school of theorists in Qi or Wu; Sun Bin. Unlike Sun Wu, Sun Bin appears to have been an actual person who was a genuine authority on military matters, and may have been the inspiration for the creation of the historical figure "Sun Tzu" through a form of euhemerism. Sun Bin was a military strategist born in what was then Juancheng of Qi State (now Yanggu county, Liaocheng, Shandong Province). He was considered by many scholars as one of the most outstanding military strategists and politicians of his time. Though, most people believe his ancestor to be Sun Tzu.

Fourth, Sun Wu and Sun Bin. Sun Tzu's historicity is uncertain. The Han dynasty historian Sima Qian and other traditional Chinese historians placed him as a minister to King Holu of Wu and dated his lifetime to 544 BC—496 BC Modern scholars accepting his historicity place the extant text of *The Art of War* in the later *Warring States period* based on its style of composition and its descriptions of warfare. Traditional accounts state that the general's descendant Sun Bin wrote a treatise on military tactics, also titled *The Art of War*. Since Sun Wu and Sun Bin could both be referred to as Sun Tzu in classical Chinese texts, some historians believed them identical. What is even more confusing is that there were two texts that could have been referred to as "Sun's Art of War", a concise one and an extended one.

Luckily, the rediscovery of Sun Bin's treatise in 1972 solved some of the confusion. In 1972, the Yinqueshan Han slips were discovered in two Han dynasty (206 BC—220 AD) tombs near the city of Linyi in Shandong Province. Among the many bamboo slip writings contained in the tombs, which had been sealed around 134 and 118 BC, respectively were two separate texts, one attributed to "Sun Tzu", corresponding to the received text, and another attributed to Sun Bin, which explains and expands upon the earlier The Art of War by Sun Tzu. The Sun Bin text's material overlaps with much of the "Sun Tzu" text, and the two may be "a single, continuously developing intellectual tradition united under the Sun name". This discovery showed that much of the historical confusion was due to the fact that there were two texts that could have been referred to as "Master Sun's Art of War", not one. The content of the earlier text is about one-third of the chapters of the modern *The Art of War*, and their text matches very closely.

There are numerous theories concerning when the text was completed and concerning the identity of the author or authors, but archeological recoveries show *The Art of War* had taken roughly its current form by at least the early Han. Because it is impossible to prove definitively when *The Art of War* was completed before this date, the differing theories concerning the work's date of completion are unlikely to be completely resolved. But it is now generally accepted that the earlier The Art of War was completed sometime between 500 and 430 BC by Sun Tzu, and the later edition was by Sun Bin.

1. Sima Qian (ca. 145 or 135 BC—86 BC), also called Ssu-ma Ch'ien, was a Prefect of the Grand Scribes (太史公) of the Han Dynasty. He is regarded as the father of Chinese historiography because of his highly praised work, *Records of the Grand Historian* (史记), a "Jizhuanti" style general history of China covering more than two thousand years from the Yellow Emperor to Emperor Han Wudi (汉武帝). His definitive work laid the foundation for later Chinese historiography.

2. *The Records of the Grand Historian*, also known by its Chinese name *Shiji*, is a monumental history of ancient China and the world finished around 94 BC by the Han dynasty official Sima Qian after having been started by his father, Sima Tan, Grand Astrologer to the imperial court. The work covers the world as it was then known to the Chinese and a 2500-year period from the age of the legendary Yellow Emperor to the reign of Emperor Wu of Han in the author's own time. The Records has been called a "foundational text in Chinese civilization".

3. Sun Bin received his name in ancient historical books because he suffered from a "Bin" (kneecap) corporal punishment in ancient China. The punishment involved the removal of one's kneecaps.

Culture Notes

1. 从汉代至唐代，对《孙子兵法》的作者一直没有人提出异议，但宋代以后，开始有人对这部兵书及其作者产生诸多疑问，大致有以下几种论断：其一，支持《史记》中的记载，认为孙武、孙膑各有其人，并分别著有"兵法"流传于世。其二，认为历史上并无孙武其人，只不过是一位战国时期"山林处士"所作的"兵法"而已，以其为吴王所用乃是夸大之词。其三，不否认历史上有孙武这个人，但《孙子兵法》不是孙武自己编著的，而为后世之人伪托"孙武"之名而作。其四，《孙子兵法》的作者是孙膑，孙武和孙膑是同一个人，"武"是其名，"膑"是绰号。其五，历史上有孙武和孙膑这两个人，但现存的《孙子兵法》作者是孙膑。其六，认为《孙子兵法》是三国的曹操所著，"兵法"中提到的"孙子"是春秋时期的伍子胥。直到1972年临沂银雀山竹简出土之前，各方各执一词，争论不休，甚至还有外国学者也参与其中。

临沂汉简本《孙子兵法》和《孙膑兵法》同时问世，使得这一场旷日持久的历史大讨论戛然而止，历史原貌不辨自明。临沂汉简的出土，向世人昭示，孙武和孙膑不但是历史上真实的两位人物，而且分别有"兵书"流传于世，同时也证明了《史记》《汉书》等早期文献记载的真实性。

2. 银雀山竹简1972年发掘出土于山东临沂银雀山两座汉墓中。简文书体为早期隶书，写于公元前140—前118年（西汉文景时期至武帝初期）。银雀山汉墓竹简共计有完整简、残简4942简，此外还有数千残片。其内容包括《孙子兵法》《孙膑兵法》《六韬》《尉缭子》《晏子》《守法守令十三篇》《元光元年历谱》等先秦古籍及古佚书。这些古籍均为西汉时手书，是较早的写本。对于研究中国历史、哲学、古代兵法、历法、古文字学、简册制度和书法艺术等方面，都提供了可贵的资料。

New Words

controversial	adj.	as the subject of intense public argument, disagreement, or disapproval	有争议的，引起争议的
subsequent	adj.	following in time or order	后来的；随后的
fertile	adj.	capable of reproducing	肥沃的；可繁殖的；想象力丰富的
notable	adj.	worthy of notice	值得注意的；显著的
prior	adj.	earlier in time	优先的；占先的；在…之前
anachronism	n.	something located at a time when it could not have existed or occurred	不合时代的事

historicity	n.	existence in history	史实性，确有其事
descendant	n.	Someone's descendants are the people in later generations who are related to them	后代；后裔
rediscovery	n.	he act of discovering again	重新发现

Exercises

I. Simple Selection

1. *Records of the Grand Historian* (*Shiji*) states that Sun Tzu was a native of _____.

    A. Qi   B. Wu   C. Lu   D. Yan

2. Scholars began to doubt the historical existence of Sun Tzu, primarily on the grounds that he is not mentioned in the historical classic _____ which mentions most of the notable figures from the Spring and Autumn period.

    A. *Records of the Grand Historian*
    B. *The Commentary of Zuo* (*Zuo Zhuan*)
    C. *Spring and Autumn Annals*
    D. *The Art of War*

3. The name "Sun Wu" does not appear in any text prior to _____.

    A. *Records of the Grand Historian*
    B. *The Commentary of Zuo* (*Zuo Zhuan*)
    C. *Spring and Autumn Annals*
    D. *The Art of War*

4. Sun Bin was a military strategist born in what was then Juancheng of _____.

    A. Wu   B. Lu   C. Yan   D. Qi State

5. In 1972, the Yinqueshan Han slips were discovered in two _____ dynasty tombs near the city of _____ in _____ Province.

    A. Tang; Liaocheng, Shandong   B. Tang; Linyi; Shandong
    C. Han; Linyi; Shandong   D. Han Liaocheng, Shandong

II. Multiple Choice

1. The name Sun Wu appears in _____.

    A. *Spring and Autumn Annals*
    B. *Wu Yue Chunqiu*
    C. *Records of the Grand Historian* (*Shiji*)
    D. *The Art of War*

2. Attribution of the authorship of *The Art of War* varies among scholars and has included _____.

A. Chu scholar Wu Zixu　　　　　B. an anonymous author
C. a school of theorists in Qi or Wu　　D. Sun Bin

3. The Yinqueshan Han slips contained two separate texts attributed to _____.
A. Sun Tzu　　B. Wu Zixu　　C. Sun Bin　　D. Sun Tzu only

III. True or False

1. The oldest available sources disagree as to where Sun Tzu was born.

2. Sun Tzu was born in the late Spring and Autumn period .

3. Spring and Autumn Annals and the Records of the Grand Historian (*Shiji*) disagree as whether Sun Tzu was a general and strategist, serving King Holu of Wu .

4. *The Spring and Autumn Annals* states that Sun Tzu was a native of Wu.

5. *The Commentary of Zuo* (*Zuo Zhuan*) has record of Sun Tzu fighting in that battle of Boju .

6. The name Sun Wu does appear in later sources such as the *Wu Yue Chunqiu*.

7. The name Sun Wu appears in the *Records of the Grand Historian* (*Shiji*).

8. Sun Bin appears to have been an actual person.

IV. Fill in the Blanks

1. _____, a time of constant war among seven ancient Chinese states – Zhao, Qi, Qin, Chu, Han, Wei, and Yan.

2. Beginning around _____ century, some scholars began to doubt the historical existence of Sun Tzu.

3. In the *Yinqueshan Han slips*, the content of the earlier text is about _____ of the chapters of the modern *The Art of War*, and their text matches very closely.

4. archeological recoveries show The Art of War had taken roughly its current form by at least the early _____.

5. It is now generally accepted that the earlier *The Art of War* was completed sometime between 500 and 430 BC by _____, and the later edition was by _____.

V. Matching

1. 夫惟无虑而易敌者，必擒于人。
2. 令素行以教其民，则民服。
3. 投之亡地然后存，陷之死地然后生。
4. 夫地形者，兵之助也。
5. 知彼知己，胜乃不殆。
6. 知天知地，胜乃不穷。
7. 兵之情主速，乘人之不及。
8. 故明君慎之，良将警之。

A. If in training soldiers commands are habitually enforced, the army will be well-disciplined.

B. If you know Heaven and know Earth, you may make your victory complete.

C. The natural formation of the country is the soldier's best ally.

D. Rapidity is the essence of war: take advantage of the enemy's uneasiness.

E. Place your army in deadly peril and it will survive; plunge it into desperate straits, and it will come off in safety.

F. If you know the enemy and know yourself, your victory will not stand in doubt;

G. He who exercises no forethought but makes light of his opponents is sure to be captured by them.

H. Hence the enlightened ruler is heedful, and the good general full of caution.

Unit 4   The Great Wall

In the north of China, there lies a long ancient wall. It was a wall like no other on earth-then or now. It has earned its name: the Great Wall. It is the largest structure that humans have ever made! It is impossible to give its exact length, that's because the Great Wall wasn't built at one time. It's a series of walls constructed over two thousand years, starting in ancient times. This ancient military fortification rises and falls with the contours of the terrain, climbing over mountains and passing through grasslands. This ancient wall experienced the vicissitudes of dynasties. The Great Wall witnessed the conflict and reconciliation between the nomadic herdsmen and the sedentary farming peoples. Amidst the billowing dust raised by the horses' hoofs and chariots, the Great Wall saw the dawn of human civilization. The Great Wall remains to this day, it heard generation after generation of the Chinese people chant in defense and search of their homes.

More than 2000 years ago, the emperor of China had workers start building a wall. Dynasty after dynasty, emperors built new walls and linked them to old ones. Some walls decayed and fell apart, so the wall we see today is but one tenth of the total length of the walls ever constructed over succeeding dynasties of China. Traditionally known as the "Long Wall of Ten Thousand Li", the massive structure takes advantage of the natural terrain for defensive purposes following the highest points and clinging to ridges. All these breathtaking fortifications, together with mountain passes, castle gates, and thousands of watch towers and signal beacons, wind their ways like a majestic dragon. With the changes of history and progress of society, the Wall today is no longer used for defensive purposes. As the largest building project ever carried out by the ancient Chinese working people, historians and amateurs have never stopped exploring the cultural and economic values inherent in this monument. Sculptors, painters and musicians are inspired to compose their masterpieces, children are interested in the folklore and ballads concerned with the Wall, architects and archaeologists are looking for clues about the ancient construction and tourists are travelling far and wide from all around the world to catch a glimpse of the human wonder. All in all, people combine the protection, exploration and study of the Great Wall Culture with the tourism development.

4.1 Timeline of the Great Wall

1046—771 BC	Continuous forts were erected to defend against Xianyun tribe.
221—207 BC	The Southern Great Wall of Qin Dynasty ran from Lintao, Min County, Gansu Province, and ended at the southern bank of the Yellow River. The Northern Wall started from Lang Mountain in the west and ended at the estuary of Qingchuan River.
202 BC—220	Great Wall of Han Dynasty spanned over north China, extending from Liaoning in the east to Lop Nur, Xinjiang in the west.
265—420	Great Wall of the Jin Dynasty traverses from today's Yangyuan County in Hubei Province to Tateishi of North Korea.
420—589	After restoring the Northern Qi Wall, the Northern Zhou Great Wall stretched from Shanhai Pass in the east to Yanmen Pass in the west.
589—618	The Wall ran from Shanhai Pass in the east to Gansu Province in the west.
618—907	It stretched from Pingcheng in modern Heshun County in Shanxi to Lukou in modern Qixian County in Shanxi.
907—1125	The Wall traversed the Inner Mongolia in China and finally reached

	Mongolia via Russia. There is also a section in today's Dalian, Liaoning that was built to defend against the neighboring Bohai Kingdom.
960—1279	To stop the incursions of Liao, Western Xia, and Jin Dynasties, the Song built a comprehensive defensive system, including forts, water walls, and stone walls.
1368—1644	The Ming Great Wall ran from Hushan by the Yalu River in the east, and ended at Jiayu Pass in China's west Gansu Province.
1644—1911	It was built in most provinces to the north of Huaihe River, especially by the Yellow River.
1984	The communist government began restoring the Great Wall.
1987	UNESCO listed the Great Wall a World Heritage Site.

The construction of the Great Wall can be traced back to the 7th century BC. According to historical records, the Great Wall of Qi was built in the Spring and Autumn period, more than 2500 years ago. That's more than 200 years before the 79-kilometer long Athens barrier built by Europeans in 459 BC and more than 400 years earlier than the Great Wall of Qin, which is called "the father of the Great Wall of China" or "the most bulwark in the world". It is the oldest military defense project.

Qi built the Great Wall with its historical origins. In the Spring and Autumn period, the emperors fought against each other. Some used rivers to defend the levees, and others placed obstacles along the mountains to ensure the stability of their states. The purpose of the war they waged is to preserve itself, destroy the enemy, expand its territory and strengthen its power. And the constant war between states pressed for the need to strengthen their fortifications. In the long and frequent war practices, Qi State got inspiration from the function of defending against the enemy, germinating the idea that building is not the closed circle of the city walls. They built tall rammed earth walls on the ground that had nothing to do with the obstruction of water, but to defend the enemy. Qi Great Wall was a large-scale project covering more than a thousand miles. It was not capable of being completed by one king in a lifetime relying completely on manpower. Starting from Qi Huangong of the Spring and Autumn period, with the efforts of several successive dynasties, the Qi Great Wall (was) completed in the reign of Qi Xuanwang of the Warring States, spanning more than 260 years.

In 221 BC, Qin Shi Huang conquered the other six rival states and became the first emperor of a unified China. To bring the minority areas such as the invading nomadic Huns in the north under his rule, also to ensure the safety of his empire and the continuity of production, he restored and extended the existing defensive walls. The resulting fortification stretched all the way from Lintao, Min County, Gansu Province in the west to Liaoning Province in the east, as long as 10000 Chinese *Li*. Historians call these sections the "Qin Wall".

Ever since Qin Shi Huang, almost all successive dynasties of the central plains had either repaired, rebuilt or expanded the wall, but no other dynasty throughout the Chinese history spent longer time repairing and building the Wall than the Han. To protect the Silk Road, also to strengthen their rule over the Hexi Corridor and North China, the ruling emperors ordered the construction of a complete defensive wall system. 10 years of hard labor extended the Wall of Han to several thousand kilometers. Today ruins of the beacons and debris of the Han Wall, the best preserved and most majestic remains of the Wall of Han, are still discernable at Wushaoling Mountain west of the Yellow River and Yumen Pass northwest of Dunhuang.

At their best times, the walls in the Han, Jin and Ming Dynasties ran as long as 5000 km to 10000 km respectively. It is fair to say that from the Spring and Autumn Period all the way down to the Qing Dynasty, the Great Wall experienced repeated repairs and extensions for over two thousand years. Of all these constructions, the wall built during the Ming Dynasty, from Shanhai Pass in the east to Jiayu Pass in the west, was commonly regarded as the best preserved sections. The Ming Wall was built under the most difficult conditions, across some of the most dangerous terrains, but with the most popular tourist attractions as well.

Notes

1. Qin Shi Huang: The founder of the Qin Dynasty and was the first emperor of a unified China. As a leader, he was a genius. Many of his reforms last to this day. As a ruler, he was a tyrant, cruel and unforgiving. During his reign, his generals greatly expanded the size of the Chinese state. He also created the world's first central government. His achievements made himself become one of the most respected and influential individuals in world's history, and a legacy among the Chinese.

2. The Qin Dynasty: Qin was the first dynasty of Imperial China, lasting from 221 to 206 BC. Named for its heartland in Qin state, the dynasty was founded by Qin Shi Huang, the First Emperor of Qin. The strength of the Qin state was greatly increased by the Legalist reforms of Shang Yang in the 4th century BC, during the Warring States period. In the mid and late 3rd century BC, the Qin state carried out a series of swift conquests, first ending the powerless Zhou dynasty, and eventually conquering the other six of the Seven Warring States. Its 15 years was the shortest major dynasty in Chinese history, consisting of only two emperors, but inaugurated an imperial system that lasted, with interruption and adaptation, until 1912.

Culture Notes

长城：又称万里长城，是中国古代用以限隔敌骑的行动军事防御工程，它的城墙、关隘、堡寨、敌台，见证了刀光剑影与炮火连天的岁月；同时，长城地处我国传统的农耕文化与游牧文化交错带，因此又成为一条经济、民族、文化的分界线。长城修筑的历史可上溯到西周时期。春秋战国时期列国争霸，互相防守，长城修筑进入第一个高潮，但此时修筑的长度都比较短。秦灭六国统一天下后，秦始皇连接和修缮战国长城，始有万里长城之称。明朝是最后一个大修长城的朝代，今天人们所看到的长城多是此时修筑。

长城资源主要分布在河北、北京、天津、山西、陕西、甘肃、内蒙古、黑龙江、吉林、辽宁、山东、河南、青海、宁夏、新疆15个省（自治区、直辖市）。1961年3月4日，长城被国务院公布为第一批全国重点文物保护单位。1987年12月，长城被列入世界文化遗产。2019年1月22日，经国务院同意，文化和旅游部、国家文物局联合印发《长城保护总体规划》。

New Words

vicissitude	n.	a variation in circumstances or fortune at different times in your life or in the development of something	变迁，盛衰
precedent	adj.	if there is a precedent for an action or event, it has happened before, and this can be regarded as an argument for doing it again	先例，在先的
fortification	n.	Fortifications are buildings, walls, or ditches that are built to protect a place and make it more difficult to attack	设防，防御工程
contour	n.	the shape of the outer edges of something such as an area of land or someone's body	外形，轮廓
terrain	n.	Terrain is used to refer to an area of land or a type of land when you are considering its physical features	地形，地势
dynasty	n.	a family of kings or other rulers whose parents, grandparents etc have ruled the country for many years	王朝，朝代
protract	v.	to lengthen or extend (a speech, etc); prolong in time	绘制，延长
reconciliation	n.	Reconciliation between two people or countries who have quarrelled is the process of their becoming friends again	和解，调和
nomadic	adj.	Nomadic people travel from place to place rather than living in one place all the time	游牧的，流浪的
herdsmen	n.	A herdsman is a man who looks after a herd of animals such as cattle or goats	牧人
sedentary	adj.	a sedentary group of people tend always to live in the same place	定居的，久坐不动的
chant	n.	A chant is a religious song or prayer that is sung on only a few notes	圣歌，赞美诗
chariot	n.	a vehicle with two wheels pulled by a horse, used in ancient times in battles and races	双轮马车，双轮战车

inscribe   v.   to carefully cut, print, or write words on something, especially on the surface of a stone or coin   题写，铭记

Exercises

I. Simple Selection

1. The Great Wall saw the protracted _____ between the nomadic herdsmen and the sedentary farming peoples.
   A. conflict and reconciliation   B. integrity and honesty
   C. safe and sound   D. alarm and quarrel

2. The great Wall witnessed the _____ of human civilization.
   A. integrity   B. dawn   C. conclusion   D. decline

3. The Great Wall we see today is but _____ of the total length of the walls ever constructed over succeeding dynasties of China.
   A. 1/4   B. 1/6   C. 1/8   D. 1/10

4. The best preserved sections of the Great wall refer to the wall built during _____.
   A. the Ming Dynasty   B. the Qin Dynasty
   C. the Song Dynasty   D. the Qing Dynasty

5. _____ was built under the most difficult conditions, across some of the most dangerous terrains, but with the most popular tourist attractions as well.
   A. The Qing Wall   B. The Ming Wall
   C. The Qin Wall   D. The Tang Wall

6. Construction of the Wall can be traced back to the _____ century BC in the Western Zhou Period.
   A. 9th B. 7th C. 8th D. 10th

7. _____, Qin Shi Huang conquered the other six rival states and became the first emperor of a unified China.
   A. In 221 BC   B. In 453 BC   C. In 476 BC   D. In 770 BC

8. Built for _____, the Wall was effective in keeping the marauding nomads and invading armies out.
   A. business convenience   B. business and trade
   C. military defense   D. commercial connection

9. In China, the Great Wall is traditionally known as "Long Wall of Ten Thousand _____".
   A. yard   B. mile   C. meter   D. Li

10. According to historical records, the Great Wall of _____ was built in the Spring and Autumn period, more than 2500 years ago.
    A. Chu   B. Qi   C. Yan   D. Wei

II. True or False

1. It was not until 221 BC that Qin Shi Huang established the first centralized, unified, feudal dynasty in Chinese history.

2. The Chinese character *chang* has two meanings: long in time and long in space.

3. Apart from Chu, the states of Qi, Wei, Zhao, Qin and Yan all constructed their own walls.

4. No other dynasty throughout the Chinese history spent longer time repairing and building the Wall than the Qin.

5. Built for military defense, the Great Wall was effective in keeping the marauding nomads and invading armies out.

6. Attacks by the nomadic tribes on the sedentary farming peoples usually resulted from natural disasters or battles between the nomads themselves.

7. Most of the ancient nomadic barbarians migrated on horseback from place to place, seeking households for their families.

8. As the largest building project ever carried out by the ancient Chinese working people, scholars have great interest in it.

9. The wall we see today is but 1/4 of the total length of the walls ever constructed over succeeding dynasties of China.

10. Ever since Qin Shi Huang, almost all successive dynasties of the Central Plains had either repaired, rebuilt, or expanded the wall.

III. Fill in the Blanks

1. Stretching from _____ Sea in the east to the deserts in the west, climbing over mountains and passing through grasslands.

2. The Great Wall witnessed the _____ of Chinese dynasties.

3. Ever since _____, almost all successive dynasties of the Central Plains had either repaired, rebuilt, or expanded the wall.

4. The best preserved sections of the Great Wall refer to the wall built during the _____ Dynasty.

5. The Ming Wall was built under the most difficult conditions, across some of the most dangerous terrains, but with the most popular _____ as well.

6. Extending from Shanhai Pass in the east to _____ Pass in the west, the Ming Wall is the longest, most complete and most splendid section of the Great Wall of China.

7. The massive structure takes advantage of the _____ for defensive purposes following the highest points and clinging to ridges.

8. To bring the minority areas under his rule, _____ sent his Great General Meng Tian on an expedition to the north.

9. The resulting fortification stretched all the way from Lintao in the west to _____ Province in the east, as long as 10000 Chinese *Li*.

10. To strengthen their rule over the Hexi Corridor and North China as well as to protect the _____, the Han's ruling emperors ordered the construction of a complete defensive

wall system.

IV. Answer the Questions

1. How will you introduce the Great Wall to foreigners?
2. Please comment on Qin Shi Huang in your own words.

4.2　Construction of the Great Wall

When it comes to the construction of the Great Wall, there is a popular folk story known as "Magic Brick". The legend goes like this that during Ming Emperor Zhengde's reign, Yi Kaizhan, a highly proficient mathematician was said to have the ability to calculate the exact building material for all construction projects needed in advance. The supervisor questioned his ability and asked him to estimate the exact number of bricks required for the whole fortress, also warned that if he miscalculated by even one brick, then all the workmen would be punished to do hard work for three years. Yi concluded that they would need 99999 bricks to build Jiayu Pass after careful calculation. When the project is finished, one brick was left over on the top of the back eaves.. At the sight of the brick, the supervisor was happy and ready to pocket a portion of the workmen's pay. Then Yi Kaizhan said, gently, "The brick was placed there by a supernatural being to keep the wall together, and even a tiny move would cause the whole structure to collapse." Therefore the brick remained in place and was never moved. It is said that very brick can still be found there today on the tower of Jiayu Pass.

The Great Wall of China has spanned different topographic features. According to the characteristics of wall construction, the Great Wall can be divided into diverse types of walls, such as rammed earth wall, piled wall, grass wall, adobe wall, stone wall, brick wall, steep-mountainous wall and oak wall. And in the construction process of the Great Wall, all the dynasties have applied the principle of "selecting local materials according to local conditions", that's why the wall of the Great Wall can still be majestically standing on the towering earth after thousands of years. Before the use of bricks, it was difficult to transport the large quantity of materials required for construction. The builders had to use local resources. They are intelligent to pack slab into walls in mountainous areas and in the plains where loess was in ready supply, walls were constructed mostly of tamped earth and gravel between board frames. And in the deserts, the fortifications were built of sandy soil sandwiched between reed mats or tamarisk branches.

When it goes to Ming Dynasty, more building materials were readily available. So many sections of the Ming Wall were built of large, locally quarried bricks held together with mortar. It's easy to imagine how hard it was to transport those heavy stones, giant bricks and mortar up the steep ways. The ancient workmen were ingenious enough to make the best of the natural terrains. In the narrow pathways, they formed human chains to pass bricks piece by piece or basket by basket up to the site. Ramps, pry bars and rolling logs would also help to transport huge blocks of stone to the top of the mountains. Sometimes, good mountain-climbers like donkeys and goats were used instead of men. On the mountain ranges, ridges and cliffs would serve as part of the foundation, faced with well-cut slabs on the sides to make the wall inaccessible. Such designs would help to reduce manpower and the cost of building materials.

Whatever, as a military defense facility, military defense must be the first priority during the construction process. Therefore, besides the local conditions, the most suitable form of wall construction for military defense should be the first choice. The body of the Juyong Pass and Badaling Wall stands about 7 to 8 meters high, lower on steep hills and the outer wall is slightly higher than the inner wall. On the inner side of such walls, placed at small intervals, were arched doors made of bricks or stones. Inside each arched door were stone or brick steps leading to the top of the battlement, where defenders could walk up and down.

On the top side facing outward stand 2-metre-high crenels called *Duokou*. The upper parts of the *Duokou* are small openings for watching out for attackers, and the lower parts are small openings or loopholes for shooting. There are also drainage holes and waterspouts in the Wall. Every 250 to 500 meters or so there is a crenellated platform rising above the top of the wall. Generally speaking, these are three categories of the platforms. *Qiangtai* is the first type, it is a terrace with crenels roughly as high as the wall-top but protruding from the side facing outward. On these platforms were installed simply structured huts to shelter the guards from wind and rain. The second type of platform is called *Ditai*, it is a two-storeyed signal tower with small brick rooms which can accommodate more than 10 soldiers. *Ditai* can be used to watch and shoot attackers or store weapons and ammunition. The third type is called *Zhantai*, usually built at strategic points, where supplies of arrows, bows, cannons and gunpowder were kept.

Signal beacons were used to send military communications. Soldiers send smoke signals in the daytime and fires or lanterns during the night. Signal beacons can also be called beacons, beacon terraces, wolf smoke mounds, or mounds. Most signal towers were self-contained high platforms, built on hilltops for maximum visibility, although some others were erected both inside and outside the Wall as outpost watchtowers. The first and foremost purpose of the signal beacon was to warn of attack and transmit military messages; the second was to ensure military-agricultural colonization; the third was to check and protect passengers, tradesmen and envoys; and the last one was to assist the defense in the neighborhood. Each beacon fire site was manned by soldiers.

During the Han Dynasty, the signal beacon was a high platform of earth and masonry with a tall stand among bundles of firewood. The guards would send signals by burning a lantern hanging from the stand if enemy attacked. The lantern full of firewood would send smoke signals in the daytime and flare the alarm at night. The strength and situation of the enemy would also be indicated by the number of fires or smoke alarms. Historical records have it that the sentries would burn wolf dung to produce thick black columns of smoke that rose to the sky, clearly visible miles away. That's why beacon sites were sometimes called wolf dung fire platforms.

Notes

1. Zhengde Emperor: Zhengde Emperor was the 11th Ming Dynasty Emperor of China between 1505—1521. Born Zhu Houzhao, he was the Hongzhi Emperor's eldest son. Zhu Houzhao took the throne at only 14 with the era name Zhengde meaning "Right virtue" or "Rectification of virtue". He was known for favoring eunuchs such as Liu Jin and became infamous for his childlike behavior. He died from anillness contracted after falling off while drunk in a boat in the Yellow River at the age of 29, leaving behind no sons and was succeeded by his first cousin Zhu Houcong.

2. The Ming Dynasty: The Ming Dynasty was widely known as the Great Ming Empire. It was the last imperial dynasty in China ruled by ethnic Han Chinese (1368—1644), following the collapse of the Mongol-led Yuan Dynasty. In 1644 the primary capital of Beijing fell to a rebellion led by Li Zicheng, who established the Shun Dynasty, but the Shun Dynasty was soon replaced by the Manchu-led Qing dynasty.

Culture Notes

长城是我国最值得骄傲与自豪的古代工程之一，更是被誉为"世界十大奇迹之一"。但是因为风吹雨蚀、游人破坏、维护不善等众多因素，中国古长城受到了严重的破坏。以明长城为例，明长城的墙体只有8.2%保存状况较为良好，而74.1%的保存状况较差，整个古长城30%已消失。长城遭到破坏有很多因素，其中风雨侵蚀、树木撑坏墙体现象非常严重。虽然长城是砖石结构，但是因为常年的风吹雨打，不少城楼已经摇摇欲坠。长在城墙缝里的树已成了这些地段对长城最大的危害，不少城墙缝里都长出了树，墙体被树撑坏的现象十分严重。第二个因素就是人为原因，例如长城砖被盗、贩卖等现象，这些都加速了古长城的破坏，尤其是部分野长城。同时长城每年都会承受大量的客流量，游客频繁的踩踏难免也会造成一些长城砖石的松动。每年的假期我们不难在新闻中看见，长城上挤满了人，其实这在一定程度上加速了对长城的破坏。

New Words

eave	n.	The eaves are the edges of the roof which overhang the face of a wall and, normally, project beyond the	屋檐

		side of a building. The eaves form an overhang to throw water clear of the walls and may be highly decorated as part of an architectural style	
collapse	v.	if a building, wall etc collapses, it falls down suddenly, usually because it is weak or damaged	倒塌，瓦解
ram	v.	force into or from an action or state, either physically or metaphorically	猛压，填塞
slab	n.	a thick flat piece of a hard material such as stone	厚板，混凝土路面
loess	n.	a light-coloured fine-grained accumulation of clay and silt particles that have been deposited by the wind	黄土
awl	n.	a pointed tool for marking surfaces or for punching small holes	钻子，锥子
rampart	n.	a wide pile of earth or a stone wall built to protect a castle or city in the past	护城墙，壁垒
tamarisk	n.	A tamarisk is a bush or small tree which grows mainly around the Mediterranean and in Asia, and has pink or white flowers	柽柳
deterrent	n.	A deterrent is something that prevents people from doing something by making them afraid of what will happen to them if they do it	妨碍物，威慑物
ingenious	adj.	Something that is ingenious is very clever and involves new ideas, methods, or equipment	有独创性的，机灵的
garrison	n.	a fortified military post where troops are stationed	驻防，守卫
crenel	n.	any of a set of openings formed in the top of a wall or parapet and having slanting sides, as in a battlement	（城墙上的）垛口
protrude	v.	if something protrudes from somewhere, it sticks out.	突出，使伸出
beacon	n.	A beacon is a light or a fire, usually on a hill or tower, that acts as a signal or a warning	烽火台，信号灯

I. Simple Selection

1. Among the legends about the Great Wall, one of the best known around Jiayu Pass is the _____ on top of the back eaves of the western Wengcheng.

A. "Magic Brick" B. "Marvellous Brick"
C. "Marginal Brick" D. "Machine Brick"

2. Before the use of bricks, the Great Wall was mainly built from _____ earth, stone, and wood.

A. rammed   B. destroyed   C. ruined   D. discarded

3. Since it was difficult to transport the large quantity of materials required for construction long ago, the builders always tried to use _____ resources.

A. internal   B. local   C. external   D. extinguished

4. In ancient times, natural _____ like high mountains, deep valleys, sandy deserts and soft grasslands made the construction work extremely difficult.

A. deterrents   B. intermittent   C. present   D. termination

5. The Great Wall we see today at _____ took advantage of the natural terrain following the highest points and clinging to ridges, some of the stone slabs measuring 3 meters long, as heavy as over 1000 kilograms.

A. Juyong Pass B. Badaling
C. Juyong Pass and Badaling D. Mutianyu Great Wall

6. Sometimes, In the narrow pathways, good mountain-climbers like _____ were used instead of men.

A. donkeys and goats B. donkeys and horses
C. horses and goats D. mules and goats

7. *Ditai* is a _____ signal tower with small brick rooms to accommodate more than 10 soldiers on the lower level.

A. four-storeyed B. three-storeyed C. two-storeyed D. one-storeyed

8. In the _____ Dynasty, the signal beacon was a high platform of earth and masonry, on top of which was a tall stand among bundles of firewood.

A. Qing   B. Song   C. Tang   D. Han

9. In case the enemy attacked, the guards on the Great Wall would send signals by burning a _____ hanging from the stand.

A. kite   B. lantern   C. straw   D. cloth

10. Historical records have it that the sentries would burn _____ dung to produce thick black columns of smoke that rose to the sky, clearly visible miles away. That's why beacon sites were sometimes called _____ dung fire platforms.

A. wolf, wolf   B. goat, goat   C. horse, horse   D. mule, mule

II. True or False

1. Before the use of bricks, the Great Wall was mainly built from rammed earth, stone, and wood.

2. During the construction of the Great Wall, the outer wall is slightly higher than the inner wall.

3. On the upper part of the Duokou are small openings used to watch out for attackers.

4. On the upper part of the Duokou are small openings or loopholes, through which

defenders could shoot.

5. There are no drainage holes and waterspouts on the Great Wall.

6. *Zhantai*, built at strategic points, is where supplies of arrows, bows, cannons and gunpowder were stored.

7. Signal beacons are also called beacons, beacon terraces, wolf smoke mounds, or mounds. They were used to send military communications.

8. Built on hilltops for maximum visibility, most signal towers were self-contained high platforms, although some others were erected both inside and outside the Wall as outpost watchtowers.

9. The first and foremost purpose of signal beacons was to warn of attack and transmit military messages.

10. Signal beacons cannot be used to check and protect passengers, tradesmen and envoys.

III. Fill in the Blanks

1. In mountainous areas where rocks were plentiful _____ were packed into walls.

2. In the plains where _____ was in ready supply, walls were constructed mostly of tamped earth and gravel between board frames.

3. To test whether the clay was rammed hard enough, supervisors would use an _____ to poke holes into the rampart.

4. In the deserts, the fortifications were built of _____ sandwiched between reed mats or tamarisk branches.

5. As more building materials were readily available during _____, many sections of the Ming Wall were built of large, locally quarried bricks held together with mortar.

6. _____ of the stone tablets found at Juyong Pass record the names of such material suppliers as brick kilns, quarries and construction departments that engaged thousands of workmen.

7. The ancient workmen, in the narrow pathways, they formed _____ to pass bricks piece by piece, or basket by basket up to the site.

8. The ancient workmen were _____ enough to make the best of the natural terrains.

9. The Great Wall is a sophisticated network of forts, castles, garrisons, and barracks that formed a _____ system with multiple functions

10. During the Ming Dynasty, the signal beacon was known as the "_____", mostly built of brick and masonry.

IV. Answer the Questions

1. What is the "Magic Brick"?

2. Please summarize the function of the Great Wall.

3. Please sum up the usage of signal beacons.

4.3 Tourist Attractions

The completion of Badaling Expressway in 2001 provides a fast and direct route to the Great Wall from Beijing. Thousands of vehicles stream northward on weekends and holiday mornings, and flow back to downtown as dusk falls. Beijing attracts millions of tourists every year. Many foreign tourists want to visit the Great Wall, as they know that "He who doesn't reach the Great Wall is not a true man".

4.3.1 Juyong Pass

Juyong Pass is a mountain pass located in the Changping District of Beijing, over 50 kilometers from central Beijing and the Cloud Platform was also built here. As early as the Jin Dynasty Juyong Pass, set amid the rolling greenery against dramatic mountains, was listed among the "Eight Sights of Yanjing". Since antiquity, Juyong Pass has been hailed as an "impregnable barrier" and a "heaven-sent barrier". Riding past Juyong Pass on horseback, Gao Shi, one of the best known Tang Dynasty frontier poets, described how inaccessible it was: *Water pounding down steep slopes; Peaks kissing the clouds. Birds refuse to fly over the mountaintops; And horses falter at the sight of icy snows.* Juyong Pass was regarded as a fort by successive dynasties. In the Ming Dynasty, for example, the ruling emperor established a border garrison, where 5000 to 6000 soldiers were stationed. The chief of the garrison had under his command all the nearby defending troops along the Wall.

The Cloud Platform at Juyong Pass is a mid-14th-century architectural feature situated in the Guangou Valley at the Juyong Pass. Although the structure looks like a gateway, it was originally the base for three white dagobas or stupas, with a passage through it, a type of structure known as a "crossing street tower". The platform is renowned for its Buddhist carvings and for its Buddhist inscriptions in six languages.

4.3.2 Badaling Great Wall

Badaling Great Wall is the site of the most visited section of the Great Wall of China, approximately 70 kilometers northwest of Beijing. Badaling Great Wall was built in the Ming Dynasty to occupy a commanding and strategic position for protecting the Juyongguan Pass on its south, further protecting the city of Beijing. The ancients said, "The danger of Juyong Pass lies not in the fort, but in Badaling". Badaling and Juyong Pass are both sited on the same natural pass through the mountains to the north of Beijing and hence heavily guarded in successive dynasties. Punctuated with watchtowers and platforms, the Wall has ramparts, crenels and loopholes that enabled the defending soldiers to fire down on their attackers. The Ming Wall is fairly firm, built of well-cut stone slabs and huge bricks. Viewed from afar, the Long Wall of Ten Thousand Li winds its way like a dragon over mountains and ridges into the distance. The endless strings of castles and watchtowers present a majestic sight. The highest point of Badaling is Beibalou, approximately 1015 metres above sea level. The portion of the wall at Badaling has undergone restoration, and in 1957 it was the first section of the wall to open to tourists, visited annually by millions.

Badaling Great Wall witnessed a great many historic events as the only passage between Beijing and the northwest, such as "Inspection Tour of Empress Dowager Xiao" of the Liao Dynasty, "Entrance of Genghis Khan into the Central Plains of China" and "Dowager Cixi fled to the west". East of the fortress lies an inconspicuously huge rock, named "Looking Back at Beijing". It is said that Empress Dowager Cixi once passed here as she fled to the west when the Eight-Power Allied Forces invaded Beijing in 1900. Standing on this rock, she looked back at the Forbidden City Badaling and Juyong Pass, which were not only major military forts in ancient times, but a strategic route between Beijing and Inner Mongolia.

It was here that President Richard Nixon and his wife, accompanied by Vice Premier Li Xiannian, visited on February 24, 1972, during his historic journey to China. Many other world leaders have made a trip to the site including Margaret Thatcher, Ronald Reagan.

4.3.3 Simatai

Simatai is a section of the Great Wall of China located in the north of Miyun County, 120 km northeast of Beijing, holds the access to Gubeikou, a strategic pass in the eastern part of the Great Wall. It was closed in June 2010 but has been reopened to tourists in 2014.

Simatai Great Wall, starting from Wangjing Tower in the east and ending at Houchuankou Pass in the west, is 5.4 km long with 35 watchtowers. This section of the Great Wall incorporated the different characteristics of each section of the Great Wall. A specialist on the Great Wall, Professor Luo Zhewen, has said that "The Great Wall is the best of the Chinese buildings and Simatai is the best of the Great Wall."

Simatai was originally built during the Northern Qi Dynasty and rebuilt during the Ming Dynasty. Having weathered storms of more than 400 years, the magic Simatai affords a more genuine impression of the original wall, complete with clusters of inscribed bricks, exquisite relief sculptures, perfect construction technology, and the majestically dancing wall itself.

Simatai Great Wall is separated by Yuanyang Lake into eastern and western parts. The western part is gently sloped with intact buttressed walls, parapets, crenels, doors, windows, rooftops, loopholes, gutters, and waterspouts. Exquisitely designed and ingeniously practical, these brickworks offer a breathtaking view. The eastern part is much steeper, following more rugged terrain that includes cliff edges and kilometre-high peaks.

4.3.4 Shanhai Pass

Shanhai Pass is one of the major passes in the Great Wall of China. It is located in Shanhaiguan District, Qinhuangdao City, Hebei province, and bordering Liaoning Province. In 1961, the pass was selected as a National Cultural Site of China. It is a popular tourist destination at the eastern terminal point of the Ming Dynasty Great Wall. The location where the wall meets the Bohai Sea is nicknamed "Old Dragon's Head". The pass lies nearly 300 kilometres east of Beijing and is linked via the Jingshen Expressway that runs northeastward to Shenyang.

Throughout Chinese history, the pass served as a frontline defensive outpost against ethnic groups. Both the Northern Qi Dynasty and the Tang Dynasty constructed passes here. In

1381, Ming general Xu Da constructed the present pass, which was named *Shanhai Guan* (literally "mountain-sea-pass") because of its position between the mountains and the sea. In the late 16th century, Ming general Qi Jiguang began fortification and construction of a military city around the pass, building cities and forts to the east, south and north, making it one of the most heavily fortified passes in China.

Currently, Shanhai Pass is a well known cultural and historical site. As a summer resort with many tourist attractions, the area offers coastal scenery and pleasant climate. In 2001, Shanhai Pass District of Qinhuangdao City was officially ranked as a "National Famous Historical and Cultural Site". The renowned site features six tourist spots: Laolongtou (Old Dragon's Head), Mengjiangnv Temple, Jiaoshan (the Wall's first high peak), The First Pass Under Heaven, Longevity Hill, and Yansai Lake.

On Shanghai Pass's east gate, Zhenyuan Tower, lies an eye-catching plaque bearing the words "First Pass under Heaven". These words were written by a renowned scholar of the Ming Dynasty, Xiao Xian. Measuring over 5 meters by 1.5 meters, the calligraphy looks fluid and spontaneous, full of vigor and strength in perfect keeping with the style of the tower. Tradition has it that the word "first" in Chinese, written as a single horizontal stroke, was not written by the calligrapher, but by the brush itself-Xiao Xian tossed the ink-soaked brush into the air, and the brush itself hit the plaque overhead, leaving its mark right there.

4.3.5 Jiayu Pass

Jiayu Pass is the first frontier fortress at the west end of the Ming Dynasty Great Wall, near the city of Jiayuguan in Gansu province, traditionally regarded as China's final outpost. The pass is located at the narrowest point of the western section of the Hexi Corridor. The pass is also known by the name "The First and Greatest Pass Under Heaven", which is corresponding to "The First Pass Under Heaven", a name for Shanhai Pass at the east end of the Great Wall near Qinhuangdao, Hebei province. The pass was a key waypoint of the ancient Silk Road.

The pass is trapezoid-shaped with a perimeter of 733 metres and an area of more than 33500 square metres. The length of the city wall is 733 metres and the height is 11 metres. There are two gates: one on the east side of the pass and the other on the west side. On each gate there is a building. An inscription of "Jiayu Pass" in Chinese is written on a tablet at the building at the west gate. The south and north sides of the pass are connected to the Great Wall. There is a turret on each corner of the pass. On the north side, inside the two gates, there are wide roads leading to the top of the pass.

Constructed of rammed earth, the fort walls are very sturdy. To further strengthen the wall structure, the gate towers, watchtowers and the crenels were faced with bricks. There's a Wengcheng extending out from the west gate, whose double gates were used to trap invading armies. Jiayu Pass consists of a triple line of defense: an inner city, an outer city and a moat. Three-story gate towers rise high above the castle-style brick turrets and corner towers, creating an imposing sight. The Ming rulers put tremendous efforts into strengthening defenses here. According to historical records, over 90000 troops were stationed in Gansu Fortressed Town. Jiayu housed a garrison of around 1000 men under an assistant commander-in-chief, responsible for 39 watchtowers. A lot of projectile weapons were installed inside the stronghold to ward off invaders.

1. Meng Jiangnv Bringing down the Great Wall with Tears

Meng Jiangnv's story is the most famous and widely spread of all the legends about the Great Wall. The story happened during the Qin Dynasty. It tells of how Meng Jiangnv's bitter weeping made a section of the Great Wall collapse. This story happened during the Qin Dynasty. There was once an old man named Meng who lived in the southern part of the country with his wife. One spring, Meng sowed a seed of bottle gourd in his yard. The bottle gourd grew up bit by bit and its vines climbed over the wall and entered his neighbor Jiang's yard. Like Meng, Jiang had no children and so he became very fond of the plant. He watered and took care of the plant. With tender care of both men, the plant grew bigger and bigger and gave a beautiful bottle gourd in autumn. Jiang plucked it off the vine, and the two old men decided to cut the gourd and divide it by half. To their surprise when they cut the gourd a pretty and lovely girl was lying inside. They felt happy to have a child and both loved her very much, so they decided to bring the child up together. They named the girl Meng Jiangnv, which means Meng and Jiang's daughter.

As time went by, Meng Jiangnv grew up and became a beautiful young woman. She was very smart and industrious. She took care of old Meng and Jiang's families, washing the clothes and doing the house work. People knew that Meng Jiangnv was a good girl and liked her very much. One day while playing in the yard, Meng Jiangnv saw a young man hiding in the garden. She called out to her parents, and the young man came out.

At that time, Emperor Qin Shi Huang announced to build the Great Wall. So lots of men were caught by the federal officials. Fan Xiliang was an intellectual man and very afraid of being caught, so he went to Meng's house to hide from the officials. Meng and Jiang liked this good-looking, honest and good-mannered young man. They decided to wed their daughter to him. Both Fan Xiliang and Meng Jiangnv accepted happily, and the couple was married several days later. However, three days after their marriage, officials suddenly broke in and took Fan Xiliang away to build the Great Wall in the north of China.

It was a hard time for Meng Jiangnv after her husband was taken away—she missed her husband and cried nearly every day. She sewed warm clothes for her husband and decided to set off to look for him. Saying farewell to her parents, she packed her luggage and started her long journey. She climbed over mountains and went through the rivers. She walked day and night, slipping and falling many times, but finally she reached the foot of the Great Wall at the present Shanhai Pass.

Upon her arrival, she was eager to ask about her husband. Bad news came to her, however, that Fan Xiliang had already died of exhaustion and was buried into the Great Wall. Meng Jiangnv could not help crying. She sat on the ground and cried and cried. Suddenly with a tremendous noise, a 400 kilometer-long section of the Great Wall collapsed over her bitter wail. The workmen and supervisors were astonished. Emperor Qin Shi Huang happened to be touring the wall at that exact time, and he was enraged and ready to punish the woman.

However, at the first sight of Meng Jiangnv, Emperor Qin Shi Huang was attracted by her beauty. Instead of killing her, the Emperor asked Meng Jiangnv to marry him. Suppressing her feeling of anger, Meng Jiangnv agreed on the basis of three terms. The first was to find the body of Fan Xiliang, the second was to hold a state funeral for him, and the last one was to have Emperor Qin Shi Huang wear black mourning for Fan Xiliang and attend the funeral in person. Emperor Qin Shi Huang thought for a while and reluctantly agreed. After all the terms were met, Emperor Qin Shi Huang was ready to take her to his palace. When the guarders were not watching, she suddenly turned around and jumped into the nearby Bohai Sea.

This story Meng Jiangnv's Bitter Weeping tells of the hard work of Chinese commoners, as well as exposes the cruel system of hard labor during the reign of Emperor Qin Shi Huang. The Ten-Thousand-Li Great Wall embodied the power and wisdom of the Chinese nation. In memory of Meng Jiangnu, later generations built a temple, called the Jiangnv Temple, at the foot of the Great Wall in which a statue of Meng Jiangnv is located. Meng Jiangnv's story has been passed down from generation to generation.

2. Empress Dowager Cixi

Empress Dowager Cixi was a Chinese empress dowager and regent who effectively controlled the Chinese government in the late Qing Dynasty for 47 years from 1861 until her death in 1908.

Selected as a concubine of the Xianfeng Emperor in her adolescence, she gave birth to a son, Zaichun, in 1856. After the Xianfeng Emperor's death in 1861, the young boy became the Tongzhi Emperor, and she became the Empress Dowager. Cixi ousted a group of regents appointed by the late emperor and assumed regency, which she shared with Empress Dowager Ci'an. Cixi then consolidated control over the dynasty when she installed her nephew as the Guangxu Emperor at the death of the Tongzhi Emperor in 1875, contrary to the traditional rules of succession of the Qing Dynasty that had ruled China since 1644.

Although Cixi refused to adopt Western models of government, she supported technological and military reforms and the Self-Strengthening Movement. She agreed with the principles of the Hundred Days' Reforms of 1898, but feared that sudden implementation, without bureaucratic support, would be disruptive and that the Japanese and other foreign powers would take advantage of any weakness. She placed the Guangxu Emperor, who she thought had tried to assassinate her, under virtual house arrest for supporting radical reformers.

After the Boxer Uprising led to invasion by Allied armies, Cixi initially backed the Boxer groups as defenders of the dynasty and declared war on all the invaders. The ensuing defeat was a stunning humiliation. When Cixi returned to Beijing from Xi'an, where she had taken the emperor, she became friendly to foreigners in the capital and began to implement fiscal and institutional reforms that began to turn China into a constitutional monarchy. The death of both Cixi and the Guangxu Emperor in 1908 left the court in the hands of Manchu conservatives, a child, Puyi, on the throne, and a restless, rebellious public.

Historians both in China and abroad have debated her reputation. The long time view portrayed her as a ruthless despot whose reactionary policies led to the fall of the Qing dynasty. Revisionists suggested that reformers and revolutionaries succeeded in blaming her for long term problems beyond her control and that she prevented political disorder, was no more ruthless than other rulers of her time, and that she was an effective reformer in the last years of her life.

Culture Notes

古北水镇：古北水镇位于北京市密云区古北口镇，坐落在司马台长城脚下。古北口自古以雄险著称，有着优越的军事地理位置，《密云县志》上描述古北口"京师北控边塞，顺天所属以松亭、古北口、居庸三关为总要，而古北为尤冲"。司马台段长城以险、密、奇、巧、全著称。险是指它建在刀削斧劈的山脊之上，惊险无比；"密"是指敌楼间的距离，两敌楼相距最近几十米，最远不过 300 米，平均间距仅 140 米；"奇"是指司马台长城山势险陡、雄奇壮丽，且山下有鸳鸯湖（冷泉与温泉交汇而成），碧波荡漾，构成湖光山色的绮丽美景；"巧"体现在步步为营的障墙上，进可攻退可守；"全"是指城楼和敌楼的建筑风格形式奇特多样。而今，古北水镇依托司马台遗留的历史文化，进行深度发掘，成为近 9 平方千米的国际旅游度假区。

New Words

adolescence	n.	Adolescence is the period of your life in which you develop from being a child into being an adult	青春期
hail	v.	If a person, event, or achievement is hailed as important or successful, they are praised publicly	称赞，招呼
impregnable	adj.	If you describe a building or other place as impregnable, you mean that it cannot be broken into or captured	牢不可破的，不可攻取的
successive	adj.	Successive means happening or existing one after another without a break	连续的，继承的
pound	v.	If you pound something or pound on it, you hit it with great force, usually loudly and repeatedly	连续重击，捣碎

facade	n.	The facade of a building, especially a large one, is its front wall or the wall that faces the street	（建筑物的）正面
portray	v.	to describe or show someone or something in a particular way, according to your opinion of them	描绘，扮演
punctuate	v.	If an activity or situation is punctuated by particular things, it is interrupted by them at intervals	不时打断
rampart	n.	The ramparts of a castle or city are the earth walls, often with stone walls on them, that were built to protect it	城墙，壁垒
crenel	n.	any of a set of openings formed in the top of a wall or parapet and having slanting sides, as in a battlement	（城墙上的）垛口
loophole	n.	a small hole in a fortified wall; for observation or discharging weapons	枪眼，漏洞
inconspicuous	adj.	Something that is inconspicuous is not easily seen or does not attract attention because it is small, ordinary, or hidden away	不显眼的，不引人注意的
exquisite	adj.	Something that is exquisite is extremely beautiful or pleasant, especially in a delicate way	精美的
cluster	n.	a group of things of the same kind that are very close together	群，簇，丛，串

I. Simple Selection

1. The late 1990s saw the dedication of an expressway in the north of Beijing, known as "_____".
   A. Badaling Expressway   B. Simatai Expressway
   C. Juyong Pass Expressway   D. Jiayu Pass Expressway

2. As early as the _____, Juyong Pass, set amid the rolling greenery against dramatic mountains, was listed among the "Eight Sights of Yanjing".
   A. Tang Dynasty B. Jin Dynasty   C. Qing Dynasty   D. Tang Dynasty

3. Riding past Juyong Pass on horseback, _____, one of the best known Tang Dynasty frontier poets, described how inaccessible it was.
   A. Gao Shi   B. Li Bai   C. Du Fu   D. Zhang Jiuling

4. The platform of Juyong Pass is pierced by a hexagonal arched gateway. Both the ceiling and facades are covered with _____ carvings.
   A. Christian   B. Catholic   C. Buddhist   D. Theravada

5. The ancients said, "The danger of Juyong Pass lies not in the fort, but in _____".
   A. Badaling   B. Jiayug   C. Simatai   D. Yumenguan

6. Viewed from afar, the Long Wall of Ten Thousand *Li* winds its way like a _____ over mountains and ridges into the distance.
   A. lion   B. dinosaur   C. lizard   D. dragon

7. As the only passage between Beijing and the northwest, Badaling Great Wall witnessed a great many historic events except _____.
   A. Inspection Tour of Empress Dowager Xiao
   B. Entrance of Genghis Khan
   C. Dowager Cixi fled to the west
   D. the First World War

8. Badaling and Juyong Pass were not only major military forts in ancient times, but a strategic route between Beijing and _____.
   A. Qinhai Province   B. Liaoning Province
   C. Inner Mongolia   D. Hebei Province

9. Situated in Gubeikou Town to the northeast of _____ County, Simatai Great Wall is 120 kilometers away from downtown Beijing.
   A. Miyun   B. Daxing   C. Huairou   D. Yanqing

10. The _____ part of Simatai is much steeper, following more rugged terrain that includes cliff edges and kilometre-high peaks.
    A. northern   B. eastern   C. southern   D. western

II. True or False

1. The west part of Simatai is relatively gentle, sporting almost intact buttressed walls, parapets, crenels, doors, windows, rooftops, loopholes, and so on.

2. Situated northeast of Qinhuangdao city, Hebei Province, and bordering Liaoning Province Shanhaiguan Pass is a walled town established in 1381.

3. Shanhaiguan features five tourist spots: Laolongtou, Mengjiangnv Temple, Jiaoshan, First Pass Under Heaven, and Longevity Hill.

4. The famous plaque at the top of the East Gate Tower of Shanhaiguan reads "First Pass under Heaven", attributed to Xiao Xian, a renowned scholar of the Ming Dynasty.

5. Jiayu Pass consists of a triple line of defense: an inner city, an outer city and a moat.

6. Jiayu Pass was nicknamed "The First Pass Under Heaven".

7. The Ming rulers put tremendous efforts into strengthening defenses of Jiayu Pass.

8. With a history of more than 1,600 years, Shanhaiguan was a major military installation in ancient China.

9. Simatai Great Wall is separated into two parts-north and south-by Yuanyang Lake.

10. The east part of Simatai Great Wall is built on the steep mountain ridges, looking like a huge dragon popping out from the lake into the clouds.

III. Fill in the Blanks

1. Since antiquity, Juyong Pass has been hailed as an "_____" and a "heaven-sent barrier".

2. _____, an eminent Ming Dynasty scholar, provided an excellent summary: "Juyong Pass, blocked by barriers upon barriers/Turns the landscape beauty into majesty".

3. An important northwestern gateway to Beijing in ancient times, Juyong Pass was regarded as a _____ by successive dynasties.

4. In the Ming Dynasty, for example, the ruling emperor of Juyong Pass established a _____, where 5000 to 6000 soldiers were stationed.

5. _____ is a fortress situated about 10 kilometers further north of Juyong Pass. They are both sited on the same natural pass through the mountains to the north of Beijing.

6. Punctuated with _____, the Badaling Wall has ramparts, crenels and loopholes that enabled the defending soldiers to fire down on their attackers.

7. Simatai Great Wall is separated into two parts-east and west-by _____.

8. Currently, Shanhaiguan is a well known _____ site. As a summer resort with as many as 90 tourist attractions, the area offers coastal scenery and pleasant climate.

9. In _____, Shanhaiguan District of Qinhuangdao City was officially ranked as a "National Famous Historical and Cultural Site".

10. Over 35 kilometers west of Jiuquan, Gansu Province, _____ is traditionally regarded as China's final outpost.

IV. Answer the Question

1. Do you know something about the calligraphy "First Pass under Heaven"?
2. Please summarize the story of Meng Jiangnv.

4.4 The Cultural Significance of the Great Wall

Why did the Chinese build the Great Wall? There must be a reason for this ancient nation to build it more than 2000 years ago. Simply put, the Great Wall was built in ancient China to keep out invaders. However, it is now regarded as one of the most important tourist spots in the People's Republic of China. Every year, it is visited by thousands of people from all over the world. The Great Wall of China has become the symbol of the Chinese nation and its culture.

4.4.1 Desire for Peace

The Great Wall is wide enough for five horses or ten men to walk side by side. Along the wall are watchtowers, where soldiers used to watch. It was very difficult to build such a wall in the ancient days without any modern machines. All the work was done by hand. The Great Wall was made not only of stone and earth, but of the flesh and blood of millions of men.

The Great Wall of China is a series of stone and earthen fortifications in northern China, built originally to protect the northern borders of the Chinese Empire against intrusions by various nomadic groups. The main sections include Badaling Great Wall, Ruined Badaling Great Wall, Juyong Pass Great Wall, Huanghuacheng Great Wall, Jiankou Great Wall, Mutianyu Great Wall, Gubeikou Great Wall, Jinshanling Great Wall and Simatai Great Wall.

Undoubtedly, the nomadic herdsmen and the sedentary farmers on two sides of the Wall represented two civilizations that had been in contact, conflict, and interdependent relationships. When a certain nomadic tribe became unified and strong enough under the command of a powerful chieftain, the next large-scale war between ethnic groups would break out anytime soon. The conquerors who had settled in the farming communities had to adapt to the local culture and economic style. Eventually, the conquerors would be assimilated by the conquered and even adopt the local language. When the farming world calmed down again toward the final stage of interracial mixing, clouds of war would be gathering far away and the next interethnic war would be building up. Conquering, migrating, blending; re-conquering, re-migrating and re-blending. Looking back at the wars around Juyong Pass that led to the fall of several dynasties, Gu Yanwu, a late Ming Dynasty scholar, sighed, knowingly: *It was not that the fort was indefensible; nor the wall too low; nor the army too small; nor the provisions inadequate. It was the poor government that had lost the confidence and support of the people.*

The war of resistance against Japan on the Great Wall was a struggle of Chinese soldiers and civilians against Japanese invaders along the Great Wall. It was an important part of the early anti-Japanese struggle of the Chinese people. In the Anti-Japanese War, tens of thousands of Chinese soldiers gave their lives for their country. This wall of blood and flesh fought against the Japanese forces for fourteen years and at long last, won the glorious victory of the Chinese patriotic war. In 1935, a movie entitled *Children of Troubled Times* became popular throughout China. The film depicts a pleasure-minded poet, Xin Baihua, who finally fell into the Anti-Japanese War because of the sacrifice of his best friend Liang Zhifu. The theme song of the movie, *The March of the Volunteers*, is composed by Tian Han and Nie Er. It is usually called the horn of the Chinese liberation. Ever since its birth in 1935, it plays a great role in motivating the patriotism of the Chinese people at the moment of national peril. On March 14, 2004, the second session of the Tenth National people's Congress adopted an amendment to the Constitution, formally stipulating the National Anthem of the people's Republic of China as "the March of the volunteers" and now it is sung every day in every corner of China by billions of the Chinese people.

There's no other structure in the world that has experienced more beacon fire and gunpowder smoke than the Great Wall, left a richer legacy of history and culture and become a more powerful symbol of national spirit. The solidarity, progress and growth of the Chinese people bear testimony to their clear vision and correct interpretation of history The peace-loving Chinese have never been taking the lead in casting away stones and never been afraid of stones cast upon them. This is arguably the Great Wall spirit embedded in the hearts of the Chinese people.

4.4.2 Stories Related to the wall

There are several fork tales concerned with the Great Wall, except the "Magic Brick" we have mentioned above, another two stories are also popular. But all these stories tend to be more fictional than factual. One of the earliest is an allusion entitled "Allies Fooled by Beacon Fires".

The last ruler of the Western Zhou Dynasty, King You, was presented a beautiful lady named Baosi. King You favored Baosi so much that he made her his prized concubine. Since she had been forced away from her parents, Baosi was downright depressed and refused to crack a smile. King You was desperate to see her smiles so he offered a prize that anyone who can think of a way to make Baosi smile will be awarded a thousand Liang of gold. A wicked court official Guo Shifu come up with an idea and took Baosi to Lishan Mountain and ordered the defenders to make beacon fires and beat the battle drums. In response to the signal of war, soldiers rushed to Xi'an, the capital of Zhou, to rescue King You, only to find out it was a joke. There was a great laugh at Baosi. King You was so happy that he lit the beacon again and again. Later, all the allies did not believe, and then gradually did not come. Several years later when the Rongdi tribe invaded and King You lit the beacon fire, all the allies thought it was just another joke. King You was killed, marking the end of the Western Zhou Dynasty.

Another allusion, "Meng Jiangnv Bringing down the Great Wall with Tears", has long been a household legend in China, widely spread in the folk in the way of oral inheritance. It was not until the beginning of the 20th century, driven by the May 4th Movement spirit, Meng Jiangnv was brought into the perspective of the researchers. Chinese famous historian Gu Jiegang said, that the original form of the legend can be traced to a story in *Zuozhuan*, an ancient Chinese narrative history commentary. *Zuo zhuan* recounts this story in order to praise Qi Liang's wife, who can still handle things with courtesy in mourning, which deserves admiration. In Yuan Dynasty, the folk opera in China was very developed, and there were many popular works. Works full of vitality and creative space as MengJiangnv was naturally became the source of creation. The plot of the story has been well laid out and the characters have becoming fuller and fuller. In Ming and Qing Dynasties, Meng Jiangnv's story continued to develop and evolve. People made various changes to this story according to different folk customs and different interests of the local people, which made Meng Jiangnv's legend have

very strong regional characteristics.In any case, the name of Mengjiangnv is tightly linked to the Wall of the Qin Dynasty. Meng Jiangnu Temple, also known as Zhennv Temple, is located in Shanhaiguan City, Hebei Province, about 6 km east of Wangfu Stone Village on the back of the hill. The construction of Meng Jiangnv Temple is the product of the folk story "Meng Jiangnv Bringing down the Great Wall with Tears" in memory of Meng Jiangnv.

4.4.3 Integration that the Great Wall brings

The geographic situation and climatic patterns of China has resulted in the two different cultures since ancient times. The south, with fertile land and a warm climate, was developed for agriculture. The north, with pastoral land and a cold climate, was developed for animal husbandry. The south had a highly developed agricultural civilization, while the north was in a less developed state. Agriculture needs stability. The northern peoples were highly mobile due to the pastoral life. While animal husbandry has limited and unstable agricultural output, which made it depend on the southern peoples. Under such circumstances, the Great wall provided a defense line. The Wall protected the agricultural economy in the South and it made the north to develop its own agricultural civilization. This made communication between the southern and northern culture possible.

Chinese history would have been changed without the Great Wall. Mr. Sun Yat-sen, who led the Revolution of 1911 once said that the Great Wall is of great benefit to the further generation. Its achievements are equivalent to those of Dayu in harnessing the water. Seen from today, if it had not been for the protection of the Great Wall, Chinese civilization would have been interrupted by the northern peoples in the late Qin or early Han Dynasties, long before the Song and Ming Dynasties. In that case, there would not have been the prosperity of the Han and Tang dynasties, or the integration of southern and northern peoples. In time, economic zones appears along the Great Wall, especially at its several dozen passes. In history, the agricultural economy in the south and the pastoral economy in the north depended on each other. The Great Wall benefited both economic structure.

4.4.4 Chinese Poems Inspired by the Great Wall

China is a country of poetry, which not only records the glorious history of this great nation, but also shows the cultural spirit of this ancient people. Throughout the history of Chinese poetry, poems about the Great Wall span the longest time, account for the largest number, and cover the most diverse themes. The image of the Great Wall appeared in ancient Chinese poetry can be traced back to the Qin Dynasty. Although in the warring States period, Zhao, Yan, Qi and other states have built the Great Wall, but only after Qin Shi Huang unified China, successive dynasties have begun to be built the Great Wall on a large scale. Among the poetry connected with the Great Wall, praying for peace and opposing war is a high theme even though there are many branches: some psalms eulogized the Great Wall as a epoch-making military project; some are the exposure of the poverty of the people during the war, criticizing the brutality of rulers; some are full of ambition; some was a sigh of regret for "great aspirations difficult to fulfill". For what it is worth, these poems all take the Great Wall as the theme or starting point, and express their feelings around the social life of war in the Great Wall area. The connotation of these poems is more profound and magnificent because of their concern about the Great Wall.

The Great Wall poetry is an important part of the frontier poetry, and the Tang dynasty frontier poems are truly the gems of the Chinese poetry, which provides valuable information for us to study the military, border defense, geography, customs and so on. The poets like Gao Shi, Cen Shen, Wang Changling, and Wang Zhihuan all have left classical poetry. The combination of the Great Wall image with the bright moon, white bone, ethnic flag, rain and snow has produced rich artistic effects, which makes the Great Wall poetry permeate the profound humanistic atmosphere and emotional connotation and their works have been passed down in the folk and lasted for a long time, featuring powerful and soulful style, the poems are largely four lines, each line containing five or seven characters.

Among all the poems concerned with the Great Wall, "Marching out to the Frontier" by Wang Changling was hailed as the "poem of poems" of all the Tang seven-character quatrains. The author associates the bright moon at the frontier pass with the numerous family tragedies resulting from continuous warfare. The poet laments the suffering of the expedition, which reflects the poet's love and protection for his family, his desire and expectation for the victory of the war, and his confidence in the good high-ranking military officer. The diction is simple and direct, with compelling images of the moon and mountain of the Qin and Han that serve to create a milieu of vast emptiness: *The moon of Qin shines yet over the passes of Han; Our men have not returned from the distant frontier. If the Winged General of Dragon City were there, No Huns horses could ever cross the Yinshan mountain.*

Perhaps no other sentences or phrases about the Great wall is more famous than *"He who has not climbed the Great Wall is not a true man"*, which is said by Mao Ze dong. Excerpted from *Mount Liupan-to the tune of Ching Ping Yueh*, the sentence inspired millions of people travel to the Great Wall. Composed in 1935 during the Red Army's Long March, the poem encouraged Chinese people generation by generation: *The sky is high, the clouds are pale. Fading into the south heaven wild geese we sacn. One is not a man if failing to reach the Great Wall. Counting, we know we've covered twenty thousand Li in all. High on the crest of Mount Liupan, red banners wave freely in the west wind. With the long cord in our hands today When shall we bind fast the Grey Dragon?*

In addition to poems, songs, tales, and allusions, the Chinese pillar couplets hung on the doorposts of towers or temples along the Great Wall are equally impressive. The most notable example is the one hung to the Mengjiangnv Temple at Shanhai Pass. These two lines include a wonderful play on homophones and homographs. The combination of shifting tides and floating clouds offer a kaleidoscopic view of the Great Wall, certainly of the whole nature.

The first two lines are the Chinese characters of the couplet, with the phonetic transliteration in Chinese pinyin in the third and fourth lines, the last two lines are the literal equivalent of English:

海水朝，朝朝朝，朝朝朝落。
浮云长，长长长，长长长消。
hǎi shuǐ cháo, zhāo zhāo cháo, zhāo cháo zhāo luò。
fú yún zhǎng, cháng cháng zhǎng, cháng zhǎng cháng xiāo。
Sea water rises, rises every morning, every day rises and ebbs.
Floating clouds gather, often gather, often gather and often go.

1. Gu Yanwu: Gu Yanwu, also known as Gu Tinglin, was a Chinese philologist and geographer. Gu began his schooling at the age of 14, spending his youth during the Manchu conquest of China in anti-Manchu activities after the Ming Dynasty had been overthrown. In the spring of 1645, Gu was recommended to get a position in the royal court at Nanjing. There he proposed many ideas. Unsatisfied with the royal court's organisation, Gu resigned and returned to his hometown. In 1655, local officials laid charges against him and threw him into prison. He was released from prison with the help of a friend. Inspired by Chen Di, who had demonstrated that the Old Chinese has its own phonological system, Gu divided the words of Old Chinese into 10 rhyme groups, the first one to do so. His positivist approach to a variety of disciplines, and his criticism of Neo-Confucianism had a huge influence on later scholars. His works include *Yinxue Wushu*, *Ri Zhi Lu* and *Zhao Yu Zhi*. Along with Wang Fuzhi and Huang Zongxi, Gu was named as one of the most outstanding Confucian scholars of the late Ming and early Qing Dynasty. In 1682, while returning from a friend's home to Huaying, Gu fell from horseback and died the next day.

2. Wang Changling: a major Tang dynasty poet. His courtesy name was Shaobo. He was originally from Taiyuan in present-day Shanxi province, according to the editors of the *Three Hundred Tang Poems*, although other sources claim that he was actually from Jiangning near modern-day Nanjing. After passing the prestigious Jinshi examination, he became a secretarial official and later held other imperial positions, including that of an official posting to Sishui, in what is currently Xingyang, in Henan province. Near the end of his life he was appointed as a minister of Jiangning county. He died in the An Lushan Rebellion. He is best known for his poems describing battles in the frontier regions of western China. He also wrote an homage to the Princess Pingyang, Lady Warrior of the early Tang Dynasty. Wang Changling was one of the competitors in the famous wine shop competition along with Gao Shi and Wang Zhihuan.

3. *Children of Troubled Times*, also known as *Feng Yun Er Nv*, is a patriotic 1935

Chinese film most famous as the origin of "The March of the Volunteers". The movie was directed by Xu Xingzhi, written by Tian Han and Xia Yan, starred by Yuan Muzhi, Gu Menghe and Wang Renmei. Yuan Muzhi plays an intellectual, Xin Baihe, who flees the trouble in Shanghai with his friend, Liang Zhifu. Liang soon joins the resistance against the Japanese invaders, but Xin chooses to pursue a relationship with a glamorous and westernized widow in Qingdao. After hearing that Liang has been killed, Xin has a change of heart and rushes to join the war effort. The theme song of the movie, "The March of the Volunteers", was sung by Gu Menghe and Yuan Muzhi and itwas selected as the provisional national anthem of the People's Republic of China in 1949. In 2004, the song was officially defined as the national anthem.

Culture Notes

1. 毛泽东《清平乐·六盘山》：天高云淡，望断南飞雁。不到长城非好汉，屈指行程二万。六盘山上高峰，红旗漫卷西风。今日长缨在手，何时缚住苍龙？

2. 王昌龄《出塞》：秦时明月汉时关，万里长征人未还。但使龙城飞将在，不教胡马度阴山。

3. 关于长城的经典诗词：

古筑城曲

[唐] 陆游

长城高际天，三十万人守。
一日诏书来，扶苏先授首。

长城

[唐] 汪遵

秦筑长城比铁牢，蕃戎不敢过临洮。
虽然万里连云际，争及尧阶三尺高。

登长城

[唐] 李益

汉家今上郡，秦塞古长城。
有日云长惨，无风沙自惊。
当今圣天子，不战四夷平。

饮马长城窟

[南北] 沈约

介马渡龙堆，涂紫马屡回。
前访昌海驿，杂种寇轮台。
旌幕卷烟雨，徒御犯冰埃。

统汉烽下
[唐] 李益
统汉烽西降户营，黄沙白骨拥长城。
只今已勒燕然石，北地无人空月明。

塞外月夜寄荆南熊侍御
[唐] 武元衡
南依刘表北刘琨，征战年年箫鼓喧。
云雨一乖千万里，长城秋月洞庭猿。

经檀道济故垒
[唐] 刘禹锡
万里长城坏，荒营野草秋。
秣陵多士女，犹唱白符鸠。

杞梁墓
[唐] 汪遵
一叫长城万仞摧，杞梁遗骨逐妻回。
南邻北里皆孀妇，谁解坚心继此来。

听筝
[唐] 张祜
十指纤纤玉笋红，雁行轻遏翠弦中。
分明似说长城苦，水咽云寒一夜风。

4. 烽火戏诸侯的传说：周宣王死后，周幽王即位。周幽王昏庸无道，骄奢淫逸，是历史上有名的昏君。周幽王有一个妃子叫褒姒，长得美若天仙。周幽王十分宠爱她，成天过着荒淫糜烂的生活。但是褒姒自打进宫后就没笑过，周幽王于是绞尽脑汁，想尽一切办法博美人一笑，可是都没能如愿。有一天，周幽王下令：谁能让褒姒笑一下，赏黄金一千两。这时，有一个大夫站了出来，百般讨好地对周幽王说："您不如把烽火台点着，诸侯们必定带着大批人马赶来，到时候您再让诸侯们回去。娘娘见了这些兵马一会儿跑过来，一会儿跑过去，肯定会笑的。"周幽王抬眼一看，认得此人名叫虢石甫。昏庸的周幽王觉得这个主意不错，他不顾其他大臣的反对，立马带着褒姒来到骊山，登上了烽火台。自古以来，烽火是敌寇入侵时的报警信号，各都在国都及边国设置烽火台。当时西周边境有强大的犬戎，为防备犬戎的侵扰，西周就在镐京附近的骊山一带修筑了二十多座烽火台，每隔几里地就是一座。一旦犬戎进犯，首先发现敌人的哨兵立刻在台上点燃烽火，邻近烽火台也相继点火，向附近的诸侯报警。诸侯见了烽火，知道天子有难，必定率兵前来救驾。周幽王命令守兵点燃烽火，一时间火光冲天，狼烟四起。邻近的诸侯看见狼烟，以为外敌入侵，赶紧带着兵马跑来救驾。诸侯们带着兵马匆匆忙忙赶到骊山下，没想到一个敌人也没看见，只听到山上一阵阵奏乐和唱歌的声音，仔细一打听，原来是周幽王和褒姒在饮酒作乐。大家你看看我，我看看你，都不知道是怎么回事。周幽王派人去对他们说："辛苦各位诸侯了，没有敌人，你们回去吧！"诸侯们这才知道上当了，虽然愤怒，但也只好各自带着兵马回去了。褒姒瞧见这么多兵马忙来忙去，嫣然一笑。周幽王终于博得美人一笑，非常高兴，重重地赏赐了虢石甫。后来，周幽王又叫人点燃烽火，诸侯们又带着兵马前来，最后又垂头丧气地回去。周幽王觉得这样很好玩，可他哪里知道，这种行为已经为整个周王朝种下了祸根。不久，犬戎前来攻打镐京，周幽王赶紧命人把骊山的烽火点了起来。诸侯们以为这又是周幽王玩的把戏，所以全都不予理睬，一个救兵也没有派出。最后周幽王和虢石甫都被犬戎杀了，褒姒也被掳走了。至此，西周灭亡。

New Words

intrusion	n.	An intrusion is something that disturbs your mood or your life in a way you do not like	侵扰；闯入
indefensible	adj.	If you say that a statement, action, or idea is indefensible, you mean that it cannot be justified or supported because it is completely wrong or unacceptable	站不住脚的；不能防卫的
provision	n.	The provision of something is the act of giving it or making it available to people who need or want it	提供；准备
legacy	n.	A legacy is money or property which someone leaves to you when they die	遗产；遗赠…
assimilate	v.	When people such as immigrants assimilate into a community or when that community assimilates them, they become an accepted part of it	吸收；使同化
interracial	adj.	conducted, involving, or existing between different races or ethnic groups	种族间的；人种混合的
tyrant	n.	You can use tyrant to refer to someone who treats the people they have authority over in a cruel and unfair way	暴君
aspiration	n.	Someone's aspirations are their desire to achieve things	志向；抱负
pastoral	adj.	A pastoral place, atmosphere, or idea is characteristic of peaceful country life and scenery	田野的；乡村的
solidarity	n.	If a group of people show solidarity, they show support for each other or for another group, especially in political or international affairs	团结一致；相互支持
testimony	n.	If you say that one thing is testimony to another, you mean that it shows clearly that the second thing has a particular quality	明证；证据

husbandry	n.	Husbandry is the raising of farm animals and plants	农牧业；耕种
envoy	n.	An envoy is someone who is sent as a representative from one government or political group to another	使者；代表
eulogize	v.	If you eulogize someone or something, you praise them very highly	称赞；颂扬

I. Simple Selection

1. Which statement about the Great Wall in not true?
    A. From the 7th century BC to the 16th century AD, many dynasties built parts of the Great Wall.
    B. The Great Wall is a series of walls constructed over two thousand years, starting in ancient times.
    C. The Great Wall experienced the ups and downs of Chinese dynasties.
    D. With advanced science and technology, we can get the exact length of the Great Wall.

2. With the basic goal of _____, the Great Wall was built.
    A. defensing home   B. safeguarding peace
    C. resisting foreign aggression D. strengthening the position of the South

3. In the age of cold steel, the Great Wall certainly served the purposes of _____.
    A. peaceful life   B. agricultural production
    C. military defense   D. resist aggression

4. With arable land and a warm climate, the south of China was suited for _____.
    A. husbandry   B. silk
    C. handicraft industry   D. agriculture

5. Stability was important for an _____ population.
    A. agricultural   B. industrial   C. educational   D. political

6. _____ provided an effective defense line for southern troops while facing the mobile northern cavalry.
    A. Guns   B. Military   C. The rivers   D. The Great Wall

7. The Great Wall of blood and flesh fought against the _____ forces for fourteen years and, at long last, won the glorious victory of the Chinese patriotic war.
    A. French   B. Britain   C. Japanese   D. Germany

8. The Great Wall has become a symbol of _____ for the Chinese people over the centuries.
    A. world peace   B. perseverance
    C. communication   D. consolidation and strength

9. Being the most precipitous part of it, _____ epitomizes the wonder of the Great Wall.

   A. Shanhai Pass B. Jiayu Pass   C. Simatai   D. Badaling

10. _____ symbolizes that great achievement can be made with a common will and concerted effort.

   A. The great wall   B. The forbidden city
   C. The summer palace   D. Temple of Heaven

II. True or False

1. The Great Wall was built in ancient China to keep out invaders.

2. The Great Wall of China has become the symbol of the Chinese nation and its culture.

3. The Great Wall is wide enough for ten horses or ten men to walk side by side.

4. The Great Wall was built with certain machines.

5. The Great Wall was made not only of stone and earth, but of the flesh and blood of millions of men.

6. The Great Wall fought against the Japanese forces for fourteen years and, at long last, won the glorious victory of the Chinese patriotic war.

7. "Let our flesh and blood become our new Great Wall!" comes from the theme song of a movie named *Children of Troubled Times*.

8. The peace-loving Chinese have never been taking the lead in casting away stones, and never been afraid of stones cast upon them. This is arguably the Great Wall spirit embedded in the hearts of the Chinese people.

9. Most of the stories related to the wall tend to be more fictional than factual.

10. The Wall protected the agricultural economy in the South and it made the north to develop its own agricultural civilization.

III. Fill in the Blanks

1. The Great Wall of China has become the symbol of the _____ and its _____.

2. The Great Wall was made not only of stone and earth, but of the _____ and _____ of millions of men.

3. Now well-known as the Great Wall of China, it starts at the _____ of Gansu Province in the west and ends at the _____ of Hebei Province in the east.

4. The majority of the existing wall was built during the _____.

5. Dr. Sun Yat-sen, said, "There would not have been the prosperity of the Han and Tang dynasties, or the _____ of southern and northern peoples without the Great Wall".

6. In history, the _____ economy in the south and the _____ economy in the north depended on each other. The Great Wall benefited both economic structure.

7. Throughout the history of Chinese poetry, _____ about the Great Wall span the longest time, account for the largest number, and cover the most diverse themes.

8. The _____ Dynasty frontier poems are truly the gems of the Chinese poetry, most notably the works of Gao Shi, Cen Shen, Wang Changling, Li Qi, Cui Hao, and Wang Zhihuan.

9. Featuring powerful and soulful style, the poems of Tang dynasty are largely four lines, each line containing _____ or _____ characters.

10. "Border Pass" by the Tang Dynasty poet _____ was hailed by the Ming Dynasty critics as the "poem of poems" of all the Tang seven-character quatrains.

IV. Answer the Questions

1. Please talk about the major categories of poem related to the Great Wall.

2. Please introduce the Great Wall in less then 200 words.

Unit 5 The Terra-cotta Warriors

5.1 Discoverer of the Terra-cotta Warriors

In March, 1974, while 6 young farmers were digging a well outside the city of Xi'an, China, to irrigate fields, a human-shaped life-size clay soldier without head was found, immediately after that the head was unearthed, then crossbows and bronze arrowheads were dug up.

Chinese authorities were notified and government archaeologists were sent to the site.

In July, 1974, organized excavation began, which later proved to be one of the greatest archaeological discoveries in the world.

They found not one, but thousands of clay soldiers, each with unique facial expressions and positioned according to rank. Though the soldiers are gray today, patches of paint still hint brightly colored clothes in the past. Further excavations have revealed swords, arrow tips, and other weapons, many in pristine condition.

The soldiers are in trenchlike, underground corridors. In some of the corridors, clay horses are aligned four abreast; behind them are wooden chariots.

All the soldiers were made of clay. They are of human's size, with commanders in the army being the tallest. The sculptures are so detailed that we can clearly see their shoelaces. It is even possible to guess the age, rank and personality of each one. To people's surprise, none of them are the same. Some of them carry weapons such as daggers, bows and arrows, swords, spears or axes.

The clay soldiers, as it is known, are part of an elaborate mausoleum created to guard the first emperor of China in the afterlife, according to archaeologists.

This vast complex of terra cotta statuary, weapons and other treasures—including the tomb of Qin Shi Huang—is now famous as the Terra Cotta Army or Terra-cotta Warriors.

There are 4 pits in the complex, one of them is empty, and the others are filled with 8000

Terra-cotta soldiers, though more might have existed. Weapons and wooden chariots drawn by life-size clay horses are also among the three pits of ruins.

The terra-cotta army was guarding the tomb of the First Emperor of China, Qin Shi Huang, who lived over 2200 years ago. However, the tomb itself remains unexcavated.

Qin's tomb itself remains unexcavated, though Sima Qian's account suggests even greater treasures. Excavation of the tomb has been delayed due to high levels of toxic mercury at the site.

The tomb is located at the northern foot of Lishan Mountain, 35 kilometers northeast of Xi'an, Shaanxi Province Ancient account has it that Qin Shi Huang mirrored the plan of his capital city, Xianyang into the tomb, with mercury the rivers and bronze the mountains. The tomb also contains replicas of fine vessels, precious stones and rarities. Precious stones such as pearls are said to represent the sun, moon, and other stars.

Chinese archaeologists are using remote sensing technology, ground-penetrating radar, and core sampling to probe the mound. They've found that the tomb complex is 38 square miles in total. The test revealed unusually high concentrations of mercury, lending credence to at least some of the historical account.

The technique revealed an underground chamber with four stairlike walls. Archaeologists guess it may have been built for the soul of the emperor. Dancers, musicians, and acrobats were also discovered; they are full of life and caught in mid-performance,

But further excavations of the tomb itself are on hold, at least for now.

Researchers believe that the conditions inside is so complex that we'd better keep the tomb untouched for now.

There has been worldwide fascination in the discovery of the Terra-cotta Army and it is now regarded as the 8th Wonder of the Ancient World. In December, 1987, the Terra-cotta army was admitted in the World Heritage List. Now, The Terracotta Army Museum is one of the must-visit attractions for all travelers to China and more than 260 overseas exhibits were organized in the 40 years after its discovery.

Notes

Xi'an: the capital city of Shaanxi Province, north-central of China. It is located in the south-central part of the province. It is noted for its historical importance. In ancient China, it was known as "Chang'an", which was the capital city of over ten dynasties. However, in the Qin Dynasty, the capital was Xianyang, which is on the west of today's Xi'an. The tomb is actually located near the capital city of its time.

Culture Notes

1. 兵马俑是古代墓葬雕塑的一个类别。古代实行人殉，奴隶是奴隶主生前的附属品，奴隶主死后奴隶要作为殉葬品为奴隶主陪葬。兵马俑即用陶土制成兵马（战车、战马、士兵）形状的殉葬品。

2. 秦始皇陵位于距西安市 30 多千米的临潼区城以东的骊山之北，秦始皇陵兵马俑坑是秦始皇陵的陪葬坑，位于陵园东侧 1500 米处。

3. 秦始皇兵马俑博物馆，是建立在兵马俑坑原址上的遗址性博物馆。1979 年 10 月 1 日开馆。

4. 2009 年 6 月 13 日，秦始皇陵兵马俑一号坑开始第三次大规模发掘。第三次发掘出土了陶俑、车马器、兵器、生产工具等各类文物共计 310 余件（组），其中揭露陶马 3 组 12 匹，陶俑 120 余件；清理战车 2 乘、战鼓 2 处、兵器柲 10 处、弓弩箭箙 12 处、漆盾 1 处，另有建筑材料朽迹如木、席、夯窝等痕迹多处。根据发掘方案的制定，秦俑一号坑第三次发掘现场采取"保护与发掘同时，展出与发掘同步"的模式，除常规保护外，已经移交实验室 10 批彩绘陶俑残片及脆弱遗迹模块，部分彩绘土样开展了回贴实验。

New Words

terracotta	n.	a brownish-red clay that has been baked and is used for making things such as flower pots, small statues, and tiles	无釉赤陶；陶瓦
irrigate	vt.	supply with water, as with channels or ditches or streams	灌溉
clay	n.	a very fine-grained soil that is plastic when moist but hard when fired	黏土，泥土
unearthed	adj.	If someone unearths facts or evidence about something bad, they discover them with difficulty, usually because they were being kept secret or were being lied about	出土的（考古）
crossbow	n.	a bow fixed transversely on a wooden stock	（昔日的）石

		grooved to direct the arrow	弓，弩
archaeologist	n.	an anthropologist who studies prehistoric people and their culture	考古学家
excavation	n.	the act of digging	挖掘；开凿
pristine	adj.	completely free from dirt or contamination	太古的，原始状态的
elaborate	adj.	marked by complexity and richness of detail	复杂的；精心制作的
mausoleum	n.	a large burial chamber, usually above ground	陵墓
emperor	n.	a man who rules an empire or is the head of state in an empire	皇帝，君主
afterlife	n.	life after death	死后的生活，来世
replica	n.	copy that is not the original; something that has been copied	复制品
rarity	n.	noteworthy scarcity	稀少；珍品
penetrate	vt.	pass into or through, often by overcoming resistance	穿透，刺入
mercury	n.	a heavy silvery toxic univalent and bivalent metallic element; the only metal that is liquid at ordinary temperatures	汞，水银
credence	n.	the mental attitude that something is believable and should be accepted as true	相信（传言）；凭证
heritage	n.	practices that are handed down from the past by tradition	遗产；继承物

I. Simple Selection

1. The Terra-cotta Warriors was discovered in the year_____.
   A. 1966　　　B. 1972　　　C. 1974　　　D. 1983
2. Organized excavation of the Terra-cotta Army began In July, _____.
   A. 1966　　　B. 1972　　　C. 1974　　　D. 1976
3. In excavation, archaeologists found not one, but thousands of clay soldiers, each with _____.
   A. the same facial expressions　　　B. unique facial expressions

        C. the same gueatures   D. unique guestures
    4. Archaeologists have excavated _____.
        A. the terra-cotta army only
        B. Qin Shi Huang's tomb only
        C. both the terra-cotta army and Qinshihuang's tomb
        D. Qin Shi Huang's coffin
    5. Qin's tomb is located at the northern foot of _____ Mountain,
        A. Wutai   B. Lu   C. Tai   D. Lishan
II. Multiple Choice
    1. Excavations of the Terracotta Army have revealed _____.
        A. clay soliders   B. swords
        C. the coffin of Qin Shi Huang   D. arrow tips
    2. Ancient account has it that Qin Shi Huang mirrored the plan of his capital, Xianyang into the tomb, with _____.
        A. mercury the rivers   B. bronze mountains
        C. replicas of fine vessels   D. precious stones and rarities
    3. Chinese archaeologists are using _____ to probe the mound.
        A. remote sensing technology   B. traditional excavating tools
        C. core sampling   D. ground-penetrating radar
    4. _____ are discovered Qin's tomb mound, and they are full of life and caught in mid-performance.
        A. Dancers   B. musicians   C. acrobats   D. concubines
    5. The Terracotta Army is now _____.
        A. admitted in the World Heritage List
        B. a museum
        C. enclosed and forbidden for visit
        D. regarded as the 8th Wonder of the Ancient World
III. True or False
    1. The Terracotta Army was discovered by coincidence.
    2. The clay soldier was first discovered by farmers.
    3. Clay soldiers are positioned according to height.
    4. The clay soldiers were in colored clothes in the past.
    5. Clay horses and wooden chariots are discovered in excavations of the Terracotta Army
    6. The sculptures of clay soldiers are rough.
    7. The tomb of Qin Shi Huang was excavated in 1974.
    8. The Terracotta Army and it is now regarded as the 8th Wonder of the Ancient World.
IV. Fill in the Blanks
    1. In the Terra-cotta Army, all the soldiers were made of _____.
    2. The Terra-cotta army was guarding the tomb of the First Emperor of China, _____, who lived over _____ years ago.

3. Sima Qian's account suggests even greater _____ in Qin's tomb.

4. Excavation of Qinshihuang's tomb has been delayed due to high levels of toxic _____ at the site.

5. Chinese archaeologists've found that the tomb complex is _____ square miles in total.

6. In December, _____, the Terra-cotta army was admitted in the World Heritage List.

V. Read the Passage about the Terra-cotta Army, and Answer the Questions:

On December 21, Michael Rohana attended a pre-Christmas party at the Franklin Institute in Philadelphia, Pennsylvania.

Around 9:15 that evening, surveillance footage shows Rohana and some friends sneaking into a closed exhibition. The exhibit, on-loan from China since September 30, 2017, contains 10 of the famous terra-cotta warriors, along with coins, gold pieces, jade, and weapons from the excavation site. Shortly after entering the exhibit, Rohana's friends left, leaving the 24-year-old alone with the frozen warriors.

In the footage, Rohana views the exhibit using the glow from his smartphone flashlight. He appears to embrace one of the soldiers—called Cavalryman—and take a selfie with it. Then, Rohana puts his hand into the left hand of the figure. He allegedly breaks something off and stashes the terra-cotta memento in his pocket. Thumb in tow, he leaves the scene.

Museum staff didn't realize the statue was missing an appendage until January 8, and they traced the alleged vandalism back to Rohana five days later. Authorities quickly showed up at his house, where he lives with his parents, and Rohana reportedly admitted that he had kept the disembodied thumb in a desk drawer in his bedroom.

On January 13, Rohana was arrested and charged with theft and concealment of a major artwork, as well as interstate transportation of stolen goods. After surrendering his passport, he was released on bail on February 16.

The Shaanxi Cultural Heritage Promotion Center, who loaned the statues out to the Franklin Institute, "strongly condemned" the museum for being "careless". The center also said it was going to send two experts to assess the damage and repair the statue with the recovered thumb. There would be a claim for compensation, it added.

But this is the first time a situation of this gravity has come to light.

"We call on the American side to severely punish the person who committed this destruction and theft of mankind's cultural heritage," an official told Beijing Youth Daily.

The Franklin Institute said in a statement that its external security contractor did not follow standard closing protocol the night of the party, and the museum has reviewed its security measures and procedures to prevent future situations like this.

1. This passage might be _____ about the Terra-cotta army.
   A. news
   B. a sutudent's composition
   C. a school text
   D. travel information

2. The best title of this passage is _____.

A. Young people not cherishing exhibition items

B. The Terra-cotta warriors in America

C. The Theft of Terra-cotta Warrior's Thumb

D. international uproar

3. Which of the following is not true about Michael Rohana?

A. He sneaked into a closed exhibition.

B. He took a photo.

C. He stole a thumb and sold it.

D. He watched the exhibit using the glow from his smartphone flashlight.

4. Which of the following is true?

A. Museum staff immediately discovered the theft.

B. Authorities showed up at his house but Rohana denied his conviction

C. Rohana was arrested and later released on bail.

D. The museum has took measures to prevent future situations like this.

5.2 The Introduction of Pit No.1, No.2, No.3, No.4

To date, four pits have been detected and three of them have been excavated. These three excavated pits are filled with the Terra-cotta soldiers, horse-drawn chariots, and weapons. The fourth pit, or Pit 4, has not been excavated and keeps empty. The other three pits were built with similar underground earth-and-wood structure but differed in layout. Archaeologists estimate the 3 pits may contain as many as 8000 figures, but the total may never be known.

The layout of these three pits shaped like a flying goose, called "Goose Formation". Pit 1, which consists of large amount of infantries and battle chariots, is more than twice bigger than Pit 2. Pit 2 is the formation lined with archery, cavalry and battle chariots. Those three pits actually is real military formation which fully reflect profound military strategy in Qin Dynasty. Pit 1 and Pit 2 are the attacking troops with different functions that obey orders from Pit 3, which was as their headquarter.

In the relic site, they were named Pit 1, Pit 2, Pit 3 and Pit 4, according to the unearthed sequence. There are 5 sloping passages with clear trail of wheels on it around the pit. The Terra-cotta figures were placed into the pottery-bricks-paved pit through the passages, then filled with rammed-earth and obturated the passages by stumpage. The pit sustained wood roof that was composed of huge and solid rafters, then covered by layers of fiber mats and earth. An underground military stronghold was finished.

Pit No.1, the largest of the 4 pits, covers 14000 square meters (the size of almost three football fields). It is believed to contain over 6000 terracotta figures of soldiers and horses, but less than 2000 are on display. The central part of Pit 1 is the main force of army which has 36 columns warriors with 178 m (584 ft) long. Totally owns 50 battle chariots and 4000 infantries, they stood in a good order according to the military formation. The whole army faces east in a rectangular array, soldiers are armed with long spear, dragger or halberd. Some warriors wore robes, some wore armors, all of this were according to their rank or army services.

The vanguard appears to be three rows of infantry who stand at the easternmost end of the army. Close behind is the main force of armored soldiers holding weapons, accompanied by 38 horse-driven chariots. Each battle chariots equipped with three warriors, one was the horse driver and other two were the warriors with weapons in hand. On the northern, southern, and western side there stand one row of figures serving as the army's defense wing. Standing in front of such a grand ancient army array, visitors would feel the ground shake to the footsteps of the advancing soldiers. The soldiers have different facial features and expressions, clothing, hairstyles, and gestures, providing abundant and detailed artifacts for the study of the military, cultural, and economic history of that period.

Pit No.2 is located about 20 meters (22 yards) to the northeast of Pit No.1 and 120 meters (130 yards) to the east of Pit No.3. Pit No. 2 is less than half its size and is L-shaped. By now, only one sixth of the pit has been fully excavated while the rest are partially unearthed to reveal the remains of wooden shelters. Pit No.2 was found in May of 1976, and opened to visitors on October 1, 1994.

Terra-cotta Army Pit 2 is the most spectacular of the three pits. Compared to Pit 1, the combat formations in Pit 2 are more complex, and the units of armed forces are more complete. According to preliminary calculations, there are over 80 war chariots, about 1300 Terra-cotta warriors and horses, and thousands of bronze weapons inside it. It is a revelation to first discover the Terra-cotta general, the kneeling archer and the cavalry warrior with saddle horse in the pit. Like Pit No. 1, its vanguard is made up largely of archers, in this case mainly carrying crossbows (unfortunately, the wooden parts are decayed). The figures in the front rows are standing up un-armored, while the ones behind are kneeling. By having one line firing, and another kneeling to reload, a steady stream of fire could be kept up on the enemy. The main force of Pit No.2 meant to overwhelm the enemy, includes about 1,300 soldiers and horses, more than 80 war chariots. Each has two riders and a charioteer and there are also some armored troops, equipped with melee weapons, intermixed. Although not as grand as Pit 1, the Terra-cotta Warriors Pit 2 is the most complete pit as it houses all types of terracotta warriors found so far, including infantries, cavalries, chariot warriors and archers.

Archaeologists discovered Pit 3 in northwest of Pit 1 on May, 11, 1976. As the smallest one, Pit 3 is the command post with high-ranking officers and a war chariot. It varies from both Pit 1 and Pit 2 in structure and content. Both warriors in Pit 1 and Pit 2 are arrayed in line of battle, but figurines in Pit 3 are standing face to face with a passageway between them. Obviously, they are the guards of the command post. These strong guards all wear heavy armors. Most outstanding characters in Pit 3 is the unearthed ancient weapons which are called

"Shu" (shaped like spear but without blade) in Pit 3. Shu is powerful weapon in hand-to-hand combat, and often used in honour guard.

In period of the Warring States (475—221 BC), the ruler often took sacrifice in order to pray for success before the war. In the rite, the augur drilled a hole on turtle shell or cattle scapula, and then burned it until crack appeared. According to this crack, augur can foresee the result of the war. Unearthed relics in Pit 3 including remains of animals just prove historians' assumption is right.

Pit No.4 is empty. 2000 years ago, it was dug but later refilled. Researchers guess the construction was ceased because of the peasants' riots at the end of the Qin Dynasty.

Notes

Goose Formation: Geese fly in V formation for a very pragmatic reason. But here it is called "Pin Formation" in Chinese language. The Chinese character Pin is "品", which is a convenient one to describe the similar lay out of things.

Culture Notes

1. 秦始皇兵马俑陪葬坑坐西向东，三坑呈"品"字形排列。最早发现的是1号俑坑，呈长方形，东西长230米，南北宽62米，深约5米，总面积14260平方米，2号坑在1号坑北侧约20米处，平面略呈曲尺形，1976年发现，是秦俑坑中的精华，2号坑的发现揭开了古代军阵之谜。东西最长处96米，南北最宽处84米，深约5米，面积约6000平方米，3号坑位于1号坑西端北侧，与2号坑东西相对，南距1号坑25米，东距2号坑120米，面积约为520平方米，整体呈凹字形，3号坑是三个坑中唯一一个没有被大火焚烧过的，所以出土时陶俑身上的彩绘残存较多，颜色比较鲜艳。4号坑有坑无俑，只有回填的泥土，据推测是因为秦末农民起义等原因未建成。

1号坑

2号坑

2号坑　　　　　　　　　　　　　　　3号坑

2. 春秋战国之前的战争，指挥将领往往要身先士卒，冲锋陷阵，所以他们常常要位于卒伍之前。春秋战国时期随着战争规模的增大，作战方式的变化，指挥者的位置开始移至中军。秦代战争将指挥部从中军中独立出来，这是军事战术发展的一大进步。指挥部独立出来研究制订严密的作战方案，更重要的是指挥将领的人身安全有了进一步的保证。这是古代军事战术发展成熟的重要标志。3号秦坑是世界考古史上发现时代最早的军事指挥部的形象资料。

3. 殳，shū，是古代的一种武器，用竹木做成，有棱无刃。可见于秦俑3号坑。

4. 钻龟，是古代一种占卜术。钻刺龟里甲，并以火灼，视其裂纹以断吉凶。

New Words

layout	n.	a plan or design of something that is laid out	布局，安排
goose	n.	web-footed long-necked typically gregarious migratory aquatic birds usually larger and less aquatic than ducks	鹅
infantry	n.	an army unit consisting of soldiers who fight on foot	步兵；步兵部队
archery	n.	the sport of shooting arrows with a bow	箭术
cavalry	n.	troops trained to fight on horseback	骑兵（队）；骑兵部队
chariot	n.	a two-wheeled horse-drawn battle vehicle	战车
headquarter	n.	main office of directors	总部
slope	vi.	be at an angle	倾斜；有斜度
passage	n.	a way through or along which someone or something may pass	通路，通道
stronghold	n.	a strongly fortified defensive structure	要塞；据点
obturate	vt.	block passage through	闭塞，封闭

stumpage	n.	the main part of a tree used to support a structure	立木，未砍伐的树；直木材
rafter	n.	someone who travels by raft	筏夫
rammed-earth	n.	condensed earth	素土夯实
rectangular	adj.	having four right angles	矩形的
array	n.	An array of objects is a collection of them that is displayed or arranged in a particular way	队列，阵列
spear	n.	a long pointed rod used as a weapon	矛；枪
halberd	n.	a pike fitted with an ax head	戟
robe	n.	any loose flowing garment	礼服
armor	n.	protective covering made of metal and used in combat	盔甲；装甲部队
vanguard	n.	the leading units moving at the head of an army	先锋，前锋
artifact	n.	a man-made object	人工制品
figurine	n.	a small carved or molded figure	小雕像
rite	n.	any customary observance or practice	典礼，礼仪
augur	n.	a religious official who interpreted omens to guide public policy	占卜师
scapula	n.	either of two flat triangular bones one on each side of the shoulder in human beings	肩胛骨

I. Simple Selection

1. Archaeologists estimate the 3 pits may contain as many as _____ figures, but the total may never be known.

    A. 8000   B. 6000   C. 10000   D. 9000

2. _____ is empty.

    A. Pit 1   B. Pit 2   C. Pit 3   D. Pit 4

3. _____ is the largest of the four pits, covers the size of almost three football fields.

    A. Pit 1   B. Pit 2   C. Pit 3   D. Pit 4

4. The Terra-cotta Army _____ Pit 2 is the most spectacular of the three pits, and its combat formations are more complex.

A. Pit 1   B. Pit 2   C. Pit 3   D. Pit 4

5. As the smallest one, _____ is the command post with high-ranking officers and a war chariot.

A. Pit 1   B. Pit 2   C. Pit 3   D. Pit 4

6. Two thousand years ago, _____ was dug but later refilled.

A. Pit 1   B. Pit 2   C. Pit 3   D. Pit 4

II. Multiple Choice

1. In Pit No. 1, Some warriors wore robes, some wore armors, all of this were according to their _____.

A. age   B. rank   C. army services   D. gender

2. Terra-cotta Army Pit 2 is the most spectacular of the three pits, with _____ in the pit.

A. the Terra-cotta general   B. the kneeling archer
C. the cavalry warrior with saddle horse   D. the headquarter

3. Pit 2 is the most complete pit as it houses all types of the Terra-cotta warriors found so far, including _____.

A. infantries   B. cavalries   C. chariot warriors   D. archers

4. Which is true of Pit No. 3? _____.

A. It is the smallest one

B. It is the command post with high-ranking officers and a war chariot

C. Figurines in Pit 3 are standing face to face

D. Ancient weapons which are called "Shu" got unearthed in it

III. True or False

1. In the Terra-cotta army, all four pits contain clay soldiers and weapons.

2. Pit No.1, No.2, and No.3 actually are real military formation.

3. The four pits have similar layout.

4. Pit 1 is more than twice bigger than Pit 2.

5. Pit No.3 is L-shaped.

6. Unearthed relics in Pit 3 including remains of animals just prove historians' assumption of rite is right.

IV. Fill in the Blanks

1. Except Pit 4, the other 3 pits were built with similar underground _____ structure.

2. The layout of these 3 pits shaped like a flying goose, called _____.

3. Pit 1 and Pit 2 are the _____ with different function that obey Pit 3's order as their _____.

4. _____ consists of large amount of infantries and battle chariots, while _____ is the formation lined with archery, cavalry and battle chariots.

5. The terracotta figures were placed into the pit paved with_____ through the passage, then filled with _____.

6. Each battle chariots in Pit 1 was equipped with three warriors, one was the _____ and other two were the warriors with _____ in hand.

5.3 Creator of the Terra-cotta Warriors

To ancient Chinese people, the social structure in the afterlife is exactly like that in the real world, especially in Qin Dynasty, the people regarded the death the same as the life. Without question, The First Qin Emperor would like to build a similar empire for his afterlife at any cost. Different from earlier rulers from the Shang and Zhou Dynasties who had soldiers, officials and other attendants buried along with the dead emperor, Qin Shi Huang had the terra-cotta figures produced to replace actual human sacrifices.

According to historical materials, there exist sun, moon, stars, rivers, mountains in his mausoleum. To protect the empire of his afterworld, an army could be a must. The Terra-cotta Army was included as one of the parts of the Mausoleum of the First Qin Emperor. Archaeologists suggest that the army was not only created to safeguard and serve the First Emperor of Qin in his afterlife, but also a show of the First Emperor of Qin's glory. It was built to remember the army he let to triumph over the Warring States and unite China. What's more, as we mentioned, it substitutes for actual human sacrifices.

The young emperor began the construction for his tomb when he was still alive in 215 BC, actually he was quite young, so that he could oversee all aspects of its construction. A total of 720 thousands men, which occupied 3.6% of the total population in Qin Dynasty, spent 39 years to construct the project which was not finished until the dead of the Emperor. The stones for building the mausoleum were carried without any mechanical appliances from some mountains which are about 97 miles away from the tomb, and the materials for molding the terra-cotta warriors and horses are the "yellow earth" easily obtained nearby the mausoleum. According to the historian Sima Qian (c.145—95 BC), workers from every province of the Empire toiled unceasingly until the death of the Emperor in 210 in order to construct a subterranean city within a gigantic mound. Most of the workmen died from exhaustion or were killed for secrecy reason after finishing their work.

Further background on the First Emperor:

Ying Zheng is considered the first emperor of China. The son of King Zhuangxiang of Qin and a concubine, Ying Zheng took the throne at the age of 13, following his father's death in 247 BC According to writings of court historian Sima Qian during the following Han dynasty, Qin ordered the mausoleum's construction shortly after taking the throne. By 221 BC, he had unified a collection of warring kingdoms and created what we now know as China, the oldest surviving political entity in the world. He became an emperor instead of a king. The name means the First Emperor of Qin Dynasty. The Qin Dynasty established the first empire in China. The empire existed only briefly from 221 to 207 BC, but the Qin Dynasty had a lasting cultural impact on the dynasties that followed.

The initial construction of the Great Wall began under Qin Shi Huang's reign and he presided over the standardization of currency and script, representing a huge step towards the development of China as a nation. In addition, during his rule, Qin standardized weights and measures and interlinked the states with canals and roads. But Qin Shi Huang is a crucial figure in China's long history. He has been seen in both positive and negative lights throughout history and his legacy is still the subject of much debate. It is precisely because of the limitations of the historical sources for the First Emperor that the archaeological evidence from his tomb is so important. These artifacts are tangible evidence of the First Emperor's existence, his great achievements and his vision. In fact, they have indeed ensured that he lives forever, although perhaps not quite as he had originally planned.

Notes

The Qin Dynasty and the state of Qin: The state of Qin was one of the most powerful states in the Eastern Zhou Dynasty, at the end of which various kingdoms fought and conquered for over 200 years and give the period the name "the Warring States Period". In 221 BC, the State of Qin conquered the last of the warring states, and united China under the Qin Dynasty. However, their dynastic rule from 221—207 BC was the shortest in Chinese history. Their empire fell apart after only 15 years but laid the foundation for 21 centuries of imperial rule.

Culture Notes

1. 据《史记》记载：秦始皇陵由丞相李斯依惯例开始主持规划设计，大将章邯监工，修筑时间长达39年之久，兵马俑是修筑秦陵的同时制作并埋入随葬坑内。

2. 制作工匠：兵马俑的制作工匠是处于秦帝国社会下层的一批陶工。这些陶工有的来自宫廷的制陶作坊，有的来自地方的制陶作坊。从陶俑身上发现的陶工名有80个，都是具有丰富实践经验的优秀陶工。

3. 制作工艺：兵马俑大部分是采用陶冶烧制的方法制成，先用陶模做出初胎，再覆盖一层细泥进行加工刻画加彩，有的先烧后接，有的先接再烧。火候均匀、色泽单纯、硬度很高。每一道工序中，都有不同的分工，都有一套严格的工作系统。当初的兵马俑都有鲜艳和谐的彩绘，发掘过程中发现有的陶俑刚出土时局部还保留着鲜艳的颜色，但是出土后由于被氧气氧化，颜色不到十秒钟瞬间消尽，化作白灰。现在能看到的只是残留的彩绘痕迹。

4. 陶俑种类：兵马俑从身份上区分，主要有士兵与军吏两大类，军吏又有低级、中级、高级之别。一般士兵不戴冠，而军吏戴冠，普通军吏的冠与将军的冠又不相同，甚至铠甲也有区别。其中的兵俑包括步兵、骑兵、车兵三类。根据实战需要，不同兵种的武士装备各异。俑坑中最多的是武士俑，平均身高1.80米左右，最高的1.90米以上，陶马高1.72米，长2.03米。秦俑大部分手执青铜兵器，有弓、弩、箭镞、铍、矛、戈、殳、剑、弯刀和钺，身穿甲片细密的铠甲，胸前有彩线挽成的结穗。军吏头戴长冠，数量比武将多。秦俑的脸型、身材、表情、眉毛、眼睛和年龄都有不同之处。

New Words

sacrifice	n.	the act of killing (an animal or person) in order to propitiate a deity	牺牲；献祭
safeguard	vt.	make safe	保护，保卫
triumph	n.	a successful ending of a struggle or contest	胜利；巨大的成就
substitute	vt.& vi.	put in the place of another	代替，替换
toil	vi.	work hard	长时间或辛苦地工作
subterranean	adj.	being or operating under the surface of the earth	地下的
gigantic	adj.	so exceedingly large or extensive as to suggest a giant or mammoth	巨大的，庞大的
throne	n.	the chair of state of a monarch, bishop, etc	御座；王位
preside	vi.	act as president	主持，指挥
legacy	n.	a gift of personal property by will	遗产
tangible	adj.	possible to be treated as fact	可触知的；确实的

I. Simple Selection

1. A total of _____ men, which occupied 3.6% of the total population in Qin Dynasty participated in building Qin Shi Huang's mausoleum.

    A. 720000   B. 620000   C. 100000   D. 150000

2. It took Qin Shi Huang _____ years to construct the project of his mausoleum which was not finished until the dead of the Emperor.

    A. 29   B. 39   C. 49   D. 59

3. Ying Zheng, the first emperor of China was he son of King _____ of Qin and a concubine.

    A. Zhuangxiang B. Xiaowen   C. Huiwen   D. Zhaoxiang

4. Ying Zheng took the throne at the age of _____.

    A. 23   B. 25   C. 13   D. 15

5. The materials for molding the terra-cotta warriors and horses are the "_____".

    A. stones from mountains faraway   B. yellow earth obtained nearby
    C. stones obtained nearby   D. yellow earth from mountains faraway

II. Multiple Choice

1. Archaeologists suggest that the army was not only created to _____, but also a _____. It was built _____. Third, as we mentioned it _____.

    A. safeguard and serve the First Emperor of Qin in his afterlife
    B. show the First Emperor of Qin's glory
    C. to remember the army he let to triumph over the Warring States and unite China
    D. substitute for actual human sacrifices

2. Which of the following is to Qin Shi Huang's credit?

    A. the initial construction of the Great Wall
    B. the standardization of currency and script
    C. the standardization of weights and measures
    D. interlinking the states with canals and roads

3. According to historical materials and modern excavation, there exist _____ _____ in Qinahihuang's mausoleum.

    A. sun, moon   B. stars   C. rivers   D. mountains

III. True or False

1. The construction of Qin Shi Huang's tomb begun immediately after his death.

2. To ancient Chinese people, the social structure in the afterlife is exactly like that in the real world.

3. Rulers from the Shang and Zhou Dynasties had soldiers, officials and other attendants buried along with the dead emperor.

4. The Terracotta Army was included as one of the parts of the Mausoleum of the First Qin Emperor.

5. Almost all of the workmen died from exhaustion in building the Mausoleum of the First Qin Emperor.

IV. Fill in the Blanks

1. Qinshihuang had the Terra-cotta figures produced to replace _____.

2. By 221 BC, Qin Shi Huang had unified a collection of _____ and created what we now know as China, the oldest surviving political entity in the world.

3. _____ established the first empire in China.

4. The Qin Dynasty existed only briefly from _____ to _____ BC.

5 _____ is considered the first emperor of China, hence named Qinshihuang.

The empire existed only briefly _____ years but had a lasting cultural impact on the dynasties that followed.

5.4 The Archaeological Significance of the Terra-cotta Army

The Terra-cotta Warriors provide information of great archaeological significance. The documentary value of a group of hyper realistic sculptures where no detail has been neglected—from the uniforms of the warriors, their arms, to even the horses' halters—is enormous.

Firstly, the information to be gleaned from the statues concerning the craft and techniques of potters and bronze-workers is immeasurable. The numerous unearthed cultural relics reflect the highest technical level of pottery, chariot assembly, metallurgy and metal processing in the Qin Dynasty.

Secondly, the grave mound, sites of constructions, burial tombs and burial pits in Qin Shi Huang Mausoleum truthfully maintain their original location, material, formation, technology and structure, which authentically reflect the constricting regulation of the Mausoleum and palace life and military systems of the Qin Dynasty. The army of statues bears unique testimony to the military organization in China at the time of the Warring Kingdoms.

Thirdly, each warrior differs in its facial features and expression, clothing, and hairstyle in accordance with its rank.

In ancient China, a person's hairstyle was not only part of his/her lifestyle, but also a reflection the social status. The hairstyles of the Terra-cotta warriors are different based on their ranks and arm of the services. Their hair was typed up with pins, ribbons or bands. The hairstyles of the figures could be divided into 2 different types. The first type includes figures wearing their hair in a bun on the right side of the head. The other type depicted figures wearing their hair in a bun at the top of the head that was then covered with a cloth cap.

The clothes of the terra-cotta figures are different. People can tell the rank and arm of military service from their dressing: Cavalrymen wear pillbox hats, neck scarves, and light body armor to the front and back. Their shoes are soft and round at the toes their mounts wouldn't be injured; Armored warriors wear heavily armored capes which were designed to protect their bodies especially their chests and backs, they also wear turtleneck robes to cover their necks; Only three generals were found in the pits (one in Pit 1 and two in Pit 2). The generals wear two layers of robes beneath an armored tunic in order to protect their chests, backs and shoulders. They also wear square-toed shoes, which are lightweight and curve upwards at the front; Chariot drivers have extra protection for their outstretched arms and hands that need to control the horses. They wear helmets to protect their head and the back of their necks.

Fourthly, to glean clues about their production, archaeologists measured a large sample of the weapons, analyzed the chemical composition of their metal, and studied small inscriptions chiseled into their surfaces. The results revealed something surprising. Initially, team members hypothesized that armorers manufactured the weapons using an assembly-line system similar to that developed by American car manufacturer Henry Ford. In this scenario, specialized workers would continuously produce one type of part—a bronze arrowhead, say, or a bamboo arrow shaft—and then send their products to an assembly line. There, workers would fit parts together to make one type of weapon.

But the chemical composition of the arrowheads pointed to a different picture. Each bundle exhibited a distinct chemical signature, slightly different from those in neighboring bundles. This strongly suggested that Qin Shi Huang's armorers worked in a "cellular production" system similar in some respects to that pioneered by Toyota to produce cars. Instead of monotonously making the same part for an assembly line, the imperial weapon makers were probably versatile artisans who worked in small, dispersed workshops making weapons from start to finish.

Each armorer was held accountable, however, for what he produced. Many of the small weapons bore chiseled symbols akin to makers' marks. Larger lances, halberds, and swords carried more detailed inscriptions that recorded the years they were made and the names of each person in the chain of command responsible for their manufacture.

This allowed imperial officials to track down anyone producing defective arms and mete out "stiff sanctions". The emperor ruled his vast realm with an iron hand.

The archaeological work towards the Terra-cotta Warriors was not confined in China. In fact, foreign historians have never stopped their research about it and contributed a lot. For example, John Komlos, a now retired German economic historian. Komlos measured 734 terra-cotta warriors and compared their heights to those of 150 Chinese men measured in the mid-19th century and reached the conclusion that the size of the Terra-cotta figures could well represent the true physical stature of the Chinese infantry". Another example, a team of archaeologists from University College London (UCL) in Britain and from Emperor Qin Shi Huang's Mausoleum Site Museum in Lintong, China, photographed and analyzed the years of 30 figures and discovered that none of them was the same as the others, which forcefully proves that every warrior is unique.

Culture Notes

1. 秦兵马俑为研究秦代军事、文化和经济提供了丰富的实物资料。它的发掘被誉为"20世纪考古史上伟大的发现之一",是考察古代建筑结构,陶俑排列,兵器配备,指挥部形制、卜占及出战仪式,命将制度等的珍贵资料。

2. 兵马俑展示了古代的颜料生产工艺水平。通过对已出土的陶俑身上服饰彩绘颜色的初步统计和分析得知粉绿、朱红、粉紫、天蓝四种颜色使用的最多,化验表明这些颜色均为矿物质。这表明2000多年前中国劳动人民已能大量生产和广泛使用这些颜料。这在世界科技史上有着重要意义。

3. 兵马俑展示了古代的冶金工艺水平。兵马俑坑内出土的青铜兵器有剑、矛、戟、弯刀以及大量的弩机、箭头等。据化验数据表明,这些铜锡合金兵器经过铬化处理,虽然埋在土里2000多年,依然刀锋锐利,闪闪发光,表明当时已经有了很高的冶金技术,可以视为世界冶金史上的奇迹。

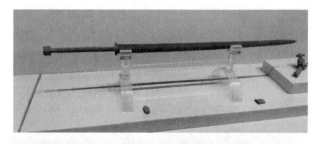

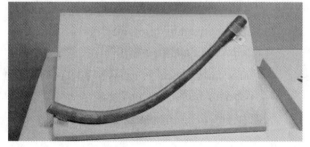

4. "物勒工名"制度,源于战国中期秦国,是秦国政府管理官府手工业、保证产品质量、控制和监督工匠生产的一种手段。这种手段运用于秦陵兵马俑的制作上,在陶俑、陶马身上打印或刻划陶工名,一方面加强了对工匠的控制与管理,另一方面也有利于作品质量的提高。在出土的陶俑、陶马身上的一些隐蔽处,考古工作者发现了一些刻划或戳印文字。字数很少,一般只有两个字,最多的一件有11个字;陶文除了编号外,都是陶工名。这些陶工名大体上可以分为四类:一是在人名前带"宫"字的,简称作宫字类;二是在人名前带"右"字或"大"字的,省称作右字和大字类;三是人名前带一地方名的；四是只有人名的，人名多数仅有一两个字，个别的为三个字。在上述四类陶工中，第一、二类是来自中央官府制陶作坊的陶工；第三类是来自地方制陶手工业作坊的陶工；第四类因文字过于简略，而对其来源尚难作出判断。

New Words

halter	n.	ope or canvas headgear for a horse	（马的）笼头
assembly	n.	a group of machine parts that fit together to form a self-contained unit	集会
metallurgy	n.	the science and technology of metals	冶金，冶金学
authentically	adv.	genuinely; with authority	确实地，真正地
testimony	n.	an assertion offering firsthand authentication of a fact	证词；证明
arm	n.	an administrative division of some larger or more complex organization	职能部门
pillbox	n.	a small round hat for a woman	（无边平顶的）筒状女帽
cape	n.	a sleeveless garment like a cloak but shorter	斗篷；披肩
chest	n.	the part of the body between the neck and the diaphragm	胸部，胸腔
turtleneck	n.	a sweater or jersey with a high close-fitting collar	高领绒衣；高翻领
helmet	n.	armor plate that protects the head	头盔；钢盔
cellular	adj.	characterized by or divided into or containing cells or compartments	由细胞组成的
monotonously	adv.	very boring because it has a regular, repeated pattern which never changes	单调地，无变化地
imperial	adj.	relating to or associated with an empire	帝国的，皇帝的
versatile	adj.	having many skills	多用途的
chisel	vt.& vi.	carve	凿，雕
lance	n.	a long pointed rod used as a weapon	长矛，标枪
stiff	adj.	lacking ease in bending	僵硬的
sanction	n.	a mechanism of social control for enforcing a society's standards	制裁，约束力

I. Multiple Choice

1. The Terra-cotta Warriors provide numerous unearthed cultural relics reflecting _____ _____ in the Qin Dynasty.
   A. technical level of pottery   B. chariot assembly
   C. metallurgy   D. metal processing

2. The _____ in Qin Shi Huang Mausoleum truthfully maintain their original form.
   A. grave mound   B. sites of constructions
   C. burial tombs   D. burial pits

3. Qin Shi Huang Mausoleum truthfully maintains its original _____.
   A. location   B. material
   C. formation   D. technology and structure

4. Qin Shi Huang Mausoleum reflects the _____ of the Qin Dynasty.
   A. constricting regulation of the mausoleum
   B. palace life
   C. military systems
   D. soldiers' life

5. Each warrior differs in its _____.
   A. facial features   B. expression
   C. clothing   D. hairstyle

6. The hairstyles of the Terra-cotta warriors are different based on their _____.
   A. ranks   B. age   C. birthplace   D. arm of the services

7. The Terra-cotta Warriors includes figures wearing their hair in a bun _____.
   A. on the right side of the head   B. on the left side of the head
   C. at the top of the head   D. at he lower part of the head

8. Many of the small weapons bore chiseled symbols akin to makers' marks. Larger lances, halberds and swords carried more detailed inscriptions that recorded _____.
   A. the years they were made
   B. the name of the weapon
   C. the names of each person in the chain of command
   D. the chemical elements of the weapon

II. True or False

1. Cavalrymen wear pillbox hats.
2. Only two generals were found in the pits.
3. To study their production, archaeologists measured a large sample of the weapons and analyzed the chemical composition of their metal.

4. Chariot drivers have turtleneck robes to cover their necks

5. Armored warriors wear heavily armored capes.

6. Archaeologists discover that armorers manufactured the weapons using an assembly-line system.

III. Fill in the Blanks

1. The army of statues bears unique testimony to _____ in China at the time of the Warring Kingdoms.

2. In ancient China, a person's hairstyle was not only part of his/her lifestyle but also a reflection the _____.

3. People watching the Terra-cotta Warriors can tell the rank and _____ service from their dressing.

4. Qin Shi Huang's armorers worked in a _____ system.

5. "Cellular production" allowed imperial officials to track down anyone producing defective arms and mete out "_____".

IV. Read the passage about the Terra-cotta Army, and answer the questions:

Recently, in a project known as Imperial Logistics: The Making of the Terracotta Army, a team of archaeologists from University College London (UCL) in Britain and from Emperor Qin Shi Huang's Mausoleum Site Museum in Lintong, China, have been using the latest imaging technology and other advanced methods to deduce the design process behind the warriors. The British-Chinese team took detailed measurements of the statues' facial features, focusing especially on the ears. Forensic research shows that ear shapes are so variable among humans that they can be used to identify individuals.

"If a thief presses an ear against a door or a windowpane, that can be as effective as a fingerprint," says team member and UCL archaeologist Andrew Bevan. If the Terra-cotta warriors portrayed real people, each statue should have distinctively shaped ears.

But taking measurements of the clay ears was a risky proposition. The fragile warriors are packed so tightly in their burial pit that moving among them with calipers could have damaged them. So the team used new digital technology known as structure-from-motion to create precise, three-dimensional reconstructions of the warriors' ears.

For the initial sample, team members picked 30 Terra-cotta warriors and photographed the left side of their heads from a safe distance and from slightly different vantage points. Then they digitally combined the photos to create 3D models of each left ear and measured the complex surface geometries of each.

Statistical analysis revealed that no two ears in the small sample group were exactly the same. Indeed, the degree of variability resembled a human population. This preliminary finding lends credence to the idea that the ancient artists were aiming for realism.

1. This passage might be _____ about the terra-cotta army.

  A. news   B. a sutudent's composition

  C. a school text   D. travel information

2. The best title of this passage is _____.

    A. Scientists and the Terra-cotta Warriors
    B. Ears of Ancient Chinese Terra-cotta Warriors Offer Clues to Their Creation
    C. the Terra-cotta Warrior's faces
    D. a ear can be as effective as a fingerprint
3. In the project, archaeologists _____.
    A. discovered a thief who presses an ear against a door or a windowpane
    B. photographed all the terra-cotta warriors
    C. aimed to get clue of the design process behind the warriors
    D. portrayed real people
4. Which of the following is true?
    A. Archaeologists are testing whether ear shape can be used to identify individuals.
    B. Archaeologists are helping in reconstructions of the warriors' ears.
    C. The research shows that it is possible that all the warriors are different from each other.
    D. Policemen will benefit from the research.

Unit 6 *Peking Opera*

6.1 The Origin of Peking Opera

With the overseas dissemination of Peking Opera, more and more foreigners are becoming interested in Chinese Opera. Peking Opera is a combination and mixture of many other dramatic forms, it absorbs mostly from the local drama '*Huiban*' which was popular in South China during the 18th century as well as *Kunqu* and *Qinqiang* which was formed much earlier. It is a scenic art integrating performance, music, literature, aria, and face-painting. Peking Opera has had many interesting names since it came into being, such as *Jinghuang*, *Pingju*, *Jingxi*, etc.

"Peking Opera" is the English term for the art form. Beijing Opera is a more recent equivalent. In China, the art form has been known by many other names in different times and places. From the earliest *Pi Huang* to *Jingju* or *Jingxi*, which reflects its start in the capital city, Jing and the form of the performance Xi. It is known that the name of Peking Opera is related to the birthplace of it. Peking Opera is a principal tradition in Chinese culture.

This attractive art form started from royal activity. In 1790, the first Anhui Opera performance was held in Beijing to celebrate the Emperor of Qianlong's 80th birthday on September 25. That was the first performance of it in Beijing. Later, some other Anhui Opera troupes went on to perform in Beijing.

In 1828, several famous Hubei troupes arrived in Beijing and performed jointly with Anhui troupes. The combination of these two forms gradually formed Peking Opera's melodies. Peking Opera was generally regarded as having fully formed by 1845. From then on, Peking Opera experienced development improvement and perfection periods.

At the end of the 19th century and the beginning of the 20th century, after merging for 10 years, Peking Opera was finally formed, and became the biggest of all operas in China. Peking Opera has a rich list of plays, artists, troupes, audiences, and wide influences, making it the foremost opera in China.

It is widely acknowledged that the end of the 18th century was the most flourishing period in the development of Peking Opera. During this time, there were lots of performances not only in folk places, but also in the palace. The noble class loved Peking Opera; the superior elements in the palace played a positive role in the performances, make-up, and stage setting. The mutual influence between palace and non-government places promoted Peking Opera's development.

From the 1920's to the 1940's of 20th century was the second flourishing period of Peking Opera. The symbol of this period was the emergence of lots of sects of the opera.

As far as we know, there are different sects, such as "*Mei*" (Mei Lanfang), "*Shang*" (Shang Xiaoyun), "*Cheng*" (Cheng Yanqiu) and "*Xun*" (Xun Huisheng). Every sect had its groups of actors and actresses. Furthermore, they were extremely active on the stage in Beijing, Shanghai and so on. The art of Peking Opera was very popular at that time.

One of the reasons why Peking Opera is unique, it is the special melody. Although it is called Peking Opera, its origins are in the southern Anhui and eastern Hubei, which share the same dialect of Xiajiang Mandarin. Peking Opera's two main melodies, Xipi and Erhuang, derived from Han Opera after about 1750. The tune of Peking Opera is extremely similar to that of Han Opera, therefore, Han Opera is widely known as the Mother of Peking Opera.

Xipi literally means shadow play, referring to the puppet show that originated in Shaanxi province. Chinese puppet shows always involve singing. Much dialogue is also carried out in an archaic form of Mandarin Chinese.

Some scholars believe that the Xipi musical form derived from the historic Qinqiang, while many conventions of staging, performance elements and aesthetic principles were retained from Kunqu, the form that preceded it as court art.

Today, Peking Opera is regarded as one of the cultural treasures of China and has also spread to other countries. It serves as a bridge through which the traditional Chinese culture is introduced to other parts of the world. In 2010, Peking Opera was listed on the World Cultural Heritage.

Notes

Peking Opera was originally performed in *Xiyuanzi*, which means "opera courtyard". Back then, people went to tea houses, sat on benches facing one another and paid only for the tea, not for the shows. Peking Opera was just some kind of side entertainment; the actors had to keep performing for up to 10 hours.

Culture Notes

京剧，曾称平剧，中国五大戏曲剧种之一，场景布置注重写意，腔调以西皮、二黄为主，用胡琴和锣鼓等伴奏，被视为中国国粹，中国戏曲三鼎甲"榜首"。

纪录片《京剧》参见网址 http://tv.cctv.com/2013/06/16/VIDE1371312186981679.shtml。

New Words

dissemination	n.	the opening of a subject to widespread discussion and debate	宣传；散播；传染（病毒）
combination	n.	a collection of things that have been combined; an assemblage of separate parts or qualities	结合；组合；联合
dramatic	adj.	suitable to or characteristic of drama	戏剧的；急剧的；引人注目的
scenic	adj.	used of locations; having beautiful natural scenery	风景优美的；舞台的；戏剧的
integrate	vt.	make into a whole or make part of a whole	使⋯完整；使⋯成整体
equivalent	adj.	equal in amount or value	等价的，相等的
reflect	vt.	manifest or bring back	反映；反射；照出；表达
attractive	adj.	pleasing to the eye or mind especially through beauty or charm	吸引人的；有魅力的
troupe	n.	organization of performers and associated personnel (especially theatrical)	剧团；一班；一团
melody	n.	a succession of notes forming a distinctive sequence	旋律；歌曲；美妙的音乐
acknowledge	vt.	declare to be true or admit the existence or reality or truth of	承认；答谢；报偿

sect   *n.*   a subdivision of a larger religious group   宗派

I. Simple Selection

1. How did Peking Opera came into being?
   A. When four Henan Opera troupes performed for the 80th birthday of the Emperor.
   B. When four Heibei Opera troupes performed for the 80th birthday of the Emperor.
   C. When four Anhui Opera troupes performed for the 80th birthday of the Emperor.
   D. When four Jiangsu Opera troupes performed for the 80th birthday of the Emperor.

2. The origin of Peking Opera was for celebration of the birthday of _____.
   A. Qian Long   B. Kang Xi   C. Yong Zheng   D. Jia Qing

3. Some scholars believe that the Xipi musical form derived from the _____.
   A. Pihuang   B. historic Qinqiang   C. Pi ying   D. Kun Qu

4. The ancestor of Peking Opera is _____.
   A. Hui Ju   B. Han Ju   C. Pi ying   D. Kun Qu

5. Peking Opera is centered in Beijing and spread all the country even the world. It is listed on World Intangible Cultural Heritage on November 16 th, _____.
   A. 2010   B. 2011   C. 2012   D. 2013

II. True or False

1. One of the reasons why Peking opera is unique, it is the special melody.

2. Han opera is widely known as the Mother of Peking opera.

3. Peking Opera serves as a bridge through which the traditional Chinese culture is introduced to other parts of the world. In 2011, Peking Opera was listed on the World Cultural Heritage.

4. Many countries design posters using Peking Opera masks to signal a "Year of Chinese Culture".

5. Peking Opera has the fame of Chinese culture essence.

6. It is widely acknowledged that the end of the 19th century was the most flourishing period in the development of Beijing Opera.

7. Most notable Peking operas with modern themes were composed before the founding of the People's Republic of China.

III. Translation

京剧，又称"东戏"，是中国文化的一个主要传统。它之所以叫京剧，是因为它是在北京形成的。京剧有200多年的历史，其源头可以追溯到古老的地方戏剧，尤其是安徽戏剧。戏剧18世纪在中国北方很流行。1790年，为庆祝皇帝的生日，安徽第一场戏剧演出在北京举行。后来，其他一些安徽剧团陆续来北京演出。安徽戏曲动作流畅，善于吸收其他戏曲的表演风格。北京积累了许多地方戏曲，使安徽戏曲发展迅速。

The Delights of Peking Opera Masks

In order to understand the charm of masks, we have to know the roles of Peking Opera. Over the past hundreds of years, the roles of Peking Opera have been simplified to today's *Sheng*, *Dan*, *Jing* and *Chou*, known as the four major roles in Peking Opera.

The S*heng* is the main male role in Peking Opera, which has numerous subtypes. For example, the *Laosheng* is a dignified older role with a gentle and cultivated disposition. Young male characters as *Xiaosheng* sing in a high, shrill voice with occasional breaks. The *Wusheng* is a martial character for roles involving combat who is highly trained in acrobatics and has a natural voice when singing.

The *Dan* refers to any female role in Peking opera. Dan roles were originally divided into five subtypes. Old women were played by *Laodan*, martial women were *Wudan*, young female warriors were *Daomadan*, virtuous and elite women were *Qingyi*, and vivacious and unmarried women were *Huadan*. A troupe will have a young Dan to play main roles, as well as an older Dan for secondary parts.

The greatest master of Peking Opera Mei Lanfang played the role of *Dan*, so this role doesn't mean the person playing the role is female, but the role on the stage is female.

The *Jing* is a painted face male role. Depending on the repertoire of the particular troupe, he will play either primary or secondary roles. *Jing* will entail a forceful character that has a strong voice and is able to exaggerate gestures. There are 15 basic facial patterns, but over 1,000 specific variations of those. Each design is unique to a specific character.

The last role is *Chou*. It is a male clown role. The *Chou* usually plays secondary roles in a troupe. Indeed, most studies of Peking Opera classify the *Chou* as a minor role. *Chou* roles can be divided into *wenchou*, civilian roles such as merchants and jailers, and *Wuchou*, minor military roles.

Chou characters are generally amusing and likable, sometimes a bit foolish. Their costumes range from simple for characters of lower status to elaborate for high status characters.

Chou has the meaning "ugly" in Chinese. It reflects the traditional belief that the clown's combination of ugliness and laughter could drive away evil spirits.

After understanding the roles of Peking Opera, let's look at Masks. China's Peking Opera radiates with the beauty of resplendent color—vivid, intense and glamorous.

This artistic beauty comes not only from the costumes, but also from the masks of exaggerated, dazzling designs, gleaming with reds, purples, whites, yellows, blacks, blues, green, every diverse color imaginable.

We know Masks, applied to the two roles of the *Jing* or painted-face role and the *Chou* or clown, but what are purposes of painting so much paints on their faces?

Actually there are two purposes. One is to indicate the identity and character of the role. For example, a "red face" means the person is loyal and brave; a "black face" signifies the person is straightforward and a "white face" identifies the person as crafty and evil.

This is demonstrated in the roles of Guan Yu, Zhang Fei and Cao Cao. They are the roles of famous novel named *The Romance of Three Kingdoms*.

The other purpose is to express people's appraisal of the roles from a moral and aesthetic point of view, such as respectable, hateful, noble, or ridiculous, etc.

So there exists the relationship between the color and characters. The main color in a facial makeup symbolizes the disposition and destiny of the character. As one of the essential elements of Peking Opera, the masks can help the audience understand the opera better. Generally speaking, different colors have different meanings.

To put it simple, red indicates devotion, bravery and uprightness; black indicates either a rough and bold character or an impartial and selfless personality; blue represents staunchness, fierceness and astuteness; a green face tells the audience that the character is impulsive and violent. Yellow signifies fierceness, ambition and cool-headedness; white suggests treacherousness, suspiciousness and craftiness; gold and silver colors are usually used for gods and spirits.

For different roles, the masks can vary a great deal. The makeup for the *Sheng* and *Dan* can be simpler, while the makeup for the *Jing* and *Chou* can be rather heavy, and for the *Jing* in particular, the pattern can be quite complex.

The Peking Opera masks often refer to the makeup of the *Jing*. For the *Chou*, they only need to powder their noses so as to form the image of a clown.

As we hardly appreciate the beauty of masks, the drawing of it must be more difficult. There is a strong nature in the art in masks. Drawing masks must also have attitudinal polytechnic nature, just like hand writing and painting. When you draw masks with a pen brush, you should do it with exactness and pithiness.

The romance should be suitable to let others see clearly where it is thick and where it is light.

Besides the meaning of colors on masks, the masks have 3 features: a combination of beauty and ugliness, an indication of the disposition of the character and the fixed pattern for drawing.

Culture Notes

京剧脸谱，是一种具有中国文化特色的特殊化妆方法。由于每个历史人物或某一种类型的人物都有一种大概的谱式，就像唱歌、奏乐都要按照乐谱一样，所以称为"脸谱"。京剧脸谱艺术是广大戏曲爱好者的非常喜爱的一门艺术，国内外都很流行，已经被大家公认为是中国传统文化的标识之一。脸谱的主要特点有三点：美与丑的矛盾统一；与角色的性格关系密切；其图案是程式化的。

New Words

cultivate	vt.	to foster the growth of	培养；陶冶；耕作
disposition	n.	the nature qualities of a person's character	处置；性情
occasional	adj.	occurring from time to time	偶然的；临时的；特殊场合的
combat	vt.	battle or contend against in or as if in a battle	反对；与…战斗；战斗；搏斗
originally	adv.	in an original manner	最初，起初；本来
warrior	n.	someone engaged in or experienced in warfare	战士，勇士；鼓吹战争的人
virtuous	adj.	morally excellent	善良的；有道德的；贞洁的
secondary	adj.	being of second rank or importance or value; not direct or immediate	第二的；中等的；次要的
repertoire	n.	the entire range of skills or aptitudes or devices used in a particular field or occupation	全部节目；计算机指令系统
particular	adj.	unique or specific to a person or thing or category	特别的；详细的；独有的
primary	adj.	of first rank or importance or value; direct and immediate rather than secondhand	主要的；初级的
exaggerate	vt.	to enlarge beyond bounds or the truth	使扩大；使增大
jailer	n.	someone who guards prisoners	狱卒，看守监狱的人
elaborate	adj.	marked by complexity and richness of detail	精心制作的；详尽的
indicate	vt.	be a signal for or a symptom of	表明；指出；预示

I. Simple Selection

1. *Qingyi* is also called_____.
   A. Zhengdan   B. Huadan   C. Laodan   D. Wudan
2. What mask should the actor of Bao Zheng wear in Peking Opera?
   A. A red one   B. A black one   C. A yellow one   D. A purple one
3. The characters of Peking Opera are divided into _____, *Dan*, *Jing* and *Chou*.
   A. *Lao sheng*   B. *Lao dan*   C. *Wu sheng*   D. *Sheng*
4. In character of *Dan*, old women were played by *Laodan*, martial women were *Wudan*, young female warriors were _____.
   A. *Qing Yi*   B. *Daoma dan*   C. *Lao dan*   D. *Dan*
5. Young male characters as _____ sing in a high, shrill voice with occasional breaks.
   A. *Lao sheng*   B. *Xiao sheng*   C. *Wu sheng*   D. *Sheng*
6. One purpose of mask is to indicate the identity and character of the role. For example, a "red face" means the person is loyal and brave; a "_____" signifies the person is straightforward; and a "white face" identifies the person as crafty and evil.
   A. black face   B. blue face   C. yellow face   D. green face
7. According to the article, what mask should the actor of Qin Hui wear in Peking Opera?
   A. A red one
   B. A black one
   C. A white one
   D. One in the shape of a butterfly

II. True or False

1. The roles in Peking Opera are divided into four types: *Sheng*, *Dan*, *Jing* and *Chou*.
2. *Sheng* is a common name of female characters.
3. A red face symbolizes loyalty and a black face signifies honesty and frankness.
4. The *Dan* refers to any female role in Peking Opera.
5. *Dan* roles were originally divided into five subtypes.
6. The role of *Dan* means the person playing the role is female, and the role on the stage is female.
7. There are 15 basic facial patterns of masks, but over 1000 specific variations of those.
8. Most studies of Peking Opera classify the *chou* as a major role.
9. Over the past hundreds of years, the roles of Peking Opera have been simplified to today's *Sheng*, *Dan*, *Jing* and *Chou*, known as the four major roles in Peking Opera.
10. The *Sheng* is the female role in Peking Opera.

III. Translate the Following Sentences into Chinese

Peking opera face-painting or Jingju Lianpu is done with different colors in accordance with the performing characters' personality and historical assessment. Roughly red-painted face means the loyalty, uprightness and intrepidity of the character's personality and characteristics such as Guan Yu. Black-painted face shows the character is upright, honest, brave even impertinent such as Bao Zheng who was the greatest clean-handed and respectable official in Song Dynasty. Yellow-painted face releases the brutality and inhumanity of the performing characters such as Dian Wei. Blue-painted or green-painted face shows the straightforwardness of the performing characters such as Dou Erdun. White-painted face shows the performing character is the evil man or illicit official such as Cao Cao and Zhao Gao.

6.3 Peking Opera Performance

To Chinese people, going to the theater to enjoy Peking Opera or other artistic performances is known as "seeing plays". In Peking Opera, "a play" is not so much the story or plot but a world of images created on stage, a wonderful arena of harmony between sentiments and settings.

The "play" or "world of images" created by Peking Opera naturally relies on the plot provided by the script, and more importantly on the performance of the actors.

However, to form a "world of images" in Peking Opera, the plot of a story provides only the framework and background, while the charm is produced by the actors' performance.

The performance of a Peking Opera actor can be summarized into four basic aspects, They are singing, speaking, acting and fighting. The core of which is a combination of song and choreography.

The uniqueness of performances in Peking Opera lies in the performance of singing, speaking, acting and fighting, all focus on one or two actors in the play.

Peking Opera and the Western Opera differ from one another in many ways. One of the main differences lies in the skills a performer needs to master, and consequently, in his training. The Peking Opera performer should be well-versed in singing, reciting, acting and acrobatics.

The first one is singing. Singing is of utmost importance in the performance of Peking Opera, because first of all, Peking Opera is a singing art. Opera boasts several wonderful arias that are well-known and popular with audiences.

The vocal music system in the West is divided into tenor, baritone and bass. It is up to the composer which vocal range he chooses for example for the role of a young man. The vocal music system in Peking Opera is entirely different. Each role has its own particular singing style and inside each role category, many other different singing patterns can be distinguished.

For example with respect to the *Dan* roles, the role of *Laodan*(elderly woman) mainly uses the real voice, whereas the role of *Qingyi* (young woman) uses mainly falsetto. A performer can play any role as long as he or she masters the singing style of that particular role. An actress can play the role of a painted face—a male character, whereas a male actor can play a *Dan* (female) role.

The second form is speaking. It refers to character monologs and dialogs, which serve to propel the development of the story. Speaking, like singing, needs to be executed in an appealing way.

The roles tell the story by speaking, whereas singing is more concerned with expression of emotions. The performer speaks in *changbai*, a speaking technique different from the daily speaking. The actor rises or muffles his voice and lengthens certain syllables to create a specific rhythm. The goal is never to imitate a conversation in a realistic way.

Acting is *Zuo* in Chinese. The Peking Opera actor possesses fine mimic skills. Without the support of complementary stage design, he has to describe the situation and the environment around him through his gestures. When the actor makes his appearance on the stage followed by a servant holding a light, the audience immediately understands that the scene takes place during the night; he opens and closes a door where there is no door at all on the stage; he mounts or dismounts a horse, boards a ship or leaves it. For example, the famous play *Picking up the Jade Bracelet*（《拾玉镯》）is an opera full of acting. In this play the actress is holding needle and thread in her hand and putting it into the hole of the needle. We can feel the movement, although without the real object. This is the charm of acting. Acting includes body movements and eye movements, solo dancing or group dancing.

The last aspect of performance is acrobatics or fighting. It's *Da* in Chinese. Acrobatics has been for long Peking Opera's most appreciated feature by Westerners. Performers' acrobatic skills are mostly displayed in the form of martial arts. Combats are often the highlight of martial plays; the audiences' interest is held by a crowded punch-up or the reckoning between two bitter enemies.

Fighting is choreographed martial arts and acrobatics (杂技) to depict fight or battle scenes. As the art of Peking Opera depends on movement to depict events, actors are given much room to perform on the stage. How to perform the art of fighting on the stage. The most famous section about it is *San Cha Kou*.

Acting and fighting serve the whole "play" or the "world of images", but at the same time they are themselves a beautiful art in both form and skill. Acting and fighting mean that actors employ physical movements to express the emotions of the characters and the circumstances.

Modern schools teach the art of performance as well as some theory. The education of a Peking Opera performer still consists in face-to-face tutoring; the teacher valuates the students and assigns them the roles of primary, secondary or tertiary characters according to their talent. Promising students perform as main characters, while students endowed with less performing talent may serve as musicians.

Notes

Since a good Peking Opera performer has to master so many different skills, the apprenticeship can be very rough and challenging. Today as in the past century, performers are first trained in acrobatics, followed by singing and acting.

Culture Notes

唱、念、做、打是戏曲表演的四种艺术手段,同时也是戏曲表演的四项基本功。通常被称为"四功"。唱指唱功,念指具有音乐性的念白,二者相辅相成,构成歌舞化的戏曲表演艺术两大要素之一的"歌",做指舞蹈化的形体动作,打指武打和翻跌的技艺,二者相互结合,构成歌舞化的戏曲表演艺术两大要素之一的"舞"。习称四功五法的四功,即指唱念做打四种技艺的功夫。

参考网址:http://tv.cctv.com/2013/06/18/VIDE1371493095160198.shtml

New Words

plot	n.	a secret scheme to do something (especially something underhand or illegal)	情节;图
arena	n.	a particular environment or walk of life	舞台;竞技场
sentiment	n.	tender, romantic, or nostalgic feeling or emotion	感情,情绪;情操;观点
script	n.	a written version of a play or other dramatic composition; used in preparing for a performance	脚本;手迹;书写用的字母
framework	n.	a hypothetical description of a complex entity or process	框架,骨架;结构
charm	n.	attractiveness that interests or pleases or stimulates	魅力,吸引力;魔力
summarize	vt.	give a summary (of)	总结;概述

aspect	n.	a distinct feature or element in a problem	方面；方向；形势
choreography	n.	a show involving artistic dancing	编舞；舞蹈艺术
uniqueness	n.	the quality of being one of a kind	独特性；独一无二
vocal	n.	music intended to be performed by one or more singers, usually with instrumental accompaniment	歌唱的；声音的
falsetto	n.	a male singing voice with artificially high tones in an upper register	假音；假声歌手
monolog	n.	speech you make to yourself	独白
execute	vt.	kill as a means of socially sanctioned	实行；执行
rhythm	n.	the basic rhythmic unit in a piece of music	节奏；韵律
complementary	adj.	of words or propositions so related that each is the negation of the other	补足的，补充的
choreograph	v.	compose a sequence of dance steps, often to music	设计舞蹈动作；为…编舞

I. Simple Selection

1. _____ is of utmost importance in the performance of Peking Opera, because first of all, Peking Opera is such kind of art.
    A. Singing   B. Speaking   C. Acting   D. Fighting

2. Speaking refers to character monologs and _____, which serve to propel the development of the story.
    A. words   B. lines   C. dialogs   D. songs

3. Which of the following is mentioned as involved with acting and fighting?
    A. Eye contract   B. Kong fu   C. Aerobatics   D. Gymnastics

4. For the basic skills of Peking Opera, which one is the closest with actor of nowadays?
    A. Singing   B. Speaking   C. Acting   D. Fighting

5. The proverb of "One minute on stage, ten years off stage" is often described for which skill of Peking Opera?
    A. Singing   B. Speaking   C. Acting   D. Fighting

II. True or False

1. Singing is not as important as acting in Peking Opera.
2. The roles tell the story by speaking, whereas singing is more concerned with expression of emotions.
3. Speaking is of utmost importance in the performance of Peking Opera, because first of all, Peking Opera is a speaking art.
4. The performance of a Peking Opera actor can be summarized into four basic aspects: singing, speaking, acting and fighting.
5. Speaking refers to character dialogs, which serve to propel the development of the story.

III. Answer the Question

1. Why is singing the most important skill in Peking Opera performance?
2. Please illustrate the performance of acting on stage according to famous opera, from the aspects of the process of acting without the real instrument on stage, such as rowing the boat or washing the coat and so on.

6.4 The Beauty of "Virtual World"

Depicting a "virtual world" is a distinctive feature of Peking Opera. Its virtuality consists of two aspects: one is virtual movements and the other virtual settings. Virtual movement refers to imitating actions onstage. For instance, riding a horse. A virtual setting means creating an imagined environment onstage. For example, rowing a boat.

Onstage, an actor can not ride a real horse, but can only hold a whip and imitate the movement by walking around the stage, turning the body, wielding the whip, and pulling the reins. A virtual setting means creating an imagined environment onstage. For example, as there is no water or boat on the stage, an actor usually takes an oar and through actions, makes the audience "see" the rowing of a boat on water.

The setting of the stage is very simple. Usually there is only one table and two chairs. The table, besides functioning as a table, may also symbolize a bed when an actor acts asleep by sitting on it with one hand upon it propping up his head. If he stands on the table and looks into the distance, it turns into a city gate tower. Simply put, changes in the stage setting follow the performance of the actors.

The effectiveness of virtual movements and virtual settings lies in their giving prominence to the actors' performance, helping the audience feel the rich connotations of the opera and its infinite appeal.

The function of the "virtual world" in the art of Peking Opera, which provides limitless room for the performances of actors; in return, performers present the audience with a world of images full of appealing wit.

Among audiences of Peking Opera there is a popular saying, "Watching a play is watching famous actors" or "Listening to an opera is listening to famous performers singing". Such remarks summarize the foremost of the main features of appreciating Peking Opera. The features of appreciating Peking Opera are decided by the characteristics of image creation in Peking Opera.

When the audiences enjoy an opera, they bear in mind not only the protagonists (主人公) of the story but also the performers who play the roles. And the performances of the actors are what they have come to the theater to enjoy, especially when the performers are well-known. This is the meaning of "Watching a play is watching famous actors".

Another observation from Peking Opera audiences is that "the more familiar an opera, the more enjoyable". When a person watches a Peking Opera, the more one is familiar with it, the further the background and plot of the story recede into the distance, the more one focuses on enjoying the performances of the actors, and feels, grasps and enjoys the deeper meaning and magic of the actors' performances.

The second characteristic of Peking Opera appreciation is that the audience always separates the beauty of the craft and form of the performance from the world of imagery. A short aria of acrobatic movement will win admiring applause from the audience. Usually, when the audience see a person performing stunts (绝技) in a film or play, they never applaud this because they only see the role; in Peking Opera, however, the same scene may bring the house down, because theatergoers pay attention to both the role and the actor, and to the beauty in form and skill of the actor's performance.

As the famous German dramatist Bertolt Brecht (1898—1956) once remarked, when we watch a Chinese actor perform onstage, we see at least three characters at the same time: one being the performer (the actor) and also the two roles being performed (the actor and the role). He thus called performance in Peking Opera a "dual performance", an important feature in the appreciation of Peking Opera. From the "dual performance", different audiences appreciate different aspects. Some prefer the entire role-centered imagery on the stage, while others enjoy the performance of the actor; and most shift between the two, gaining double enjoyment from the "dual performance".

The famous actors in Peking Opera are called *MingJuer* in Chinese. Besides the talents the actors possesses and actors diligence what is more important is the supporting or sponsoring from audiences. It's called *Peng Juer* in Chinese.

Bertolt Brecht，贝尔托·布莱希特，也译做贝托尔德·布

莱希特（1898年2月10日—1956年8月14日）。是一位著名的德国戏剧家与诗人。1898年2月10日，贝尔托·布莱希特生于德国巴伐利亚奥格斯堡镇。他年轻时曾任剧院编剧和导演，也曾投身工人运动。1933年后流亡欧洲大陆。1941年经苏联去美国，但战后遭迫害，1947年返回欧洲。1948年起定居东柏林。1951年因对戏剧的贡献而获国家奖金。1955年获列宁和平奖金。1956年8月14日布莱希特逝世于柏林。

New Words

virtual	adj.	being actual in almost every respect	虚拟的；实质上的
setting	n.	the context and environment in which something is set	环境；安装
imitate	vt.	reproduce someone's behavior or looks	模仿，仿效
row	vt.	propel with oars	划船；使…成排
whip	n.	an instrument with a handle and a flexible lash that is used for whipping	鞭子；抽打
rein	n.	one of a pair of long straps (usually connected to the bit or the headpiece) used to control a horse	缰绳；驾驭；统治
symbolize	vt.	to express indirectly by an image, form, or model; be a symbol	象征；用符号表现
prop	n.	a support placed beneath or against something to keep it from shaking or falling	支柱，支撑物
effectiveness	n.	power to be effective; the quality of being able to bring about an effect	效力
connotation	n.	an idea suggest by a word in addition to its main meaning	内涵；含蓄；暗示
infinite	adj.	having no limits or boundaries in time or space or extent or magnitude	无限的，无穷的
appeal	vt.	to take a court case to a higher court for review	呼吁，恳求
remark	n.	a statement that expresses a personal opinion or belief	注意；言辞
protagonist	n.	a person who backs a politician or a team etc.	主角，主演，主要人物
observation	n.	the act of making and recording a measurement	观察；监视

enjoyable	*adj.*	affording satisfaction or pleasure	快乐的；有乐趣的
background	*n.*	a person's social heritage: previous experience or training	背景；隐蔽的位置
craft	*n.*	the skilled practice of a practical occupation	工艺；手艺
aria	*n.*	an elaborate song for solo voice	咏叹调，独唱曲
acrobatic	*adj.*	vigorously active	杂技的；特技的
stunt	*n.*	a difficult or unusual or dangerous feat; usually done to gain attention	噱头，手腕；绝技
dramatist	*n.*	someone who writes plays	剧作家，剧本作者
dual	*adj.*	consisting of or involving two parts or components usually in pairs	双的；双重的

I. Simple Selection

1. A virtual _____ means creating an imagined environment onstage. For example, Rowing a Boat.
  A. setting   B. movement   C. stage   D. role

2. The function of the "_____" in the art of Peking Opera, which provides limitless room for the performances of actors; in return, performers present the audience with a world of images full of appealing wit.
  A. virtual setting   B. virtual world
  C. lines   D. acting

3. What is special about the performance *At the Crossroad* is that, although the fight happens _____, the stage is brightly lit; yet the audience is able to sense it is a pitch-dark night from the actors' performance, which feature stealthy movements typical of people in darkness.
  A. in the morning   B. in the afternoon
  C. at night   D. at noon

4. In *Picking up the Jade Bracelet*, Sun Yujiao was selecting one pattern to embroidery on her cloth. She acted on the stage without _____.
  A. knife and fork   B. cloth and clothes
  C. needle and thread   D. paper and pen

5. In Peking Opera, "a play" is not so much the story or plot but a world of images created onstage, a wonderful arena of harmony between _____ and settings.

    A. sentiments   B. players   C. settings   D. stages

6. Which of the following statements is true of Peking Opera?

    A. The real charm of Peking Opera is created by the actors.

    B. The actors usually stand at the center of the stage.

    C. There must be famous arias in any Peking Opera.

    D. Speaking is designed to attract the audience's attention.

7. What is implied but not stated about the setting of Peking Opera?

    A. The setting is all virtual without any real props.

    B. The setting of the stage is very complex.

    C. One prop can serve different purposes.

    D. Actors are in charge of changing the stage setting.

8. According to the examples, the benefits of virtual movements and settings are that _____.

    A. they save the cost of the performance

    B. they save the labor force of changing the stage

    C. actors have more room on the stage for their performance

    D. they highlight the actors' performance

9. What can we learn about Peking Opera through the saying "watching a play is watching famous actors"?

    A. The viewers go to the theater to see the actors instead of the play.

    B. The famous actors are good-looking and perform well.

    C. The actors are good at all of the four basic aspects of Peking Opera.

    D. The performances of the actors are as important as the play itself.

10. Which of the following is the distinct feature of watching a Peking Opera as compared with seeing a film?

    A. The Peking Opera theatergoers pay more attention to the roles.

    B. The Peking Opera theatergoers applaud from time to time while watching a performance.

    C. The audience of a film applaud when a person performing stunts.

    D. The audience of a film value the beauty of the craft so that they ignore the world of imagery.

II. True or False

1. Tables and chairs and can be used for different purposes in Peking Opera.

2. There are lots of props on the stage to indicate different situations.

3. The virtuality of Peking Opera consists of two aspects: one is virtual movements, and the other virtual settings.

4. Virtual movement refers to imitating actions onstage. For instance, rowing a boat.

5. The "play" or "world of images" created by Peking Opera naturally relies on the plot

provided by the script.

III. Translation

唱、念、做、打是戏曲表演中的四种艺术手段，同时也是戏曲演员表演的四种基本功。通常被称为"四功"。"唱"指的是唱功。"做"指的是做功，也就是表演。"念"指的是音乐性念白。而"打"则指的是武功。戏曲演员从小就从这四个方面进行训练培养的，虽然有的演员擅长唱功，有的行当以做功为主，有的以武打为主。但是要求每一个演员必须有过硬的唱、念、做、打四种基本功，才能充分发挥作为歌舞剧的戏曲艺术表演的功能。

6.5 The Appreciation of Famous Peking Operas

Picking up the Jade Bracelet (Shi Yuzhuo)

The young woman Sun Yujiao and the young scholar fell in love with each other, and their eyes affixed on each other as if a thread connected them. In this section we will see Sun Yujiao was selecting one pattern to embroidery on her cloth. The most famous section is how she acted on the stage without needle and thread.

At the Crossroad（三岔口）

This opera describes the story of two yamen runners escorting Jiao Zan to prison. On the way they stay at an inn for the night. "ren" Tanghui, whose task is to protect Jiao Zan, checks in at the same time. The owner of the inn, however, suspects "ren" Tang hui is planning to murder Jiao Zan, so he gropes his way into "ren"'s room at night. Thus a fight stars.

What is special about the performance is that, although the fight happens at night, the stage is brightly lit; yet the audience is able to sense it is a pitch-dark night from the actors' performance, which feature stealthy movements typical of people in darkness. Sometimes, one man's sword swishes down, only a few inches away from the other's face, yet the latter feels nothing, thus producing a breathtaking yet meaningful and humorous effect.

Autumn River

This play transplanted from Sichuan Opera. This story describes a young nun, Chen Miaochang who leaves the nunnery to pursue her lover Pan Bizheng. On stage, there is neither water nor boat, but through the performance of the young woman and the old boatman, the audience is able to obviously see that the stage is a river. The boat sways forward; all the way there the girl complains about the boat for being slow, while the old boatman keeps teasing her about her anxiety to see her lover. The performance is full of wit and humor.

The Lance of the Universe

In this play, a woman named Zhao Yanrong pretended to have gone mad. She resisted and expressed her complain and innocence from the emperor. This play is a traditional play, Mei Lanfang's representative work. Some people describe it as a Mei school graduate level play. Mei Lanfang attached great importance to this play in his lifetime and changed it again and again. For example, the performance artistic conception and unique abstract freehand brushwork in the "revised version" against Erhuang can not only improve the performance level of the actors, but also enhance the audience's appreciation and understanding. Master Mei said "I admit that this play is what I put most effort on stage in my life".

Mei Lanfang transformed the reality of life into the sense of rhythm of opera and pursued the beauty of image in opera performance. Looking at Mei Lanfang's preparation for acting crazy on the stage, throwing her sleeves, turning right, pulling her left sleeve in and lifting her shoulders  back, she ran quickly into the stage door, which gave the audience great psychological expectations. Then we can see the performance after that, expose the right sleeve lined with green folds, right hand with left sleeve cover, tremble, turn to the small side of the stage, open the door to sing. Such costumes and performances lead the stage atmosphere to the "crazy" rhythm all of a sudden.

Culture Notes

《宇宙锋》是中国戏曲的传统剧目，而梅兰芳（京剧）、陈素真（豫剧）、陈伯华（汉剧）三位大师的《宇宙锋》并称为"宇宙三锋"。秦腔表演艺术家、教育家马蓝鱼的《宇宙锋》是梅兰芳亲排。同样，马蓝鱼老师又传授给了得意弟子梅花奖得主齐爱云。秦腔还有为数不多的演员在演。

京剧选段网址参考：www.boosj.com/5391877.html.www.ixigua.com/i64080996617808942091.

New Words

bracelet	n.	a band of cloth or leather or metal links attached to a wristwatch and wrapped around the wrist	手镯；手链
scholar	n.	a learned person (especially in the humanities); someone who by long study has gained mastery in one or more disciplines	学者；奖学金获得者
affix	vt.	attach to	粘上；署名
connect	vt.	fasten, or put together two or more pieces	连接；联合

select	vt.	pick out, or choose from a number of alternatives	挑选；选拔
embroidery	n.	elaboration of an interpretation by the use of decorative (sometimes fictitious) detail	刺绣；刺绣品
escort	n.	someone who escorts and protects a prominent person	护卫队；护送者
suspect	n.	someone who is under suspicion	嫌疑犯
murder	vt.	kill intentionally and with premeditation	谋杀，凶杀
grope	vi.	feel about uncertainly or blindly	摸索；探索
pitch	n.	the property of sound that varies with variation in the frequency of vibration	倾斜；投掷
sword	n.	a cutting or thrusting weapon that has a long metal blade and a hilt with a hand guard	刀，剑；武力
swish	n.	a brushing or rustling sound	鞭打；使作沙沙声
nun	n.	a woman religious	修女，尼姑
nunnery	n.	the convent of a community of nuns	尼姑庵；女修道院
wit	n.	a message whose ingenuity or verbal skill or incongruity has the power to evoke laughter	智慧；才智

Exercises

I. Fill the Blanks

1. The famous play of Peking Opera *at the Crossroad* is the illustration of art form of _____.

2. The famous play of Peking Opera Picking up the Bracelet is the illustration of art form of _____.

3. The performance of famous play of Peking Opera Autumn River belongs to the virtual _____.

4. Scholars believe the play of _____ is the graduated level representative art works in Mei school.

5. _____ put the most effort on stage in the opera The Lance of the Universe in his life.

II. Match the Following English Name of Plays with the Chinese Translation

( ) 1. *Orphan of Zhao Family*   A. 元宵谜

( )　2. *King Chu Bids Farewell to His Concubine*　　B. 拾玉镯

( )　3. *The Lance of the Universe*　　C. 秋江

( )　4. *The Ruse of Empty City*　　D. 游园惊梦

( )　5. *The Drunken Concubine*　　E. 宇宙锋

( )　6. *Fifteen Strings of Coppers*　　F. 贵妃醉酒

( )　7. *Picking up the Jade Bracelet*　　G. 霸王别姬

( )　8. *Autumn River*　　H. 赵氏孤儿

( )　9. *Sweet Dream in the Garden*　　I. 空城计

( )　10. *The legend of Yuanxiao*　　J. 十五贯

III. Please illustrate the details of performance in the opera The Lance of the Universe, and how Mei Lanfang acted the role through acting

 Great Peking Opera Artist-Mei Lanfang

For those foreigners who pay a visit to Beijing, three things are recommended to do. Climbing the Great Wall, tasting the Beijing Roast and appreciating Peking Opera. As the quintessence of our country, it has been the cynosure of all eyes.

In the history of Peking Opera, there have arisen many celebrated performers, including certain legendary artists of great accomplishment. One of them is Mei Lanfang who was known by all the foreigners and also the first actor to transmit Peking Opera to the world. He had the reputation of Peking Opera master. Born in Beijing in 1894 in a family full of Chinese opera performers, Mei Lanfang was the best known Chinese Peking Opera master. At that time, he was so famous and rich that all the people were eager to have a visit to his home.

The actors of Peking Opera emphasize the group or tutor. Mei Lanfang was the most influential and successful actor thanks to his team and support from them. They were called *Mei Pai* in Chinese. His 50-year stage career, his exclusive skills of female characters playing has won him a worldwide acclaim.

Mei Lanfang was an actor who played the role of *Dan*. Together with Cheng Yanqiu, Shang Xiaoyun and Xun Huisheng, they were acclaimed the "four famed Peking Opera female-role performers."

Mei Lanfang had a melodious voice, a beautiful stage appearance, with elegant dancing and movements onstage. He crafted a noble and natural image, reaching the zenith of female-role performance.

Mei Lanfang made innovations to the art of Peking Opera in different aspects. He composed many new melodies, introduced facial expressions, movements and the technique of dancing to the accompaniment of singing, from *Kunqu* Opera to Peking Opera; he also created various dances, such as the silk dance, sword dance, sleeve dance and duster dance.

In his representative opera *King Chu Bids Farewell to His Concubine*, artist Mei Lanfang performed a sword dance in a miraculously skillful way, which became very popular with audiences.

He was the first to use *Erhu* to support *Jinghu* (traditional stringed instruments), to accompany singing by the female role, thus musically enriching Peking Opera. He also made innovations to mask, hairstyles and costumes. There are many famous and unforgettable roles he played on the sage, such as *The Drunken Concubine*(《贵妃醉酒》), *The Lance of the Universe*(《宇宙锋》) *and Women General Mu Guiying*(《穆桂英挂帅》).

Mei Lanfang's appearance, costumes, dance, movements and singing onstage are all extremely striking. *The Drunken Concubine*(《贵妃醉酒》) depicts a woman's graceful appearance and conduct in an inebriated state. *The Lance of the Universe* describes a woman named Zhao Yanrong pretending to have gone mad, who yet presents a beautiful image despite her insanity.

In 1930, Mei Lanfang went to United States to demonstrate Chinese classical beauty with everlasting allure. His perfect and attractive performance not only presented the traditional and specific art form, but also introduced this mysterious oriental opera to the West even to the world.

Under such circumstance, Mei Lanfang's performance achieved extraordinarily successful. He is worthy of the title of "master artist of Peking Opera".

Forming friendships with western artists and showing the harmony and beauty in Chinese performance had played an important role to eliminate the bias between China and West in that era. This has been winning an international reputation for Peking Opera.

Notes

Mei Lanfang was the first Peking Opera master who participated in cultural exchanges with foreign countries in his contemporary time in China. During the period from 1919 to 1935, he paid visits to Japan, United States and other regions, spreading Peking Opera to foreign countries. From then on, foreigners have been understanding the brilliant and excellent art based on Peking Opera.

Culture Notes

梅兰芳（1894—1961年），名澜，又名鹤鸣，乳名裙姊，字畹华，别署缀玉轩主人，艺名兰芳。祖籍江苏泰州，生于北京的一个梨园世家。梅兰芳是近代杰出的京昆旦行演员，"四大名旦"之首，"梅派"艺术创始人；同时也是享有国际盛誉的表演艺术大师。

其表演被推为"世界三大表演体系"之一。在西方人的眼中，梅兰芳就是京剧的代名词，他的代表剧目有《贵妃醉酒》《霸王别姬》等；昆曲有《游园惊梦》《断桥》等。所著论文编为《梅兰芳文集》，演出剧目编为《梅兰芳演出剧本选集》。

New Words

recommend	vt.	push for something	推荐，介绍
quintessence	n.	the fifth and highest element after air and earth and fire and water; was believed to be the substance composing all heavenly bodies	精华；典范
cynosure	n.	something that provides guidance	指针；众人瞩目的焦点
arise	vi.	come into existence; take on form or shape	出现；上升；起立
legendary	adj.	so celebrated as to having taken on the nature of a legend	传说的，传奇的
transmit	vt.	transfer to another	传输；传播
reputation	n.	the state of being held in high esteem and honor	名声，名誉
tutor	n.	a person who gives private instruction (as in singing or acting)	导师；家庭教师
exclusive	adj.	not divided or shared with others	独有的；排外的
melodious	adj.	having a musical sound; especially a pleasing tune	悦耳的；旋律优美的
innovation	n.	a creation (a new device or process) resulting from study and experimentation	创新，革新
compose	vt.	form the substance of	构成；写作
representative	n.	a person who represents others	代表；典型
accompany	vt.	be associated with	陪伴，伴随
insanity	n.	relatively permanent disorder of the mind	疯狂；精神错乱
demonstrate	vt.	show or demonstrate something to an interested audience	证明；展示
oriental	n.	a member of an Oriental race; the term is regarded as offensive by Asians	东方人
eliminate	vt.	terminate or take out	消除；排除

I. Simple Selection

1. Which of the following is NOT true about Mei Lanfang?
    A. He wrote some plays for Peking Opera.
    B. He created various dances.
    C. He composed many new melodies.
    D. He enriched Peking Opera by introducing *Erhu*.

2. _____ had the reputation of Peking Opera master.
    A. Mei Lan Fang
    B. Shang Xiao yun
    C. Cheng Yan qiu
    D. Xun Hui Sheng

3. Which play is not the representative play of Mei Lan Fang in Peking Opera?
    A. *The Drunken Concubine*（《贵妃醉酒》）
    B. *The Lance of the Universe*（《宇宙锋》）
    C. *Women General Mu Guiying*（《穆桂英挂帅》）
    D. *At Crossroad*（《三岔口》）

4. The actors of Peking Opera emphasize the group or tutor. Mei Lanfang was the most influential and successful actor thanks to his team and support from them. They were called _____ in Chinese.
    A. Mei Xi   B. Mei Pai   C. Mei Zu   D. Mei Tuan

II. Multiple Choice

1. Mei Lanfang was an actor who played the role of *dan*. Together with _____, they were acclaimed the "four famed Peking Opera female-role performers".
    A. Cheng Yanqiu
    B. Shang Xiaoyun
    C. Xun Huisheng
    D. Zhang Erkui

2. Mei Lanfang composed many new melodies, and introduced facial expressions, movements and the technique of dancing to the accompaniment of singing, from Kunqu Opera to Peking Opera. He also created various dances, such as _____ and duster dance.
    A. drunk dance
    B. silk dance
    C. sword dance
    D. sleeve dance

3. During the period from 1919 to 1935, Mei Lanfang paid visits to _____ and other regions, spreading Peking Opera to foreign countries. From then on, foreigners have been understanding the brilliant and excellent art based on Peking Opera.
    A. Russia   B. England   C. Japan   D. United States

4. Mei Lanfang also made innovations to _____.
    A. mask   B. hairstyle   C. makeup   D. costume

5. In China, Peking opera has been known by many other names in different times and

places. Which are the names for it once?

    A. *Pi Huang*   B. *Pi Ying*   C. *Jing Xi*   D. *Jing Qu*

III. True or False

1. Xun Huisheg was known by all the foreigners and also the first actor to transmit Peking Opera to the world.

2. Mei Lanfang was the most influential and successful actor thanks to his team and support from them. They were called Mei Pai in Chinese.

3. The Four Famous Players of Peking Opera were: "Mei" (Mei Lanfang)、"Shang" (Shang Xiaoyun)、"Cheng" (Cheng Yanqiu) and "Xun" (Xun Huisheng).

4. Mei Lanfang was an actor who played the role of *Sheng*.

5. Mei Lanfang also created various dances, such as the silk dance, sword dance, sleeve dance and duster dance.

IV. Translation

梅兰芳在 50 余年的舞台生活中，发展和提高了京剧旦角的演唱和表演艺术，形成一个具有独特风格的艺术流派，世称"梅派"。京剧中把女性统称为"旦"，其中按照人物的年龄、性格又可细分为许多行当。梅兰芳通过不断的努力，终于集京剧旦角艺术之大成，融青衣、花旦、刀马旦行当为一炉，创造出独特的表演形式和唱腔，影响很大。梅兰芳所创新的京剧梅派艺术，不仅是中国京剧与整个中国戏曲艺术的高峰，而且还位列世界三大表演体系之一。梅兰芳的一生，体现了不断革新、精益求精的敬业精神，他将诸多艺术领域的创作思想融于了京剧艺术舞台表演之中，使京剧旦行的唱腔、表演艺术臻于完美的境界，成为旦行中影响深远的流派。

Unit 7　Folk Arts

Chinese folk arts are artistic forms inherited from a regional or ethnic scene in China. It is an important part of the country's extremely rich cultural and art heritage. Usually there are some variations between provinces. Individual folk arts have a long history, and many traditions are still practiced today. Folk art is put forward in accordance with the concept of academic art and literati art. Broadly speaking, folk art is an art created by laborers to meet their own life and aesthetic needs, including folk arts and crafts, folk music, folk dance, opera and other art forms. In a narrow sense, folk art refers to folk plastic arts, including folk arts and crafts in various forms. Chinese folk art has won recognition and praise from experts both at home and abroad for its great variety, sincere rural content, rich flavor of life, distinctive local style, and its artistic approaches of romanticism.

According to the materials, there are various kinds of folk handicrafts made of different materials such as paper, cloth, bamboo, wood, stone, leather, metal, surface, clay, ceramics, grass, willow, palm rattan and lacquer. They are mainly made of natural materials with local materials and traditional handmade methods. They have strong local characteristics and ethnic styles and are closely related to folk activities and life. The festivals in a year are accompanied by folk art, the life etiquette from birth to death, the daily life of daily necessities.

From the perspective of creators, folk art is a kind of artisanal art product mainly made by farmers and handicraftsmen to meet the needs of creators, supplement family income or even take it as a source of livelihood, and it is usually inherited from generation to generation by taking one family as the production unit and passing on children from father to son and teachers to apprentices.

When it comes to function, it includes folk art works focusing on appreciation and spiritual pleasure, as well as implements and decorations focusing on practicality and function. The theme and content of the works fully reflect the aesthetic needs and psychological needs of the public in the civil society. The shape is full and rough, with bright and strong colors. It is not only beautiful and practical, but also has the spiritual function of seeking auspicious and exorcising evil and avoiding harm.

Here we present an introduction to a select few.

7.1 Embroidery, Dyeing and Hollow-out Printing

7.1.1 Traditional Embroidery

Chinese embroidery has a long history since the Neolithic age. Most Chinese fine embroideries are made in silk because of the texture of silk. Some ancient vestiges of silk production have been found in various Neolithic sites dating back 5000~6000 years in China. Currently the earliest real sample of silk embroidery discovered in China is from a tomb in Mashan in Hubei province identified with the Warring States Period. After the opening of Silk Route in the Han dynasty, the silk production and trade flourished. In the 14th century, the Chinese silk embroidery production reached its high peak. Suzhou embroidery, Hunan embroidery, Sichuan embroidery, and Cantonese embroidery are regarded as the four most distinguished embroidery styles in China. Today, most handwork has been replaced by machinery, but some very sophisticated production is still hand-made. Modern Chinese silk embroidery still prevails in southern China.

Suzhou embroidery, or Su embroidery, is crafted in areas around Suzhou, Jiangsu Province, having a history dating back 2000 years. It is famous for its beautiful patterns, elegant colours, variety of stitches, and consummate craftsmanship.

Its stitching is meticulously skillful, coloration subtle and refined. Suzhou artists are able to use more than 40 needlework and a 1000 different types of threads to make embroidery, typically with nature and environment themes such as flowers, birds, animals and even gardens on a piece of cloth. A rare subset is Su double-sided embroidery which requires ultimate skill and artistry. The front and back of the piece may have different designs, but the ends are not knotted but woven in so the back can't be distinguished.

Hunan embroidery, or Xiang embroidery, uses pure silk, hard satin, soft satin, transparent gauze and nylon as its materials as well as a variety of colorful silk threads. Traditional Xiang Embroidery uses threads in a very distinctive way-the thread is firstly boiled with Gleditsia and then wiped with bamboo paper, which prevents the thread from pilling and thus is convenient for embroidering.

In Xiang Embroidery, there is a special type of thread-in one thread dyed one color with different shades of that color, by which the sfumato effect can be presented after the embroidering finished. In addition, Xiang Embroidery is also renowned for its careful thread splitting technique, making the thread as thin as hair. And people call the embroidery using this kind of thread "Yang Mao Xi Xiu". The proficient manipulation of different shades of grey, black and  white and the natural chiaroscuro in Xiang Embroidery both enhance its texture and stereoscopic effect; the combination of the void and the solid in its structure makes a good use of emptiness on the embroidery cloth, thus highlighting the subject. In addition, borrowing skills of traditional painting, Xiang Embroidery has also given full play to the embroidery technology. Therefore, it finally forms a realistic, bright and simple style strongly affected by the local culture of Hunan and has the simplicity and elegance of Chinese wash painting on the other hand. In 2006, Hunan embroidery was selected into the first batch of national intangible cultural heritage list.

Sichuan embroidery, also known as Shu embroidery, is one of the embroidery types with the longest inheritance of Chinese embroidery, Shu embroidery has formed its own unique charm with its bright and beautiful colors and exquisite stitching, ranking the first among the four famous embroideries in terms of richness.

 Shu embroidery has a long history dating back to the civilization of Sanxingdui. Shu embroidery is mainly made of soft satin and colored silk with 12 categories and 122 stitches. It is characterized by precise stitching, even stitching, rich variety, vivid image and three-dimensional sense.

Cantonese embroidery, or Yue embroidery, is a style of embroidery folk art of the Pearl River Delta region. Cantonese embroidery is highly regarded for its full composition, vivid images, bright colors, multiple embroidery techniques, smoothness, and evenness. This style usually use

nature or auspicious symbols as the subject matters.

Located in a subtropical region with plenty of sunshine and rainfall, Cantonese have had access to a diverse set of flora and fauna, resulting nature being an important source of inspiration for Cantonese embroidery's aesthetics. Cantonese embroidery can be further divided into four styles: woolen needlepoint tapestry, bead embroidery, machine embroidery and "Ding Gum Sau" (the use of silver and gold threads). Cantonese embroidery can be founded on all kinds of objects: hanging screen, clothes, shoes, etc.

7.1.2 Folk Dyeing

Batik is a technique of wax-resist dyeing applied to whole cloth, or cloth made using this technique. Batik is made either by drawing dots and lines of the resist with a spouted tool called a canting, or by printing the resist with a copper stamp called a cap. The applied wax resists dyes and therefore allows the artisan to colour selectively by soaking the cloth in one colour, removing the wax with boiling water, and repeating if multiple colours are desired. Batik is done by the ethnic people in the South-West of China, with diverse patterns influenced by a variety of cultures, and is the most developed in terms of pattern, technique, and the quality of workmanship. The Miao and Bouyei people use a dye resist method for their traditional costumes.

The traditional costumes are made up of decorative fabrics, which they achieve by pattern weaving and wax resist. Almost all the Miao decorate hemp and cotton by applying hot wax then dipping the cloth in an indigo dye. The cloth is then used for skirts, panels on jackets, aprons and baby carriers. And their traditional patterns also contain symbolism, the patterns include the dragon, phoenix, and flowers.

Tie-dye is a traditional and unique dyeing process in Chinese folk art in which a fabric is partially ligated during dyeing so that it cannot be dyed. The following picture is the representative product "Panda" made by Zhang Xiaoping, master of tie-dye in Zigong, Sichuan province.

Tie-dye process is divided into two steps: tie-knot and dyeing. It is the dyeing after binding, sewing, tying, affixing, or clamping the fabric by yarn, thread, rope and other tools. The fabric is dyed after being twisted, only when the dyeing process in finished, will the knotted thread be dismantled. The tool for tie-dyeing is simple, a needle and a thread is enough.

As long as you follow the arrangement on the cloth, you can dye beautiful pattern alone. The technique of tie-dyeing can produce lasting appeal, especially in the course of dyeing, the combination of certainty and chance will produce unexpected effects. What is more surprising is the flowers being tied, even if there are thousands, it will not appear the same after dyeing. In 2006 and 2008, the tie-dye skills of Bai nationality in Dali, Yunnan and Zigong tie-dye skills in Sichuan were listed as national intangible cultural heritage by the ministry of culture.

7.1.3 Hollow-out Printing

Hollow-out printing is one of the most ancient dyeing art, began in the Qin and Han Dynasties, flourished in Tang and Song Dynasty. Emperor Sui Yang once ordered artisans to print and dye the colorful skirt with valerian flowers and gave them to the maids of honor and the wives and daughters of officials. During the Tang Dynasty, the color of valerian was so prevalent that officers and soldiers' uniforms were also marked with "valerian".

The fabric is clamped between the hollow plate to be tightened, and the clamped fabric is immersed in the dye vat. The groove that allows the dye to flow into the vat is reserved for the fabric to be dyed, while the clamped part retains its original color. The ancient Chinese character for "xie" refers to the printing and dyeing of patterns and patterns on silk fabrics. As the name suggests, it is the use of carved board in silk wool and other things on the clip dyed a predetermined effect. Chinese Etymology interprets the skill as "the printing and dyeing method in Tang dynasty is to carve the same pattern with two wooden plates, fold the silk cloth in half and clip it into the two plates, and then dye in the carving space to make a symmetrical pattern".

1. Miao: The Miao is an ethnic group belonging to South China, and is recognized by the

government of China as one of the 55 official minority groups. The Miao live primarily in southern China's mountains, in the provinces of Guizhou, Yunnan, Sichuan, Hubei, Hunan, Guangxi, Guangdong and Hainan.

2. Bouyei: The Bouyei people is an ethnic group living in southern mainland China. Numbering 2.5 million, they are the 11th largest of the 56 ethnic groups officially recognized by the People's Republic of China. Some Bouyei also live in Vietnam. The Bouyei live in semi-tropical, high-altitude forests of Guizhou province, as well as in Yunnan and Sichuan provinces.

Culture Notes

四大名绣：四大名绣是中国民族传统刺绣工艺中的苏绣、湘绣、粤绣和蜀绣的统称。苏绣是江苏地区刺绣产品的总称，其历史长达2000多年，因图案秀丽、技巧精湛、绣工精细而被誉为"东方明珠"。湘绣是以湖南长沙为中心的刺绣产品的总称，其图案借鉴了中国画的长处，所绣内容多为山水、人物、走兽等，尤其是湘绣的狮、虎题材，形象逼真，栩栩如生。粤绣是以广东省潮州市和广州市为生产中心的刺绣产品的总称，粤绣构图饱满，装饰性强，色彩浓郁鲜艳，绣制平整光滑。粤绣在清朝发展到顶峰，产品畅销欧洲、美洲、亚洲各国。蜀绣是以成都为中心的四川刺绣产品总称，蜀绣以软缎和彩丝为主要原料，针法多达100多种，具有浓厚的地方风格。

New Words

artisanal	adj.	having natural skill in any of the fine arts	手工艺性的
embroidery	n.	Embroidery is the activity of stitching designs onto cloth	刺绣，刺绣品
vestige	n.	A vestige of something is a very small part that still remains of something that was once much larger or more important	残留部分，遗迹
Neolithic	adj.	relating to the last period of the stone age, about 10,000 years ago, when people began to live together in small groups and make stone tools and weapons	新石器时代的，早期的
stitch	n.	If you sew or knit something in a particular stitch, you sew or knit in a way that produces a particular pattern	针织法，一针
meticulous	adj.	very careful about small details, and always making sure that everything is done correctly	一丝不苟的，注重细节的
sfumato	n.	a gradual transition between areas of different	渲染层次

		colour, avoiding sharp outlines	
manipulation	n.	the action of touching with the hands (or the skillful use of the hands) or by the use of mechanical means	操作，处理
chiaroscuro	n.	Chiaroscuro is the use of light and shade in a picture, or the effect produced by light and shade in a place	明暗的使用，明暗的配合
auspicious	adj.	showing that something is likely to be successful	吉祥的，吉利的
batik	n.	a way of printing coloured patterns on cloth that involves putting wax over some parts of the cloth	蜡染法
dyeing	n.	the process or industry of colouring yarns, fabric, etc	染色，染色工艺
tie-dye	n.	A tie-dye is a garment or piece of cloth that has been tie-dyed	扎染，扎染法
valerian	n.	any of various Eurasian valerianaceous plants of the genus Valeriana, esp. officinalis, having small white or pinkish flowers and a medicinal root	缬草属植物

I. Simple Selection

1. Suzhou embroidery, Hunan embroidery, Sichuan embroidery, and _____ embroidery are regarded as the four most distinguished embroidery styles in China.

  A. Cantonese B. Liaoning C. Shanxi D. Shandong

2. In _____, the fabric is clamped between the hollow plate to be tightened, and the clamped fabric is immersed in the dye vat.

  A. tie-dye   B. Hollow-out printing
  C. Batik   D. traditional dyeing

3. Batik is done by the ethnic people in the _____ of China. The Miao, Bouyei and Gejia people use a dye resist method for their traditional costumes.

  A. north-east B. south-west C. north-west D. south-east

4. Almost all the _____ decorate hemp and cotton by applying hot wax then dipping the cloth in an indigo dye.

  A. Miao B. Yi C. Bai D. Dai

5. _____ is a traditional and unique dyeing process in Chinese folk art in which a fabric is partially ligated during dyeing so that it cannot be dyed.

  A. Engraving   B. Hollow-out Printing

C. Batik   D. Tie-dye

6. Shu embroidery is mainly made of soft satin and colored silk with _____ categories and _____ stitches.

    A. 12;122   B. 14;144   C. 16;166   D. 18;188

7. Located in a subtropical region with plenty of sunshine and rainfall, Cantonese have had access to a diverse set of flora and fauna, resulting _____ an important source of inspiration for Cantonese embroidery's aesthetics.

    A. peacocks   B. elephants   C. human being   D. nature being

8. Because of the quality of silk fibre, most Chinese fine embroideries are made in _____.

    A. silk   B. wood   C. cotton   D. linen

9. Suzhou artists are able to use more than 40 needlework and a 1000 different types of threads to make embroidery, typically with _____ themes.

    A. animals and plants   B. human beings
    C. nature and environment   D. flowers and plants

10. Traditional Xiang Embroidery uses threads in a very distinctive way—the thread is firstly boiled with Gleditsia and then wiped with _____, which prevents the thread from pilling and thus is convenient for embroidering.

    A. bamboo paper   B. linen paper
    C. lotus leaf   D. licorice

II. True or False

1. Chinese folk art are artistic forms inherited from a regional or ethnic scene in China and there are no variations between provinces.

2. Broadly speaking, folk art is an art created by laborers to meet their own life and aesthetic needs.

3. In a narrow sense, folk art refers to folk plastic arts, including folk arts and crafts in various forms of expression.

4. According to the materials, there are various kinds of folk handicrafts made of different materials.

5. Folk products are mainly made of natural materials with local materials and traditional handmade methods.

6. Folk crafts have strong local characteristics and ethnic styles and are closely related to folk activities and life.

7. From the perspective of creators, folk art is a kind of artisanal art product mainly made by farmers and handicraftsmen to meet the needs of creators, supplement family income or even take it as a source of livelihood.

8. Folk arts are usually inherited from generation to generation by taking one family as the production unit and passing on children from father to son and teachers to apprentices.

9. When it comes to function, folk art works focus on appreciation and spiritual pleasure, as well as implements and decorations focusing on practicality and function.

10. Chinese embroidery has a long history since the Neolithic age.

III. Fill in the Blanks

1. Suzhou embroidery is famous for its beautiful _____, elegant colours, variety of _____, and consummate craftsmanship.

2. Traditional Xiang Embroidery uses threads in a very distinctive way—the thread is firstly boiled with Gleditsia and then wiped with _____, which prevents the thread from pilling and thus is convenient for embroidering.

3. Xiang Embroidery is renowned for its careful _____, making the thread as thin as hair.

4. In Xiang Embroidery, the combination of _____ and _____ in its structure makes a good use of emptiness on the embroidery cloth, thus highlighting the subject.

5. Shu embroidery is characterized by precise stitching, even stitching, rich variety, vivid image and _____ sense.

6. Cantonese embroidery, or Yue embroidery, is a style of embroidery folk art of the _____ region.

7. Cantonese embroidery is highly regarded for its full _____, vivid images, bright colors, multiple embroidery techniques, smoothness, and evenness.

8. _____ is a technique of wax-resist dyeing applied to whole cloth, or cloth made using this technique.

9. _____ is a traditional and unique dyeing process in Chinese folk art in which a fabric is partially ligated during dyeing so that it cannot be dyed.

10. During the Tang dynasty, the color of valerian was so prevalent that officers and soldiers' uniforms were also marked with "_____".

IV. Answer the Questions

1. Please talk about the four most distinguished embroidery styles and their characteristics in China.

2. Please talk about the Batik of the Miao people.

7.2 Plastic Art

7.2.1 Clay Sculpture

Clay sculpture is an important category of plastic art, with Fengxiang clay sculpture as a representative, which is called "Ni Huo" by local people.

Clay sculpture are made from a special local clay, found only in Fengxiang County, northwest of Xi'an. The clay is well-suited for making sculptures because it is very sticky and doesn't crack easily after it dries. The figurines are made of this local clay mixed with pulp, then painted after shaping. The craft of making the painted clay-figurines of Fengxiang has a recorded history of more than three hundred years. According to folklore, however, the figurines first appeared some 600 years ago.

Broadly speaking, Fengxiang painted clay sculpture can be divided into 3 types, the first is the clay toy, mainly animal and twelve Chinese Zodiac; The second is pendants, such as tiger head, cow head, lion head, unicorn to send children and eight immortals crossing the sea; The third is mainly figure sculpture from Chinese folklore and historical stories.

The subjects of the figurines span a wide range of bold and brief shapes of wild exaggeration and bright colours with a strong local flavour. They are well received by the local people, who put them as toys and symbols of good fortune and happiness. Every time when the lunar New Year draws near, the local handicraftsmen, with the beautifully painted clay-figurines on shoulders or in hand, would converge on the market and set up stalls in meandering lines. This makes the country fair during the festival more flourishing and exciting. Infused with simple and sincere feelings of the laboring people, the painted clay-figurines reflected the superb creative ability in art of the peasants and are typical articles of folk art. They not only attract the attention of artists, but also appeal very much to people of various fields both at home and abroad.

Large clay tiger for hanging are frequent examples of Fengxiang's clay sculpture works. Tiger is believed to protect families from evil spirits and bring fortune and safety to children. Large in size and rich in colors, it looks powerful and majestic. Auspicious designs like peony (wealth), pomegranate (having lots of children), "Buddha's hand" (happiness and kindness), lotus (holy symbol of Buddhism), golden fish (surplus), peach (longevity), and fylfot, or swastika (endless happiness) are drawn on its body, and followed by bright colors. Frog design sculpture with "Five Poisons" is a unique design popular in rural areas. Ancient Chinese generally called the scorpion, centipede, snake, gecko, and toad the "Five Poisons". The frog is of the same family as the toad in the "Five Poisons". People put this hanging frog with "Five Poisons" on children's beds, with their venomous powers, to keep away evil spirits and disaster from children.

7.2.2 Dough Modeling

Dough modeling, commonly known as "kneading people", is one of the traditional Chinese folk art from Shandong, Shanxi and Beijing. According to historical records, China's dough figurines were written down as early as the Han dynasty. After thousands of years of inheritance and management, they have a long history and have long been an important part of Chinese culture and folk art. In terms of pinching style, the Yellow River basin is simple, rough, bold and deep; The Yangtze valley is delicate, beautiful and exquisite.

Inferring from the terra-cotta figures and piglets from the Astana Tang Tomb, dough modeling may date back to at least 1340 years. The Southern Song dynasty also have records about kneading people: "to make a smile people with oil molasses". At that time, all the dough can be eaten, that is "fruit food". There is a legend among the people that Zhugeliang of The *Three Kingdoms* invaded Nanman. When he was crossing the Lujiang river, he was suddenly confronted by a strong wind. The clever Zhugeliang then worshiped the God Jiang by making the head and animal with the dough.

Simply speaking, artists shape the body, hand, head by picking up the materials, kneading, rubbing, lifting, then put on hair ornaments and clothes, instantly, lifelike artistic image will be out of hand. In the old society, the dough figurines artists "just to make a living, went everywhere with tears in their eyes", carrying cases, going from town to town, doing sculpture in the streets. Nowadays, the art of dough figurines is valued as a precious intangible cultural heritage, and small toys have entered the art hall.

7.2.3 Puppet Art

Chinese puppet art reflects the broad and profound characteristics of Chinese culture from different aspects. A puppet is an object, often resembling a human, animal or mythical figure, that is animated or manipulated by a person called a puppeteer. The puppeteer uses movements of their hands, arms, or control devices such as rods or strings to move the body, head, limbs, and in some cases the mouth and eyes of the puppet. The puppeteer often speaks in the voice of the character of the puppet, and then synchronizes the movements of the puppet's mouth with this spoken part. The actions, gestures and spoken parts acted out by the puppeteer with the puppet are typically used in storytelling. Puppetry is a very ancient form and there are many different varieties of puppets, and they are made from a wide range of materials, depending on their form and intended use. They range from very simple in construction and operation to very complex.

Two simple types of puppets are the finger puppet, which is a tiny puppet that fits onto a single finger, and the sock puppet, which is formed and operated by inserting one's hand inside a sock, with the opening and closing of the hand simulating the movement of the puppet's "mouth". The sock puppet is a type of hand puppet, which is controlled using one hand that occupies the interior of the puppet and moves the puppet around. A "live-hand puppet" is similar to a hand puppet but is larger and requires two puppeteers for each puppet. A Marionette is a much more complicated type of puppet that is suspended and controlled by a number of strings connected to the head, back and limbs, plus sometimes a central rod attached to a control bar held from above by the puppeteer.

7.2.4 Shadow Play

Shadow play, or shadow puppetry is a kind of traditional folk drama in China. It is a traditional form of storytelling and entertainment which uses flat articulated cut-out figures that are held between a source of light and a translucent screen or scrim. It is an indispensable treasure in China's folk custom culture. It was listed by UNESCO as a world intangible cultural heritage protection list at the end of 2011. The cut-out shapes of the puppets sometimes include translucent color or other types of detailing. Various effects can be achieved by moving both the puppets and the light source. A talented puppeteer can make the figures appear to walk, dance, fight, nod and laugh.

Legend has it that Emperor Wu of the Western Han was depressed with the death of his favourite concubine Lady Li. To help him get over the sadness, an occultist sculptured a wooden figure in the likeness of the lady and projected its shadow on a curtain for the emperor to see, bringing him consolation with the belief that the shadow was her spirit. This has been thought to be the beginning of the shadow show.

Today's shadow puppets are made of leather instead of wood for the simple reason that leather is much lighter, easier to manipulate and carry round. The process for making the puppets is as follows: sheep or donkey skin with hair removed is cleaned and treated chemically to become thin enough to be translucent. Coated with tung oil and dried, it is carved into various parts of dramatic figures. The trunk, head and limbs of a puppet are separately carved but joined together by thread so that each part may be manipulated by the operator to simulate human movements. The leather puppets are painted with various colours to show their different qualities—kind or wicked, beautiful or ugly. During the performance, the 'actors' are held close to a white curtain with their coloured shadows cast on it by a strong light from behind. Moved by guiding sticks, they play the roles, accompanied by music, with their parts or singing done by the operators. The plays can be quite dramatic and, when it comes to fairy tales or kungfu stories, the 'actors' may be made to ride on clouds or perform unusual feats, to the great enjoyment of the audience, especially children.

The shadow show became quite popular as early as the Song Dynasty when holidays were marked by the presentation of many shadow plays. During the Ming, there were 40 to 50 shadow show troupes in the city of Beijing alone. In the 13th century the shadow show became a regular recreation in the barracks of the Mongolian troops. It was spread by the conquering Mongols to distant countries like Persia, Arabia and Turkey. Later, it was introduced to Southeastern Asian countries, too. And Chinese shadow puppetry is also shown in the 1994 Zhang Yimou's film *To Live*.

Notes

1. Fengxiang: Fengxiang, called YongZhou in ancient times, was an ancient town in Shaanxi Province. Before Qin Shi Huang, the first emperor of the Qin dynasty, unified China in 221 BC, the town was the capital of the Qin Kingdom for more than three hundred years.

2. Five Poisons: The fifth day of the fifth month or Duanwu in ancient Chinese folklore symbolised the beginning of the Summer, this day also known as 'Double 5th day' was seen as one of the most inauspiciously and dangerous days of the year, this was because all the poisonous animals and bugs would then began to appear. The Ancient Chinese believed that the only way to combat poison was with poison, and one way they believed that they could protect themselves on this day was by drinking realgar wine which contains arsenic sulfide, another way to protect themselves on this day was by hanging pictures of Zhong Kui, another custom holds that the Chinese should mix mercury (cinnabar) with wine, or using Gu poison to combat these creatures, however the far most common way of protecting themselves was using "Five poison" charms and amulets, it was also customary for Chinese parents to let their children wear these amulet that have pictures of the 5 poisons or otherwise hang small pouches filled with mugwort around the necks of these children. The five poisons in this context don't refer to five actual toxins but to five animals that were perceived to be "poisonous", these animals according to various historical sources usually included: snakes, scorpions, centipedes, toads and spiders.

Culture Notes

十二生肖：又叫属相，是中国与十二地支相配的十二种动物，即（子）鼠、（丑）牛、（寅）虎、（卯）兔、（辰）龙、（巳）蛇、（午）马、（未）羊、（申）猴、（酉）鸡、（戌）狗、（亥）猪。十二生肖在中国传统文化中有独特的历史地位，自产生以来即与人们的社会文化生活密切相关，从纪历到推算年命，到推算人的一生的命运，生肖在人们头脑中的影响可谓深矣，其影响人们的时间可谓久矣。生肖文化是我国先民的智慧结晶，其起源受到原始社会复杂社会环境中多重因素的影响，在漫长的发展过程中，不断变化发展，直至最终定型。

New Words

clay	n.	a kind of earth that is soft when it is wet and hard when it is dry	黏土，粘土
crack	v.	If something hard cracks, or if you crack it, it becomes slightly damaged, with lines appearing on its surface	破裂
figurine	n.	a small model of a person or animal used as a decoration	小塑像，小雕像
folklore	n.	the traditional stories, customs, and habits of a particular community or nation	民间传说，民俗
infuse	v.	to fill something or someone with a particular feeling or quality	使充满，向…灌输
pendant	n.	A pendant is an ornament on a chain that you wear around your neck	坠饰，挂件
pomegranate	n.	A pomegranate is a round fruit with a thick reddish skin. It contains a lot of small seeds with juicy flesh around them	石榴
synchronize	v.	to happen at exactly the same time, or to arrange for two or more actions to happen at exactly the same time	使同时发生，使同步
translucent	adj.	If a material is translucent, some light can pass through it	透明的，半透明的
molasses	n.	a thick dark sweet liquid that is obtained from raw sugar plants when they are being made into sugar	糖浆，糖蜜
knead	v.	When you knead dough or other food, you press and squeeze it with your hands so that it becomes smooth and ready to bake	揉，揉捏
puppet	n.	A puppet is a doll that you can move, either by pulling strings that are attached to it or by putting your hand inside its body and moving your fingers	木偶
puppeteer	n.	someone who performs with puppets	操作木偶的人
mulberry	n.	a dark purple fruit that can be eaten, or the tree on which this fruit grows	桑树，桑葚

I. Simple Selection

1. _____ is an important category of plastic art, with Fengxiang clay sculpture as a representative.

   A. Embroidery   B. Clay sculpture   C. Paper cutting   D. Dough modelling

2. Which one is not an auspicious design of traditional clay sculpture?

   A. pomegranate   B. peony   C. snake   D. Buddha's hand

3. A _____ is an object, often resembling a human, animal or mythical figure, that is animated or manipulated by a person called a puppeteer.

   A. dough   B. puppet   C. plastic art   D. paper cutting

4. Although there are many earlier records of all kinds of puppetry in China, clear mention of Chinese shadow play does not occur until the _____.

   A. Northern Song Dynasty   B. Southern Song Dynasty
   C. Tang Dynasty   D. Yuan Dynasty

5. Fengxiang clay sculpture is an important category of plastic art, which is called "_____" by local people.

   A. Ni Yi   B. Ni Kuan   C. Ni Ren   D. Ni Huo

6. The Fengxiang clay is well-suited for making sculptures because it is very _____ and doesn't crack easily after it dries.

   A. stubborn   B. smooth   C. sticky   D. strong

7. Which statement about "Five Poisons" is wrong?

   A. It is a unique design popular in rural areas.
   B. Ancient Chinese generally called the scorpion, centipede, snake, gecko, and toad the "Five Poisons".
   C. People put this hanging frog with "Five Poisons" on children's beds.
   D. People want to keep away evil spirits and disaster from children.

8. Broadly speaking, which category does not belong to Fengxiang painted clay sculpture?

   A. clay toy   B. pendants   C. figure sculpture   D. cultural supplies

9. Which statement about shadow play is not true?

   A. The storytellers generally used the art to tell events between various war kingdoms or stories of Buddhist sources.
   B. The earliest shadow theatre screens were made of white paper.
   C. During the Ming Dynasty there were 40 to 50 shadow show troupes in the city of Beijing alone.
   D. Shadow theatre became quite popular as early as the Song Dynasty when holidays were marked by the presentation of many shadow plays.

10. Which statement about puppet art is not true?

A. The puppeteer often speaks in his own voice, without imitating any figure.

B. The puppeteer uses movements of their hands, arms, or control devices such as rods or strings to move the body, head, limbs, and in some cases the mouth and eyes of the puppet.

C. A puppet is an object, often resembling a human, animal or mythical figure, that is animated or manipulated by a person called a puppeteer.

D. Chinese puppet art reflects the broad and profound characteristics of Chinese culture from different aspects.

II. True or False

1. Every time when the lunar New Year draws near, the local handicraftsmen, with the beautifully painted clay-figurines on shoulders or in hand, would converge on the market and set up stalls in meandering lines.

2. Infused with simple and sincere feelings of the laboring people, the painted clay-figurines reflected the superb creative ability in art of the peasants and are typical articles of folk art.

3. Large clay lion for hanging are frequent examples of Fengxiang's clay sculpture works.

4. According to historical records, China's dough figurines were written down as early as the Tang dynasty.

5. In terms of pinching style, the Yellow River basin is simple, rough, bold and deep; The Yangtze valley is delicate, beautiful and exquisite.

6. Nowadays, the art of dough figurines is valued as a precious intangible cultural heritage, and small toys have entered the art hall.

7. A puppet is an object, often resembling a human, animal or mythical figure, that is animated or manipulated by a person called a puppeteer.

8. Finger puppet and sock puppet are two simple types of puppets.

9. Today, puppets made of leather and moved on sticks are used to tell dramatic versions of traditional fairy tales and myths.

10. A Marionette is a much more complicated type of puppet that is suspended and controlled by a number of strings connected to different body parts.

III. Fill in the Blanks

1. Clay sculptures are well received by the local people, who put them as _____ and _____ of good fortune and happiness.

2. In clay sculpture, _____ is believed to protect families from evil spirits and bring fortune and safety to children.

3. The _____ uses movements of their hands, arms, or control devices such as rods or strings to move the body, head, limbs, and in some cases the mouth and eyes of the puppet.

4. The _____ is a type of hand puppet, which is controlled using one hand that occupies the interior of the puppet and moves the puppet around.

5. _____ is a traditional form of storytelling which uses flat articulated cut-out figures that are held between a source of light and a translucent screen or scrim.

6. And Chinese shadow puppetry is also shown in the 1994 Zhang Yimou's film _____.

7. _____ is a tiny puppet that fits onto a single finger.

8. The figurines are made of this local clay mixed with _____, then painted after shaping.

9. Dough modeling, commonly known as "_____", is one of the traditional Chinese folk art from Shandong, Shanxi and Beijing.

10. A _____ is an object, often resembling a human, animal or mythical figure, that is animated or manipulated by a person called a puppeteer.

IV. Answer the Questions

1. Please shortly introduce the paper cutting.

2. Please briefly introduce the shadow play.

7.3 Cutting and Engraving

7.3.1 Paper Cutting

The paper cutting is a special folk art in China, with a history of nearly 1000 years. The materials used are ordinary paper and a pair of scissors or a cutting knife. A skilled paper-cutting craftsperson cuts paper into designs like doing magic tricks. A piece of red paper is folded and then cut several times, before being unfolded into an attractive picture.

Some craftspeople do not even set their eyes on what they are doing; they can even place a piece of paper inside a baggy sleeve and cut it into a beautiful pattern. Paper cutting is a type of improvised art with powerful expression: a papercut artist does not need a model picture to copy from, but relies on a pair of scissors to produce a work of art, each time with slight difference. Paper cuttings are very popular in rural areas. In the city of Xi'an, Shanxi Province, people once used paper instead of glass as window-coving. As white paper was monotonous and considered inauspicious, clever and deft young women started to cut pieces of red paper into joyous baby images or beautiful butterflies, which they put on the windows to add liveliness to ordinary windows.

In ancient China, people enjoyed the tradition of making and hanging lanterns for festivals and joyous occasions. The shapes of lanterns varied, from red lanterns hung in midair, running-horse lanterns, lotus lanterns on the surface of water, and lion lanterns loved by children. People sometimes drew pictures on the lanterns but more often would prefer to paste papercuts of different patterns, which, set off by the lantern light, became even more vivid and interesting.

7.3.2 Wood Engraving

Chinese wood carving has a long history. Wood carving is a form of woodworking by means of a cutting tool in one hand or a chisel by two hands or with one hand on a chisel and one hand on a mallet, resulting in a wooden figure or figurine, or in the sculptural ornamentation of a wooden object. The phrase may also refer to the finished product, from individual sculptures to hand-worked mouldings composing part of a tracery.

The making of sculpture in wood has been extremely widely practiced, but survives much less well than the other main materials such as stone and bronze, as it is vulnerable to decay, insect damage, and fire. It therefore forms an important hidden element in the art history of many cultures. Outdoor wood sculptures do not last long in most parts of the world, so it is still unknown how the totem pole tradition developed. Many of the most important sculptures of China are in wood, it is light and can take very fine detail so it is highly suitable for masks and other sculpture intended to be worn or carried. It is also much easier to work on than stone.

Now there are four popular Chinese wood carvings, namely Dongyang wood carving, Huangyang wood carving, Chaozhou wood carving and Longan wood carving. The four major wood carvings have their own characteristics, distinct regional features in techniques and materials.

7.3.3 Jade Carving

Many countries have jadeware culture, but none of them has as long a history as China has. China's jadeware culture has undergone a long process of development from the New Stone Age 10000 years ago to the present. There is ample evidence that the earliest jadeware found in China was a piece of serpentine stoneware unearthed in Haicheng, Liaoning Province dating back to the New Stone Age more than 12000 years ago. The second was a small hanging jade article excavated in the site of Hemudu in Zhejiang Province dating back more than 7000 years. In Shang Dynasty, craftsmen used metal tools to make new progress in jadeware models and sculpture. Round jade articles increased in number and jadeware was often given as gifts. By Qin and Han Dynasties, jadeware became more practical and objects such as jade tablets fell out of use. Right at that time, people began to believe in the power of jadeware to increase longevity. They thought they would live forever like gods if they had jadeware. Therefore, the practice of burying the dead with jadeware became common. Invaluable jade figures and clothes sewn with gold threads have been found in tombs dating back to the Han Dynasty.

The patterns of China's jadeware have rich connotations showing strong auspicious colours. Bats and gourds were often used as a basis for more than 100 patterns because their Chinese pronunciations sound like "good fortune". When a bat was carved on an ancient coin with a hole, it meant fortune was at hand. All these reflected the ancient Chinese people's yearning for a happy life and revealed the essence of China's traditional culture.

Jade in China is varied and can be divided into two categories: hard and soft. Good materials provide strong basics for jadeware carving, but the value of a jade object depends on the skills and reputation of craftsmen, the dates of carving, peculiar modelling and the owner's status. Certainly, different people will have various views on the value of the same jade object. It is difficult to have a unanimous standard. In 2008, jade carvings were included in the second batch of national intangible cultural heritage list.

7.3.4 Sugar People and Sugar Painting

Sugar people is a traditional Chinese form of folk art using hot, liquid sugar to create three-dimensional figures. These fragile, plump figures have a distinct brownish-yellow colour, usually with yellow or green pigment added. They are mainly purchased for ornamental purposes and not for consumption, due to sanitary concerns. Popular figures include animals such as dragons, roosters and pigs, and such objects machetes and spears. This art form has been practiced in public places for hundreds of years, and can still be seen today. Traditionally, artists set up their point of production and sale in areas such as markets, and outside schools, as the figures appeal to children. These days, this art form is practiced in tourist areas. Prices can range from ten to tens of RMB, depending on the piece. However, during difficult economic times, artists would exchange figures for metal scraps, broken shoes, old clothing, and notably, toothpaste.

Using a small charcoal stove, sugar is heated in a metal vessel. When at the correct temperature, a ball is extracted. It is then kneaded in the artist's hands to product consistency and pliability. A thin straw is then inserted into the ball, and the artist begins to blow air into it, in order to slowly inflate it. Simultaneously, the artist pinches and pulls parts of the ball, by hand, or sometimes with tools such as tweezers, to produce limbs, and various shapes. Before the figure has completely cooled, colours, typically red or green, are added to the surface, and a wooden stick is inserted into the underside. The straw is then extracted, and the figure put on display for sale.

Sugar painting is a traditional Chinese form of folk art using hot, liquid sugar to create two dimensional figures. This snack is popular among children. Selecting a figure is normally determined by spinning the arrow on a wheel which will randomly land on such popular figures as a dragon, fish, monkey, dog, bird, or flower basket. Sugar painting may have originated during the Ming Dynasty when small animals made of sugar were created in molds for religious rituals. This art form then became more popular during Qing Dynasty. After that period techniques improved, and a more diverse range of patterns emerged. In Sichuan, further developments were made in production, seeing the replacement of the molds with the now-common small ladle, often bronze or copper.

Although techniques vary, normally the hot sugar is drizzled from a small ladle onto a flat surface, usually white marble or metal. The outline is produced with a relatively thick stream of sugar. Then, supporting strands of thinner sugar are placed to attach to the outline, and fill in the body of the figure. These supporting strands may be produced with swirls, zigzags, or other patterns. Finally, when completed, a thin wooden stick, used to hold the figure, is attached in two or more places with more sugar. Then, while still warm and pliable, the figure is removed from the surface using a spatula-like tool, and is sold to the waiting customer, or placed on display.

7.3.5 Bamboo Weaving

Bamboo weaving is a form of bambooworking and a traditional craft of China. It involves manipulating bamboo into various traditional knit and woven patterns to create both useful and decorative objects.

Woven bamboo goods with an age of up to 7000 years unearthed at the Hemudu cultural ruins show that bamboo weaving has been a part of Chinese cultural history since very early periods of development. By the Warring States period, technique had substantially improved and examples of many types of bamboo wares have been found, such as boxes and bowls. During the Qin and Han Dynasties these techniques were applied to create new types of bamboo wares such as mats and curtains. A notable example from this period would be bamboo weaving patterns represented in bronze from a chariot found in the mausoleum of Qin Shi Huang.

By the Tang and Song Dynasties, bamboo weaving had expanded beyond practical objects and into creation of toys. During the middle Ming Dynasty, bamboo weaving was mostly used for boxes and storage containers. After the founding of the People's Republic of China, efforts have been made by the government to encourage and preserve the cultural history and skill of bamboo weaving, awarding titles to particularly accomplished masters of the craft, as well as designating some regions as recognized for their long history of practicing the art. Anji County is particularly important to the production of bamboo crafts due to both the great variety and quantity of bamboo grown, and a high concentration of history and expertise in bamboo crafts.

7.3.6 Chinese Knotting

Chinese knotting is a decorative handicraft art that began as a form of Chinese folk art in the Tang and Song Dynasty in China. The technique was later popularized in the Ming and spread to Japan and Korea. The art is also referred to as "Chinese traditional decorative knots". In other cultures, it is known as "decorative knots". Chinese knots are usually lanyard type arrangements where two cords enter from the top of the knot and two cords leave from the

bottom. The knots are usually double-layered and symmetrical.

Archaeological studies indicate that the art of tying knots dates back to prehistoric times. Recent discoveries include 100000 years old bone needles used for sewing and bodkins, which were used to untie knots. However, due to the delicate nature of the medium, few examples of prehistoric Chinese knotting exist today. Some of the earliest evidence of knotting have been preserved on bronze vessels of the Warring States period, Buddhist carvings of the Northern Dynasties period and on silk paintings during the Western Han period.

Further references to knotting have also been found in literature, poetry and the private letters of some of the most famous rulers of China. In the 18th century, one novel that talked extensively about the art was *Dream of the Red Chamber*.

The phenomenon of knot tying continued to steadily evolve over the course of thousands of years with the development of more sophisticated techniques and increasingly intricate woven patterns. During the Qing Dynasty knotting finally broke from its pure folklore status, becoming an acceptable art form in Chinese society and reached the pinnacle of its success. Knotting continued to flourish up until about the end of imperial China and the founding of the Republic of China in 1911 when China began its modernization period.

1. Dongyang: Dongyang is a county-level city in the center of Zhejiang Province. Dongyang county was first set up in A.D. 195 and known as Wuning. In A.D. 688, the name was changed to Dongyang which means "Eastern Sun". Now it is part of the Yangtze River Delta Economic Region. Dongyang Woodcarving enjoys a long history of development, it came into being early in Tang Dynasty. And in Song Dynasty, it became state of the art. During the Ming and Qing Dynasties, Dongyang woodcarving flourished. Now its products sell well both abroad and at home.

2. Virgin boy eggs: Dongyang has been honored as the hometown of woodcarving since ancient time. But there is also a famous local tradition in Dongyang, which surprise the tourists, the virgin boy egg. It is an annual tradition that in early spring time, the urine of boys, who were presumably peasants, preferably under the age of ten, are collected. Then the eggs, which have official cultural significance status, are boiled in the urine, first with their shells on and then with them off for a day and a night before they're ready to be eaten. It is said that "It tastes like spring". In 2008, Dongyang recognized the eggs as "local intangible cultural heritage".

Culture Notes

中国元素：中国元素是在中华民族融合、演化与发展过程中逐渐形成的、由中国人创造、传承、反映中国人文精神和民俗心理、具有中国特质的文化成果，包括有形的物质符号和无形的精神内容。优秀的中国元素是指凡是被大多数中国人认同的、凝结着华夏民族传统文化精神，并体现国家尊严和民族利益的形象、符号或风俗习惯。中国元素由三部分组成：第一是中国固有元素，比如中国的领土，中国的人种，中国的气候等；第二是中国传统文化元素，比如本章提及的民间艺术形式；第三是中国的现代文化元素，比如北京的奥运精神，中国的航天精神，中国的电影文化，中国著名企业的文化等。中国传统文化都是中国元素，但中国元素不全等于中国传统文化，还包括中国现代文化。

New Words

improvise	v.	When performers improvise, they invent music or words as they play, sing, or speak	即兴创作，临时拼凑
monotonous	adj.	Something that is monotonous is very boring because it has a regular, repeated pattern which never changes	单调的，无变化的
deft	adj.	A deft action is skilful and often quick.	灵巧的，机敏的
chisel	n.	a tool that has a long metal blade with a sharp edge at the end for cutting and shaping wood and stone	凿子
mallet	n.	a wooden hammer with a square head	木槌，棒
moulding	n.	a strip of plaster or wood along the top of a wall or around a door, which has been made into an ornamental shape or decorated with a pattern	装饰线条
exquisite	adj.	extremely beautiful and very delicately made	精美的，精致的
scrap	n.	pieces of unwanted food which are thrown away or given to animals	残羹，剩饭
charcoal	n.	a black substance made of burned wood that can be used as fuel	木炭
pliability	n.	the property of being easily bent without breaking	柔软，易曲折
simultaneous	adj.	Things which are simultaneous happen or exist at the same time	同时的，同时发生的
strand	n.	A strand of something such as hair, wire, or thread is a single thin piece of it	缕，线
swirl	n.	v. If you swirl something liquid or flowing, or if it swirls, it moves around and around quickly	漩涡，打旋

| substantially | adv. | If something changes substantially or is substantially different, it changes a lot or is very different | 很大程度地，充分地 |

I. Simple Selection

1. The _____ is a special folk art in China, with ordinary paper and a pair of scissors as the material.

    A. jade engraving   B. wood carving

    C. paper cutting   D. puppet

2. Which statement about Paper Cutting is not true?

    A. A papercut artist must have a model picture to copy from.

    B. In the city of Xi'an, people once used paper instead of glass as window-coving.

    C. White paper was monotonous and once considered inauspicious.

    D. Clever and deft young women cut pieces of red paper into joyous baby images or beautiful butterflies and put on the windows to add liveliness to ordinary windows.

3. Which statement about Wood Sculpture is not true?

    A. The making of sculpture survives much better well than the other main materials such as stone and bronze.

    B. Wood sculpture forms an important hidden element in the art history of many cultures.

    C. Outdoor wood sculptures do not last long in most parts of the world.

    D. It is still unknown how the totem pole tradition developed.

4. Which statement about jade carving is not true?

    A. Jade carving is one of the oldest carvings in China.

    B. There are many kinds of jade carvings, including figures, utensils, birds and animals, flowers and other large works.

    C. In the process of making, according to the natural color and natural shape of different jade materials, the jade stone were make into exquisite handicraft after careful design, repeated pondering.

    D. In 1998, jade carvings were included in the first batch of national intangible cultural heritage list.

5. Many countries have jadeware culture, but none of them has as long a history as _____ has.

    A. China   B. America   C. Korea   D. Vietnam

6. Which statement about bamboo weaving is not true?

    A. Bamboo weaving has been a part of Chinese cultural history since very early periods of development.

B. By the Warring States period, technique had substantially improved and examples of many types of bamboo wares have been found

C. During the Qin and Han Dynasties techniques were applied to create new types of bamboo wares such as mats and curtains.

D. A notable example of bamboo weaving pattern was a sedan found in the mausoleum of Qin Shi Huang.

7. Chinese knotting is a decorative handicraft art that began as a form of Chinese folk art in the Tang and Song Dynasty in China. The technique was later popularized in the Ming and spread to _____.

   A. Japan and Korea B. Japan and Vietnam
   C. Laos and Burma D. Korea and Vietnam

8. Which statement about Sugar People is not true?

   A. Sugar people is a traditional Chinese form of folk art using hot, liquid sugar to create two-dimensional figures.

   B. Sugar people are mainly purchased for ornamental purposes and not for consumption, due to sanitary concerns.

   C. Popular figures include animals such as dragons, roosters and pigs, and such objects machetes and spears.

   D. Traditionally, artists set up their point of production and sale in areas such as markets, and outside schools, as the figures appeal to children.

9. Which statement about Sugar Painting is not true?

   A. Sugar painting is a traditional Chinese form of folk art using hot, liquid sugar to create two dimensional figures.

   B. Sugar painting is popular among children.

   C. Sugar painting may have originated during the Yuan Dynasty when small animals made of sugar were created in molds for religious rituals.

   D. Selecting a figure of sugar painting is normally determined by spinning the arrow on a wheel which will randomly land on such popular figures as a dragon, fish, monkey, dog and so on.

10. Sugar people are mainly purchased for ornamental purposes and not for consumption, due to _____.

    A. sanitary concerns B. religious concerns
    C. cultural concerns D. historical concerns

II. True or False

1. A skilled paper-cutting craftsperson cuts paper into designs like doing magic tricks.

2. The shapes of lanterns varied, from red lanterns hung in midair, running-horse lanterns, lotus lanterns on the surface of water, and lion lanterns loved by children.

3. The making of sculpture in wood has been extremely widely practiced, but survives much less well than the other main materials such as stone and bronze.

4. Many of the most important sculptures of China are in wood, it is light and can take

very fine detail so it is highly suitable for masks and other sculpture intended to be worn or carried.

5. A piece of red paper is folded and then cut several times, before being unfolded into an attractive picture.

6. Now there are three popular Chinese wood carvings, namely Dongyang wood carving, Huangyang wood carving and Longan wood carving.

7. Bamboo weaving involves manipulating bamboo into various traditional knit and woven patterns to create both useful and decorative objects.

8. After the founding of the People's Republic of China, efforts have been made by the government to encourage and preserve the cultural history and skill of bamboo weaving, awarding titles to particularly accomplished masters of the craft.

9. Anji County is particularly important to the production of bamboo crafts due to both the great variety and quantity of bamboo grown.

10. Some craftspeople do not even set their eyes on what they are doing; they can even place a piece of paper inside a baggy sleeve and cut it into a beautiful pattern.

III. Fill in the Blanks

1. A papercut artist does not need a _____ to copy from, but relies on a pair of scissors to produce a work of art, each time with slight difference.

2. People sometimes _____ on the lanterns but more often would prefer to paste papercuts of different patterns,

3. The making of sculpture in wood survives much less well than the other main materials such as _____ and _____, as it is vulnerable to decay, insect damage, and fire.

4. Wood sculpture is light and can take very fine detail so it is highly suitable for _____ and other sculpture intended to be worn or carried.

5. There is ample evidence that the earliest jadeware found in China was a piece of serpentine stoneware unearthed in Haicheng, Liaoning Province dating back to the New Stone Age more than _____ years ago.

6. By the Tang and Song Dynasties, bamboo weaving had expanded beyond practical objects and into creation of _____.

7. _____ is a decorative handicraft art that began as a form of Chinese folk art in the Tang and Song Dynasty in China. The technique was later popularized in the Ming and spread to Japan and Korea.

8. Chinese knots are usually lanyard type arrangements where two cords enter from the top of the knot and two cords leave from the bottom. The knots are usually double-layered and _____.

9. Archaeological studies indicate that the art of tying knots dates back to _____ times.

10. Chinese knotting has been mentioned in literature, poetry and the private letters of some of the most famous rulers of China. One novel that talked extensively about the art was _____.

IV. Answer the Questions

Please shortly introduce the Chinese knot.

7.4 Cloisonné, New Year Pictures and Face-changing

7.4.1 Cloisonné

Cloisonné is an ancient technique for decorating metalwork objects, in which the colors of the design are kept apart by thin metal strips. Major work processes include: making the red-copper roughcast, forming patterns on the roughcast with thin copper strips, filling patterns with enamel of different colors, firing, and polishing. The making of Cloisonné integrates bronze and porcelain-working skills, traditional painting and etching. It is the pinnacle of traditional Chinese handicraft.

Beijing is where Cloisonné making originated. The earliest extant Cloisonné was made in the Yuan Dynasty and the best was made during the Xuande period of the Ming Dynasty. During the Jingtai period of the Ming, handicraftsmen found a dark-blue enamel which gave Cloisonné a gorgeous, solemn look and is still used today. During the Qianlong period of the Qing Dynasty, the skills of making Cloisonné reached their pinnacle when pure copper began to be used for roughcasts. A Qing-dynasty Cloisonné vase with a peach-and-bat design is a famous artifact. Its mouth, belly and base are welded together instead of being originally one piece. Its surface is first inlaid with copper wires, before the colorful glaze is applied. The nine peaches and bats have the symbolic meaning of happiness, longevity and peace.

Chinese people like to decorate their homes with Cloisonné articles. They are often used as gifts, too. People are attracted by their blue beauty and glittering thin copper strips. In Beijing, most shops in hotels as well as tourist stores sell Cloisonné articles, which can be as big as sacrificial utensils, screens tables and chairs, and as small as chopsticks, earrings, candy boxes, toothpicks and smoking tools. They are works of art as well as articles with use value. Handicraftsmen have of late developed a multi-coloring technique for the making of Cloisonné which has resulted in more refined and gorgeous products.

7.4.2 New Year Pictures

A New Year picture, literally "Year Picture", is a popular Banhua in China. It is a form of Chinese colored woodblock print, for decoration during the Chinese New Year holiday, then later used to depict current events. Its original form was a picture of a door god fashioned during the Tang Dynasty. Later, more subjects, such as fairs, the Kitchen God, women and babies were included. Customarily, as each Chinese New Year arrives, every family replaces its New Year picture in order to 'say goodbye to the Past and welcome the Future'.

New Year pictures are an indispensible part of this celebration for each and every household. People put up New Year pictures in their homes to enhance the lively festival atmosphere. Most New Year pictures feature designs symbolizing good fortune, auspiciousness and festivity. A popular New Year picture entitled Surplus in Successive Years depicts a cute plump baby holding a big carp in his arms and a bouquet of lotus flowers in his hand.

The most famous production places for New Year Pictures in China are Sichuan, Tianjin, Shandong and Suzhou. Among the best four, Yangliuqing from Tianjin was regarded as the greatest, which were first produced between 1573 and 1620. Yangliuqing is a small town located in the southwestern outskirts of Tianjin. About 300 years ago, its New Year pictures began to enjoy great fame, with every family adept at creating this particular genre of painting—Yangliuqing. New Year pictures adopt the method of xylograph overprinting combined with hand-painted color; hence establishing its distinctive feature of "half printing, half painting".

The process goes like this: to carve designs out of wood; to print the pictures; to color the pictures; and to mount the pictures. All pictures are handmade paintings rather than mass-produced products, and all evoke traces of the woodcut and the feel of brushwork. With exquisite craftsmanship, Yangliuqing New Year Pictures are very popular with Chinese people. The lively festive atmosphere is best reflected in the Yangliuqing New Year pictures. Fresh and effervescent, each picture reproduces an interesting scene from everyday life. For example, Mother and Son depicts a lakeside countryard, inside which are rock formations and flowers. The mother stands at a window, fan in hand, calling out to her son frolicking outside. The plump son in a bellyband holds a wooden stick with a bird perching on it. The whole picture brims with an affectionate, loving atmosphere of family life.

New Year pictures usually print with simple lines and bright and warm color. Also make people feeling happy. The art of New Year pictures have very long history in China, but also reflects the history of Chinese society, life, beliefs and customs. Every Lunar New Year, people bought few pictures posted on the door, and almost every home is same. Every family, from the front door to the private room and all covered with a variety of colorful symbol of auspicious and wealth of New Year pictures. The reason of the Chinese New Year filled with happily and lively, the New Year pictures is a main element and also the New Year pictures is an important role in the New Year. New Year pictures is not only a kind of colorful decoration, but also a kind of cultural circulation, education of moral, a kind of Chinese art. For the kind of events of the theme, it's also a kind of media.

7.4.3 Face-changing

Face-changing, or "bian lian" in Chinese, is an ancient Chinese dramatic art that is part of the more general Sichuan opera. Performers wear brightly colored costumes and move to quick, dramatic music. They also wear vividly colored masks, typically depicting well-known characters from the opera, which they change from one face to another almost instantaneously with the swipe of a fan, a movement of the head, or wave of the hand.

Face-changing is an important subgenre of Chinese Sichuan opera. Sichuan opera is one of the Han Chinese operas, popular in eastern and central Sichuan, Chongqing and Guizhou Province, Yunnan Province. Sichuan Opera masks are the important part of the Sichuan Opera performing, they are treasures that the ancient opera artists work together to create and pass down. The secret of the face change has been passed down from one generation to the next within families. Traditionally only males were permitted to learn Bian Lian, the theory being that women do not stay within the family and would marry out, increasing the risk the secret would be passed to another family.

Since the cultural basis of the opera are not well known outside of China, international performers have been making efforts to inform and increase the entertainment value for Westerners who do not know the context and meaning of the different faces. Generally speaking, there are four ways of face-changing. The first one is "Blowing Dust", that is the actor blows black dust hidden in his palm or close to his eyes, nose or mouth, so that it obscures his face; the second is "Beard Manipulation", that is beard colours can be changed while the beard is being manipulated, from black to grey and finally to white, expressing anger or excitement; the third is "pulling-down masks", that is the actor can pull down a mask which has previously been hidden on top of his head, changing his face to red, green, blue or black to express happiness, hate, anger or sadness, respectively; and the last one is "face-dragging", that is the actor drags greasepaint hidden in his sideburns or eyebrows across his face to change his appearance.

Notes

1. Yangliuqing is a market town in Xiqing District, in the western suburbs of Tianjin. Despite its relatively small size, it has been named since 2006 in the "famous historical and cultural market towns in China". It is best known in China for creating new year picture or Yangliuqing Nian Hua. For more than 400 years, Yangliuqing has in effect specialised in the creation of these woodcuts for the New Year.

2. Sichuan opera: Sichuan opera is a type of Chinese opera originating in China's Sichuan province around 1700. Regionally Chengdu remains to be the main home of Sichuan opera, while other influential locales include Chongqing, Guizhou, Yunnan, Hubei and Taiwan. Overall the art form is well known for its singing, which is less constrained than that of the more popular Peking opera form. Sichuan opera is more like a play than other forms of Chinese opera, and the acting is highly polished. The music accompanying Sichuan opera utilizes a small gong and an instrument called a Muqin, which is similar to the Erhu. The traditional formula is quite systematic with a combination of stunts like face-changing, sword-hiding, fire-spitting and beard-changing with the plot and different characters.

Culture Notes

景泰蓝：又称"铜胎掐丝搪瓷""嵌搪瓷"，俗称"珐蓝"，是一种在铜质的胎型上，用柔软的扁铜丝掐成各种斑纹焊上，然后把搪瓷质的色釉填充在斑纹内烧制而成的器物。因其在明朝景泰年间盛行，制造技艺比较老练，运用的搪瓷釉多以蓝色为主，故而得名"景泰蓝"。景泰蓝是北京工艺品四大名旦之一，同时也是燕京八绝之首。2006年，景泰蓝的制作工艺被列入第一批国家级非物质文化遗产名录。

New Words

Cloisonné	n.	a design made by filling in with coloured enamel an outline of flattened wire put on edge	景泰蓝
vitreous	adj.	made of glass or resembling glass	玻璃的，玻璃般的
enamel	n.	Enamel is a substance like glass that can be heated and put onto metal, glass, or pottery in order to decorate or protect it.	搪瓷，珐琅
gemstone		a jewel or stone used in jewellery	（经雕琢的）宝石
inlay	n.	a material which has been set into the surface of furniture, floors etc for decoration, or the pattern made by this	镶嵌物，镶嵌图案
geometric	adj.	having or using the shapes and lines in geometry, such as circles or squares, especially when these are arranged in regular patterns ornamental shape or decorated with a pattern	几何学的，几何图形的
schematic	adj.	showing the main parts of something in a simple way	图解的，概要的
glaze	v.	to cover plates, cups etc made of clay with a thin liquid that gives them a shiny surface	给…上釉
filigree	n.	delicate designs or decorations made of gold or silver wire	金银丝工艺品
concave	adj.	A concave surface is curved inwards in the middle.	凹的，凹面的
porosity	n.	the property of being porous; being able to absorb fluids	有孔性，多孔性
bouquet	n.	an arrangement of flowers, especially one that you give to someone	花束
surplus	n.	an amount of something that is more than what is needed or used	剩余，过剩
homophony	n.	the linguistic phenomenon whereby words of different origins become identical in pronunciation	同音异义

I. Simple Selection

1. Cloisonné is a traditional art widely known in and outside China. It is a kind of superb local expertise from _____.
   A. Tianjin   B. Shanghai   C. Guangzhou   D. Beijing

2. Possibly the most challenging step of the procedure of Filigree Welding is heating to _____ degrees centigrade to firm the metal.
   A. 700   B. 500   C. 900   D. 1000

3. To the _____ Dynasty, New Year pictures gradually matured with the development of the commercial economy as well as the citizen culture, providing a huge market.
   A. Southern Song   B. Eastern Jin
   C. Western Jin   D. Northern Song

4. About _____ years ago, Yangliuqing New Year pictures began to enjoy great fame, with every family adept at creating this particular genre of painting.
   A. 300   B. 400   C. 500   D. 600

5. Cloisonné combines the skills of bronze art, carving, _____, and other types of folk arts.
   A. painting   B. porcelain   C. carving   D. knitting

6. During the reigns of Emperors _____ and _____ of the Qing Dynasty, Cloisonné improved and reached its artistic summit.
   A. Kangxi and Qianlong   B. Kangxi and Yongzheng
   C. Yongzheng and Qianlong   D. Qianlong and Xianfeng

7. Shandong's New Year pictures as well have a rich content. The collocation of colors is usually exaggerated, bold, intense, and _____ in contrast.
   A. bold   B. violent   C. ambiguous   D. extravagant

8. Face-changing is an important subgenre of Chinese Sichuan opera. It is popular in the following provinces except _____.Sichuan opera is one of the Han Chinese operas, popular in eastern and central Sichuan, Chongqing and,.
   A. Chongqing municipality   B. Guizhou Province
   C. Yunnan Province   D. Liaoning Province

9. Which statement about face-changing is not true?
   A. Face-changing is an important subgenre of Chinese Sichuan opera.
   B. Sichuan opera is one of the Han Chinese operas, popular in Pearl River Delta.
   C. Sichuan Opera masks are treasures that the ancient opera artists work together to create and pass down.
   D. The secret of the face change has been passed down from one generation to the next within families.

10. Which statement about new year pictures is not true?

A. New Year pictures are an indispensible part of this celebration for each and every household.

B. People put up New Year pictures in their homes to enhance the lively festival atmosphere.

C. Most New Year pictures feature designs symbolizing good fortune, auspiciousness and festivity.

D. A popular New Year picture entitled *Surplus in Successive Years* depicts a cute plump baby holding a big pig in his arms and a bouquet of lotus flowers in his hand.

II. True or False

1. The making of Cloisonné first appeared during the Jingtai reign of the Ming Dynasty.

2. It was the emperor of the Chenghua reign that improved the color process, and created the bright blue that appealed to the Oriental aesthetic sense.

3. Through the interesting procedure of Enamel Filling, the cloisonné wears a colored wrap.

4. During the Yuan Dynasty, specific markets and workshops appeared, and New Year pictures evolved into an independent art form.

5. Taohuawu New Year pictures once spread to Japan and exerted certain influence on Japanese ukjyoe paintings, or paintings from the "floating world".

6. Cloisonné is a traditional art widely known in and outside China. It is a kind of superb local expertise from Tianjin.

7. A Qing-dynasty Cloisonné vase with a peach-and-monkey design is a famous artifact.

8. In face-changing, performers wear brightly colored costumes and move to show and soothing music.

9. Performers of face-changing change from one face to another almost instantaneously with the swipe of a fan, a movement of the head, or wave of the hand.

10. The secret of the face change has been passed down within and outside the families.

III. Fill in the Blanks

1. A New Year picture is a form of Chinese colored woodblock print, for decoration during the Chinese New Year Holiday, then later used to depict _____.

2. _____, or "bian lian" in Chinese, is an ancient Chinese dramatic art that is part of the more general Sichuan opera.

3. Performers of face-changing wear vividly colored masks, typically depicting _____ from the opera.

4. Traditionally only _____ were permitted to learn Bian Lian, avoiding the risks that the secret would be passed to another family.

5. Since the cultural basis of the opera are not well known outside of China, international performers have been making efforts to inform and increase the _____ for Westerners who do not know the context and meaning of the different faces.

6. _____ is one way of face-changing, that is the actor blows black dust hidden in

his palm or close to his eyes, nose or mouth, so that it obscures his face.

7. _____ is one of the four ways of face-changing, that is beard colours can be changed while the beard is being manipulated, from black to grey and finally to white, expressing anger or excitement.

8. Face-changing is an important subgenre of Chinese _____.

9. In the process of face-changing, the actor can pull down a mask which has previously been hidden on _____, changing his face to red, green, blue or black to express happiness, hate, anger or sadness, respectively.

10. Generally speaking, Chinese folk art are artistic forms inherited from a _____ or _____ scene in China.

IV. Answer the Questions

1. Please shortly introduce the Chinese New Year Picture.
2. Please shortly introduce Face-changing.

Unit 8 The Silk Road

8.1 The Origin of the Silk Road

The Silk Road was noted down by the German geographer Ferdinand von Richthofen in the book of "Chinese geology" at the end of 19th Century. It refers to the route between China and Central Asia and between China and India, as the medium of trade from 114 BC to 127. This term was soon accepted in academic circles and by the public formally. Later, the German historian Horman in a book published in early 20th Century, *The Ancient Silk Road between China and Syria*, extended the category of the Silk Road, according to the newly discovered archaeological data. It was extended to the west Mediterranean and Asia Minor. After that, the connotation of the Silk Road referred to the land trade, starting from ancient China through Central Asia ; South and West Asia, to the North Africa and Europe .

The ancient Silk Road stated from Chang' an, the ancient capital of China, and reached the Mediterranean through Central Asian countries such as Afghanistan, Iran, Iraq, Syria and Rome, with a total length of 6440 km. This road is considered to be the intersection of ancient Eastern and Western civilizations linking Asia and Europe. As the silk is the most representative goods for trade, this route was called the Silk Road. For thousands of years, nomads, or tribes, merchants, thoughts, diplomats, soldiers and academic investigators have been conducting along the silk road.

Along with the development of the times, the silk road has become a general term of all political, economic and cultural activities between ancient China and the west. There are several silk roads or routes. In the West, there was the northwest silk road. This route was opened officially by Zhang Qian in Western Han Dynasty. In the north, there was the prairie silk road through the Mongolia plateau, then to the West of Tian shan Mountains into the Central Asia. In the southwest, there was the Southwest Silk Road from Chang' an to Chengdu and to India. There was maritime Silk Road from Guangzhou, Quan zhou, Hangzhou, Yang zhou and other coastal areas, starting from the Nan yang City, to the sea of Arabia, even as far as the east coast of Africa.

In the pre Qin period, the communication channel connecting the eastern countries and the western countries already existed. But in the western Han Dynasty it originated officially to the western regions, starting from the trail of Zhang Qian. During this period, it was documented in the historical materials that the route was very clear, the communication was frequent, the trade activities were organized officially, so the real silk road opened in the Western Han Dynasty.

During the Wei, Jin, Northen and Southen Dynasties, the silk road continued to develop, mainly including the northwest Silk Road (also known as the oasis silk road or desert Silk Road), the Southwest Silk Road and the maritime Silk Road. It has three characteristics: it was the transition from the Han Dynasty to the Sui and Tang Dynasties, the maritime Silk Road further developed, and the exchanges with the western regions were frequent in both the Northen and Southen Dynasties.

The most prosperous period of the Silk Road established in Tang Dynasty after Sui Dynasty. In the Northen Song Dynasty, the actual layout of territory substantially reduced, and the government failed to control the He xi Corridor. In the Southen Song Dynasty, more regions can not be covered in the northwest regions. The Silk Road declined generally, but the Maritime Silk Road was more prosperous seeming to replace the Silk Road.

In Yuan Dynasty, this route just played the role of communication. Most diplomatic missions were about the religious or cultural exchanges instead of having business as the leading factor, which reflected the decline of the Silk Road to some extent.

After Ming Dynasty, the government adopted the closed door policy, at the same time, with the continuous development of shipbuilding and navigation technology, maritime traffic caused the Silk Road trade to decline.

Notes

Silk is a natural protein fiber, some forms of which can be woven into textiles. The protein fiber of silk is composed mainly of fibroinand produced by certain insect larvae to form cocoons. The best-known silk is obtained from the cocoons of the larvae of the mulberry silkworm Bombyx mori reared in captivity (sericulture). The shimmering appearance of silk is due to the triangular prism-like structure of the silk fibre, which allows silk cloth to refract incoming light at different angles, thus producing different colors.

Culture Notes

丝绸之路，简称丝路，一般指陆上丝绸之路，广义上讲又分为陆上丝绸之路和海上丝绸之路。陆上丝绸之路起源于西汉（前202—8年）汉武帝派张骞出使西域开辟的以首都长安（今西安）为起点，经甘肃、新疆，到中亚、西亚，并连接地中海各国的陆上通道。"海上丝绸之路"是古代中国与外国交通贸易和文化交往的海上通道，该路主要以南海为中心，所以又称南海丝绸之路。海上丝绸之路形成于秦汉时期，发展于三国至隋朝时期，繁荣于唐宋时期，转变于明清时期，是已知的最为古老的海上航线。

New Words

origin	n.	the place where something begins, where it springs into being	起源；原点；出身
geographer	n.	A geographer is a person who studies geography or is an expert in it	地理学者
route	n.	an established line of travel or access	路线；航线；通道
medium	n.	a means or instrumentality for storing or communicating information	方法；媒体；媒介
academic	adj.	associated with academia or an academy	学术的；理论的
extend	vi.	stretch out over a distance, space, time, or scope; run or extend between two points or beyond a certain point	延伸；扩大；推广
category	n.	a collection of things sharing a common attribute	种类，分类
connotation	n.	what you must know in order to determine the reference of an expression	内涵；含蓄；暗示
intersection	n.	a junction where one street or road crosses another	交叉；十字路口；交集
civilization	n.	a society in an advanced state of social development	文明；文化
representative	n.	an item of information that is representative of a type	代表；典型
diplomat	n.	an official engaged in international negotiations	外交家，外交官
investigator	n.	a scientist who devotes himself to doing research	研究者；调查者
prairie	n.	A prairie is a large area of flat, grassy land in North America. Prairies have very few trees	大草原；牧场
originate	vi.	come into existence; take on form or shape	发源；发生
transition	n.	the act of passing from one state or place to the next	过渡；转变
prosperous	adj.	in fortunate circumstances financially; moderately rich	繁荣的；兴旺的

| mission | n. | an organization of missionaries in a foreign land sent to carry on religious work | 使命，任务；代表团 |

I. Simple Selection

1. There are several silk roads or routes. In the West, there was the northwest silk road. This route was opened officially by Zhang Qian in _____ Dynasty.
   A. Western Han　　　　　　B. Eastern Han
   C. Tang　　　　　　　　　　D. Qin

2. There was _____ from Guangzhou, Quanzhou, Hangzhou, Yangzhou and other coastal areas, starting from the Nanyang City, to the sea of Arabia, even as far as the east coast of Africa.
   A. the Northwest Silk Road　　B. the prairie Silk Road
   C. the Southwest Silk Road　　D. maritime Silk Road

3. The western region is divided into two parts of the South and the north with the Mountains as the boundary.
   A. QiLian　　B. Tianshan　　C. Hua Shan　　D. Tai Shan

4. The Silk Road was noted down by the _____ geographer Ferdinand von Richthofen in the book of "Chinese geology" at the end of nineteenth Century.
   A. German　　B. British　　C. American　　D. Roman

5. The ancient silk road stated from _____, the ancient capital of China, and reached the Mediterranean through Central Asian countries such as Afghanistan, Iran, Iraq, Syria and Rome, with a total length of 6,440 km.
   A. Kaifeng　　B. Luoyang　　C. Beijing　　D. Changan

6. Silk Road is considered to be the intersection of ancient Eastern and Western civilizations linking Asia and _____.
   A. Africa　　B. Europe　　C. Atlantic　　D. Indian

7. As _____ is the most representative goods for trade, this route was called the Silk Road.
   A. the silk　　B. the china　　C. the tea　　D. the jade

II. True or False

1. The Silk Road refers to the route between China and Central Asia and between China and India, as the medium of trade from 114 BC to 127.

2. The ancient Silk Road stated from BeiJing , the ancient capital of China, and reached the Mediterranean through Central Asian countries such as Afghanistan, Iran, Iraq, Syria and Rome, with a total length of 6,440 km.

3. The expression "Silk Road" was not recorded until about 1,700 years after its

appearance.

4. In the north, there was the prairie silk road through the Mongolia plateau, then to the North of Tianshan Mountains into the Central Asia.

5. The most prosperous period of the silk road established in Sang Dynasty after Tang Dynasty.

6. After Ming Dynasty, the government adopted the closed door policy, at the same time, with the continuous development of shipbuilding and navigation technology, maritime traffic caused the Silk Road trade to decline.

7. The western region is divided into two parts of the South and the north with the Tianshan Mountains as the boundary.

III. Translation

丝绸之路，简称丝路，一般指陆上丝绸之路，广义上讲又分为陆上丝绸之路和海上丝绸之路。陆上丝绸之路起源于西汉。汉武帝派张骞出使西域开辟的以首都长安为起点，经甘肃、新疆，到中亚、西亚，并连接地中海各国的陆上通道。它的最初作用是运输中国古代出产的丝绸。"海上丝绸之路"是古代中国与外国交通贸易和文化交往的海上通道，该路主要以南海为中心，所以又称南海丝绸之路。海上丝绸之路形成于秦汉时期，发展于三国至隋朝时期，繁荣于唐宋时期，转变于明清时期，是已知的最为古老的海上航线。

8.2 Zhang Qian, Trail Blazer

The pioneer who blazed the trail of the Silk Road was Zhang Qian, a general of the Western Han Dynasty. In Zhang Qian's time, the Chinese had little knowledge about Central and West Asian countries, Africa or Europe, although they were aware of the existence of many different countries and cultures in faraway places to the west.

The western region is divided into two parts of the South and the north with the Tian shan Mountains as the boundary. Most of the people live around the Tarim basin. In the early years of the Western Han Dynasty, there were "thirty-six states", which were small in size, mostly desert oases, and also had valleys or basins.

The general population, twenty thousand or thirty thousand, the largest Kucha is 80000, only one thousand or two thousand small. Residents engaged in agriculture and animal husbandry. In addition to the production of grain, in some places there were abundant fruits such as grapes and best forage alfalfa. There are donkeys, horses and camels in animal husbandry. In addition, there are jade, copper, iron and other mineral resources, some local residents have learned to use copper and iron casting weapons. In the north and south of the Tian shan, although the states were very small, they owned their own territories. Under the kings of all countries there are offices and a large proportion of the army. In the 2nd Century, before Zhang Qian was sent to the western regions, the Huns extended to the western regions and enslaved and exploited small countries.

The emperor Wu in Han Dynasty was a great emperor in history with gifts and strategies. When he ascended the throne, he was only 16 years old. At that time, the Han Dynasty had established more than 60 years, after several generations of the early Han Dynasty emperors. With the reducing taxes and prospering economy policy, especially "*Wen jing zhi zhi*", the unity of politics was centralized and economic was recovered. The whole country entered into a prosperous situation, and the national strength had been quite abundant. Emperor Wu of the Han Dynasty, by means of this powerful material and financial resources, promptly attacked the *Xiongnu* invasion, and fundamentally relieved the the northern threat. That was the circumstance when Zhang Qian set out to the west.

When the Western Han Dynasty was founded, the North was faced with the threat of a powerful nomadic nation. This nation, collectively referred to as "Huns", after the spring and autumn, its king was called "*Kehan*". During the Wu emporer period, the invasion from the Huns made a serious threat to the safety of the Western Han Dynasty.

Under such circumstances, Emperor Wu appointed Zhang Qian to lead a team of more than 100 envoys (使者) to the Western Regions. The mission was to unite the Indo-Scythic people against the Huns, who once killed their chieftain. Zhang Qian's team set out in 138 BC. They were captured by the Huns and held under house arrest for over 10 years. Zhang Qian and only one other remaining envoy managed to escape and return to Chang'an in 126 BC. Their accounts about the Western Regions were a revelation the Han emperor and his ministers.

In the next decades, Emperor Wu launched three major campaigns against the Huns, forcing them to retreat from the Western Regions. In 119 BC, the emperor sent Zhang Qian on a second mission to the Western Regions. This time Zhang Qian went further west, while his deputies reached more than a dozen countries in South and West Asia, and the Mediterranean. This is the ancient route in history.

Zhang Qian's tow missions to the Western Regions opened up the road to the west. Emperor Wu adopted a series of measures to strengthen ties with the Western Regions, including encouraging Han people to trade there. Soon the route was bustling with caravans of camels carrying goods of all types bells.

The significance of Zhang Qian's two missions to the Western Regions are:

Through the Silk Road, trade flourished between China and Central, South and West Asian countries, Africa, and Europe. In 166, envoys from Rome arrive via the Silk Road in Chang'an, where they set up an embassy. Which proved the central role of ancient China.

The Silk Road also facilitated active trade between India, Southeast Asia, West Asia, Africa and Europe. The exchange of new goods and technologies from different continents greatly helped to promote the development of all the civilizations involved.

Zhang Qian's mission to the western regions was not only an extremely difficult diplomatic trip, but also an effective scientific expedition. Zhang Qian carried out on-the-spot investigation and Research on the vast western regions. He not only personally visited Xinjiang and Middle Asian countries, but through these places to have a preliminary understanding of present Iran Irap and India. After returning to Changan, Zhang Qian made a detailed report to the emperor about the location, population, city, military products and so on . Up to now, it is still the most precious material for studying the geography and history of the above-mentioned regions and countries in the world.

Notes

Zhang Qian, born in Chenggu (present-day Chenggu county, Shaanxi Province), was a famous explorer and imperial diplomat during the period referred to as the Western Han Dynasty.

Culture Notes

匈奴是中国古代北方游牧民族，兴起于今内蒙古阴山山麓。据《史记·匈奴列传》中记载，匈奴，其先祖夏后氏之苗裔也，曰淳维。唐虞以上有山戎、猃狁、荤粥，居于北蛮，随畜牧而转移。中国古籍中的匈奴是秦末汉初称雄中原以北的强大游牧民族。

New Words

trail	n.	a track or mark left by something that has passed	小径；痕迹；尾部
blazer	n.	lightweight single-breasted jacket; often striped in the colors of a club or school	燃烧体；宣布者
pioneer	n.	someone who helps to open up a new line of research or technology or art	先锋；拓荒者
boundary	n.	the line or plane indicating the limit or extent of something	边界；范围；分界线
valley	n.	a long depression in the surface of the land that	山谷；流域；溪谷

		usually contains a river	
resident	n.	someone who lives at a particular place for a prolonged period or who was born there	居民；住院医生
husbandry	n.	the practice of cultivating the land or raising stock	饲养；务农
abundant	adj.	present in great quantity	丰富的；充裕的
cast	vt.	put or send forth	投，抛
territory	n.	a region marked off for administrative or other purposes	领土，领域
proportion	n.	the quotient obtained when the magnitude of a part is divided by the magnitude of the whole	比例，占比
enslave	vt.	make a slave of; bring into servitude	束缚；征服
ascend	vi.	travel up	上升；登高
centralize	vt.	make central	使集中；使成为⋯的中心
promptly	adv.	with little or no delay	迅速地；立即地
invasion	n.	the act of invading; the act of an army that invades for conquest or plunder	入侵，侵略
nomadic	adj.	(of groups of people) tending to travel and change settlements frequently	游牧的；流浪的
envoy	n.	a diplomat having less authority than an ambassador	使者；全权公使
capture	n.	the act of forcibly dispossessing an owner of property	俘获；夺得
revelation	n.	the speech act of making something evident	启示；揭露
retreat	vi.	pull back or move away or backward	撤退；退避
deputy	n.	someone authorized to exercise the powers of sheriff in emergencies	代理人，代表

I. Simple Selection

1. Who was the pioneer blazing the trail of the Ancient Silk Road?
   A. Zhang Qian   B. Huo Qubing   C. the Huns   D. Zheng He

2. When the Western Han Dynasty was founded, the North was faced with the threat of a powerful nomadic nation. This nation, collectively referred to as "_____".
   A. Races   B. Hans   C. Huns   D. Minors

3. Zhang Qian's team set out in _____. They were captured by the Huns and held under house arrest for over ten years.

  A. 138 BC B. 138 AD C. 119 BC D. 119 AD

4. In the early years of the Western Han Dynasty, there were _____ states, which were small in size, mostly desert oases, and also had valleys or basins.

  A. 35 B. 37 C. 36 D. 32

5. The emperor _____ in Han dynasty was a great emperor in history with gifts and strategies.

  A. Wu B. Wen C. Jing D. Hui

6. Emperor Wu of the Han Dynasty, by means of this powerful material and _____ resources, promptly attacked the Huns invasion, and fundamentally relieved the northern threat. That was the circumstance when Zhang Qian set out to the west.

  A. mineral B. natural C. cultural D. financial

7. In 119 BC, the emperor sent Zhang Qian on a _____ mission to the Western Regions.

  A. second B. first C. third D. forth

II. True or False

1. With the reducing taxes and prospering economy policy, especially "WenJingzhizhi", the unity of politics was centralized and economic was recovered.

2. In 119 BC, the emperor sent Zhang Qian on a third mission to the Western Regions. This time Zhang Qian went further west, while his deputies reached more than a dozen countries in South and West Asia, and the Mediterranean.

3. In 166, envoys from India arrive via the Silk Road in Chang'an, where they set up an embassy, which proved the central role of ancient China.

4. Zhang Qian was sent on the first mission to the Western Regions to join with the Indo-Scythic People in fighting against the Huns.

5. On his second mission, Zhang Qian went to more than a dozen countries in South and West Asia, and the Mediterranean.

6. In the Eastern Han Dynasty it originated officially to the western regions, starting from the trail of Zhang Qian.

7. In the second Century, before Ban Gu was sent to the western regions, the Huns extended to the western regions and enslaved and exploited small countries.

III. Translation

张骞，中国汉代杰出的外交家、旅行家、探险家，丝绸之路的开拓者。张骞富有开拓和冒险精神，公元前139年，奉汉武帝之命，率领一百多人出使西域，打通了汉朝通往西域的南北道路，即赫赫有名的丝绸之路。史学家司马迁称赞张骞出使西域为"凿空"，意思是"开通大道"。张骞被誉为伟大的外交家、探险家，是"丝绸之路的开拓者""第一个睁开眼睛看世界的中国人"。他将中原文明传播至西域，又从西域诸国引进了汗血马、葡萄、苜蓿、石榴、胡麻等物种到中原，促进了东西方文明的交流。

8.3 The Significance of the Silk Road

The Silk Road functioned not only as a trade route, but also as a bridge that linked the ancient civilizations of China, India, the Mesopotamian plains, Egypt and Greece.

It also helped to promote the exchange of science and technology between east and west. The Silk Road served as the main channel for ancient China to open up to the outside world, as well as for fresh impulses from other cultures to enter the country, which contributed a significant share to the shaping of Chinese culture.

Together with the economic and political exchange between the East and West, religions of the West were introduced into China via the world-famous route. Buddhism, Zoroastrianism, Manicheism, Nestorianism and Islam were cultural treasure of the ancient west, which were bestowed upon China during the old times.

In the first century BC, Buddhism was introduced into Yutian (now Hetian). From there, it quickly spread throughout the vast Western Regions. It was not until the Eastern Han Dynasty (25—220) that Buddhism infiltrated the inland of China. In the following centuries, many monks played important roles in the development of Buddhism in China. One of them is Xuan Zang in the Tang Dynasty (618—907). He traveled on the route to ancient India to study sutras, contributed greatly to the propagation of Buddhism.

The cultural exchange between China and the West offered mutual benefit and achieved common progress. The Chinese Four Great Inventions (Papermaking, Printing, Gunpowder and Compass) as well as the skills of silkworm breeding and silk spinning were transmitted to the West. This greatly sped up the development of the entire world. Apart from Chinese exquisite goods, many Chinese advanced technologies were also exported to the west, such as the silkworms breading, silk spinning, paper making, printing with movable type and gunpowder.

In Han Dynasty (206 BC—220 AD), China had a monopoly on silk trade by keeping the silks production technology a secret. A Han princess smuggled silkworms and mulberry seedlings as well as skilled workmen into Yutian. It was not until the 12th century AD that this technology reached to West Europe.

In Tang Dynasty, Printing Technique had been introduced into the Central Asia. In the 13th century, many European travelers reached China through the Silk Road and brought back Printing Technique to Europe. In 1444, Gutenberg, a German inventor of letterpress printing, printed the Bible using a similar printing technique.

During the early period of the thirteenth century, Mongolian hordes used gunpowder to flatten resistance against them in their westward conquests. That was equivalent to weapons of mass destruction in those days.

From the Three Kingdoms (220—280) to the Tang Dynasty (618—907), the music, dance, acrobatics and arts of West Asia and Central Asia spread into China. The Kung-hou (23stringed instrument) and lute of Persia joined Chinese traditional musical instruments in the Han Dynasty (206 BC—220 AD).

Material culture exchange was also underway on this long trade road. A large number of products of the West flowed into China, such as grapes, clover, walnuts, carrots, peppers, beans, spinach, cucumbers, pomegranates, rare animals, medicinal materials, flavorings and jewelry. Chinese porcelains and lacquers were traded into the West as well.

The Silk Roads have connected civilizations and brought people and culture into contact with each other from across the world for thousands of years, permitting not only an exchange of goods but an interaction of ideas and culture that has shaped our world today.

The historic Silk Roads were a network of trade routes across land and sea that spanned much of the globe from prehistoric times until the present day, along which people of many different cultures, religions and languages met, exchanged ideas and influenced each other.

Notes

The Four Great Inventions are inventions from ancient China that are celebrated in Chinese culture for their historical significance and as symbols of ancient China's advanced science and technology. The Four Great Inventions are: Compass, Gunpowder, Papermaking and Printing. These four discoveries h ad a profound impact on the development of civilization throughout the world. However, some modern Chinese scholars have opined that other Chinese inventions were perhaps more sophisticated and had a greater impact on Chinese civilization–the Four Great Inventions serve merely to highlight the technological interaction between East and West.

Culture Notes

佛教：佛教也是世界三大宗教之一。佛，意思是"觉者"。佛又称如来、应供、正遍知、明行足、善逝、世间解、无上士、调御丈夫、天人师、世尊。佛教重视人类心灵和道德的进步和觉悟。佛教信徒修习佛教的目的即在于依照悉达多乔达摩所悟到修行方法，发现生命和宇宙的真相，最终超越生死和苦、断尽一切烦恼，得到究竟解脱。

New Words

function   *n.*   what something is used for   功能

link	vt.	make a logical or causal connection	连接，连结
promote	vt.	contribute to the progress or growth of	促进；提升
channel	n.	a path over which electrical signals can pass	通道；频道
impulse	n.	an instinctive motive	冲动
contribute	vt.	bestow a quality on	贡献，出力
religion	n.	a strong belief in a supernatural power or powers that control human destiny	宗教；宗教信仰
treasure	n.	accumulated wealth in the form of money or jewels	财富，财产
bestow	vt.	give as a gift	使用；授予
infiltrate	vt.	cause (a liquid) to enter by penetrating the interstices	使潜入；使渗入
propagation	n.	the spreading of something (a belief or practice) into new regions	传播；繁殖
transmit	vt.	transfer to another	传输；传播
exquisite	adj.	intense or sharp	精致的；细腻的
monopoly	n.	exclusive control or possession of something	垄断；垄断者
smuggle	vt.	import or export without paying customs duties	走私；偷运
flatten	vt.	make flat or flatter	击败，摧毁；使…平坦
resistance	n.	the action of opposing something that you disapprove or disagree with	阻力；电阻；抵抗
equivalent	adj.	equal in amount or value	等价的，相等的
prehistoric	adj.	belonging to or existing in times before recorded history	史前的；陈旧的

I. Simple Selection

1. Through the Silk Road, trade flourished between China and Central, South and West Asian countries _____ and Europe.

  A. India B. Africa C. Atlantic D. America

2. The Chinese Four Great Inventions as well as the skills of _____ and silk spinning were transmitted to the West.

A. silkworm growing B. silkworm treating
C. silkworm breeding D. silkworm counting

3. In _____ Dynasty, Printing Technique had been introduced into the Central Asia.

A. Tang B. Han C. Song D. Sui

4. Which one is not the Great Four Inventions in ancient China?

A. Paper making B. Gun powder
C. Printing D. Planting

5. Which one does not flow into China via ancient Silk Road?

A. Grapes B. Silk C. Clover D. Walnuts

II. True or False

1. In the first century BC, Buddhism was introduced into China via the Silk Road.

2. The Chinese Four Great Inventions (Papermaking, Printing, Gunpowder and Compass) as well as the skills of silkworm breeding and silk spinning were transmitted to the West.

3. Thanks to the Silk Road, the ancient Greeks had known a lot about eastern civilizations before 700 BC.

4. The Silk Road not only promoted the economic exchange between east and west, but also helped with the shaping of Chinese culture.

5. Rome was probably the first country to set up its embassy in Chang'an.

6. The Silk Road helped with the setting up of the open policy from the Han to Tang Dynasties.

7. For thousands of years, nomads or tribes, merchants, thoughts, diplomats, soldiers and academic investigators have been conducting along the silk road.

III. Translation

四大发明，是关于中国科学技术史的一种观点，是指中国古代对世界具有很大影响的四种发明，是中国古代劳动人民的重要创造，是指造纸术、指南针、火药及印刷术。这四种发明对中国古代的政治、经济、文化的发展产生了巨大的推动作用，且这些发明经由各种途径传至西方，对世界文明发展史也产生了很大的影响。中国的四大发明在欧洲近代文明产生之前陆续传入西方，对西方科技发展产生一定影响。火药和火器的采用摧毁了欧洲中世纪天主教的思想枷锁。指南针传到欧洲航海家的手里，使他们有可能发现美洲和实现环球航行，为西方奠定了世界贸易和工场手工业发展的基础。

8.4 One Belt and One Road

The Silk Road Economic Belt and the 21st-century Maritime Silk Road, better known as the One Belt and One Road. It is a development strategy proposed by Chinese chairman Xi Jinping that focuses on connectivity and cooperation between Eurasian countries, primarily the

People's Republic of China, the land-based Silk Road Economic Belt and the oceangoing Maritime Silk Road.

The strategy underlines China's push to take a larger role in global affairs with a China-centered trading network. It was unveiled in September and October 2013 for Silk Road Economic Belt and Maritime Silk Road respectively. It was initially called One Belt and One Road, but in mid-2016 the official English name was changed to the Belt and Road Initiative .

When Chinese leader Xi Jinping visited Central Asia and Southeast Asia in September and October 2013, he raised the initiative of jointly building the Silk Road Economic Belt and the 21st Century Maritime Silk Road.

The Maritime Silk Road, also known as the "21st Century Maritime Silk Road" is a complementary initiative aimed at investing and fostering collaboration in Southeast Asia, Oceania, and North Africa, through several contiguous bodies of water—the South China Sea, the South Pacific Ocean, and the wider Indian Ocean area.

Once proposed, the strategy has received positive responses from the related countries along the road. The situation in countries along the Belt and Road is complicated, with different culture language and industrial levels, but each country has its own advantages. Internal cooperation can help them achieve their own dreams. In recent years, China has been developing rapidly in the aspects of economy, culture, science and technology. In the 21st century, a series of important and significant achievements proved that.

In Chairman Xi Jinping's speech , he said:

"I proposed the Belt and Road Initiative in the hope that with a focus on connectivity, the free and convenient flow of all elements of production will be encouraged, multidimensional cooperation platforms developed and mutual gains and shared development achieved. The Belt and Road Initiative draws inspirations from the ancient Silk Road, and aims to help realize the shared dream of people worldwide for peace and development. Shining with wisdom from the East, it is a plan that China offers the world for seeking common property and development. The Belt and Road Initiative is based on the principle of extensive consultation, joint contribution and shared benefits. It's not exclusive but open and inclusive. The Initiative will not be solo for China, but a chorus of all countries along the routes.

The Chinese economy is deeply integrated with the global economy and forms an important driving force of the economy of Asia and even the world at large. China's investment opportunities are expanding. Investment opportunities in infrastructure connectivity as well as in new technologies, new products, new business patterns, and new business models are constantly springing up. China's foreign cooperation opportunities are expanding.

For more than 3 years, over 100 countries and international organization has responded positively and offered support for the Initiative. The 'friend circle' of the Initiative has kept widening. A great cause should be pursued for common good."

Notes

The Belt and Road Initiative (BRI), also known as the One Belt One Road (OBOR) (Chinese: 一带一路) or the Silk Road Economic Belt and the 21st century Maritime Silk Road (Chinese: 丝绸之路经济带和 21 世纪海上丝绸之路), is a development strategy adopted by the Chinese government involving infrastructure development and investments in countries in Europe, Asia and Africa. "Belt" refers to the overland routes for road and rail transportation, called "the Silk Road Economic Belt"; whereas "road" refers to the sea routes, or the 21st century Maritime Silk Road.

Culture Notes

2013 年 9 月 7 日，习近平主席在哈萨克斯坦纳扎尔巴耶夫大学发表演讲时表示：为了使各国经济联系更加紧密、相互合作更加深入、发展空间更加广阔，我们可以用创新的合作模式。共同建设"丝绸之路经济带"，以点带面，从线到片，逐步形成区域大合作。2013 年 10 月 3 日，习近平主席在印尼国会发表演讲时表示：中国愿同东盟国家加强海上合作，使用好中国政府设立的中国—东盟海上合作基金，发展好海洋合作伙伴关系，共同建设 21 世纪"海上丝绸之路"。

New Words

strategy	n.	an elaborate and systematic plan of action	战略，策略
propose	vt.	make a proposal, declare a plan for something	建议；打算，计划；求婚
connectivity	n.	the property of being connected or the degree to which something has connections	连通性；互联互通；连接
cooperation	n.	joint operation or action	合作，协作

primarily	adv.	for the most part	首先；主要地，根本上
underline	n.	a line drawn underneath (especially under written matter)	下划线
global	adj.	involving the entire earth; not limited or provincial in scope	全球的；总体的；球形的
unveil	vt.	remove the veil from	使公之于众，揭开；揭幕
respectively	adv.	in the order given	分别地；各自地，独自地
initiative	n.	readiness to embark on bold new ventures	主动权；首创精神；新方案
complementary	adj.	of words or propositions so related that each is the negation of the other	补足的，补充的
invest	vt.	make an investment	投资；覆盖；耗费
foster	vt.	promote the growth of	培养；养育，抚育
collaboration	n.	act of working jointly	合作；勾结；通敌
contiguous	adj.	very close or connected in space or time	连续的；邻近的；接触的
response	n.	a result	响应；反应；回答
complicated	adj.	difficult to analyze or understand	难懂的，复杂的
multidimensional	adj.	having or involving or marked by several dimensions or aspects	多维的；多面的
platform	n.	a raised horizontal surface	平台；月台，站台

inspiration	n.	arousal of the mind to special unusual activity or creativity	灵感；鼓舞；吸气
wisdom	n.	accumulated knowledge or erudition or enlightenment	智慧，才智；明智
consultation	n.	a conference (usually with someone important)	咨询；磋商
solo	n.	any activity that is performed alone without assistance	独奏；独唱
chorus	n.	any utterance produced simultaneously by a group	合唱队；齐声
infrastructure	n.	the basic structure or features of a system or organization	基础设施；公共建设
constantly	adv.	seemingly uninterrupted	不断地；时常地

I. Multiple Selection

1. Along with the development of the times, the silk road has become a general term of all _____ activities between ancient China and the west.
    A. political   B. economic   C. cultural   D. martial

2. The Strategy of The Belt and Road should promote policy coordination, _____ and people-to-people bonds as their five major goals and strengthen cooperation.
    A. friendly communication   B. facilities connectivity
    C. unimpeded trade   D. financial integration

3. There was maritime Silk Road from _____ and other coastal areas, starting from the Nanyang City, to the sea of Arabia, even as far as the east coast of Africa.
    A. Guangzhou   B. Quanzhou   C. Hangzhou   D. Yangzhou

II. True or False

1. The Silk Road Economic Belt and the 21st century Maritime Silk Road, better known as the One Belt and One Road.

2. It is a development strategy proposed by Premier Li Keqiang.

3. It was initially called One Belt and One Road, but in mid-2016 the official English name was changed to the Belt and Road Initiative .

4. The Maritime Silk Road, also known as the "21st century Maritime Silk Road" is a

complementary initiative aimed at investing and fostering collaboration in West Asia, Oceania and North Africa.

III. Fill in the Blanks

1. The Silk Road Economic Belt and the 21st century Maritime Silk Road, better known as _____ .

2. It was initially called One Belt and One Road, but in mid-2016 the official English name was changed to _____ .

3. The Maritime Silk Road, also known as the "21st century Maritime Silk Road" is a complementary initiative aimed at investing and fostering collaboration in Southeast Asia, Oceania, and North Africa, through several contiguous bodies of water – the South China Sea, _____ and the wider Indian Ocean area.

IV. Translation

The Chinese economy is deeply integrated with the global economy and forms an important driving force of the economy of Asia and even the world at large. China's investment opportunities are expanding. Investment opportunities in infrastructure connectivity as well as in new technologies, new products, new business patterns, and new business models are constantly springing up. China's foreign cooperation opportunities are expanding. For more than 3 years, over 100 countries and international organization has responded positively and offered support for the Initiative. The "friend circle" of the Initiative has kept widening. A great cause should be pursued for common good.

8.5 The Significance of the Strategy of the Belt and Road

In the 21st century, a new era marked by the theme of peace, development, cooperation and mutual benefit, it is all the more important for us to carry on the Silk Road Spirit in face of the weak recovery of the global economy and complex international and regional situations.

Countries along the Belt and Road have their own resource advantages and their economies are mutually complementary. Therefore, there is a great potential and space for cooperation. They should promote policy coordination, facilities connectivity, unimpeded trade, financial integration and people-to-people bonds as their five major goals, and strengthen cooperation in the following key areas:

8.5.1 Facilities connectivity

In the sky, overland and sea, countries are well connected . In the future, what will the Asia be? What is the vision for Africa and Europe? What will the world look like? Road can help close the distance between people. Since ancient times, Asia and Europe were never apart, and are now getting closer and closer.

Improving the transportation infrastructure will reduce logistics costs and giving back the profit to the trade partner. In order to increase economic growth, the countries along the Belt and Road are busy developing their infrastructure.

We should promote cooperation in the connectivity of energy infrastructure, work in concert to ensure the security of oil and gas pipelines and other transport routes, build cross-border power supply networks and power-transmission routes, and cooperate in regional power grid upgrading and transformation.

The road was opened up to promote trade. However, the development of a country lies not only in trade but in industrialization. Most countries along the Belt and Road are in the early stage of industrialization. Their industrial base is not solid. Over-relying on resources keeping them in a relatively backward position in the world economic system. To reach industrialization, these countries need more power. The mission of The Belt and Road Initiative is to help countries along the way achieve industrialization through the international cooperation.

Interconnection is just around the corner. Wind power, hydropower thermal power, photovoltacic, the total amount of equipment China is exporting to countries along the Belt and Road equals the power installed in Beijing. At the same time, the hidden energy sources under the ancient Silk Road are being excavated. From East Asia to West Asia, from the southeast coast of China to the Mediterranean, from the Pacific Ocean to Indian Ocean, energy is flowing. The Silk Road has become a power transmission road to boost the development of countries along the way.

8.5.2 Unimpeded trade

Investment and trade cooperation is a major task in building the Belt and Road. We should strive to improve investment and trade facilitation and remove investment and trade barriers for the creation of a sound business environment within the region and in all related countries. We will discuss with countries and regions along the Belt and Road on opening free trade areas so as to unleash the potential for expanded cooperation.

In 1988, China set up its first economic development zone in Dalian. Since then, more than 200 zones were established in suburban areas of big cities throughout China. Economic development zones are a new model of urban management. That gives birth to a new area in the city bringing industry, the zones provide platforms for companies, manpower policies and funds also create jobs and revenue for local countries and local cities. It's among the 30 years of success, China's reform and opening up. In 2016, 56 economic and trade cooperation zones were established with 20 other countries around the world with an investment of 18.5 billion dollars from China.

Cooperation zones between Xinjiang and Central Asia, between Yunnan and South Asia, between Guangxi and Southeast Asia, from port trade to pilot free trade zone, from inland to the sea, has gradually become reality, generating regional production networks around China.

8.5.3 Financial integration

Capital is the driving force of development. For a long time, the global institutions funding for infrastructure were the World Bank, Asian Development Bank, European Bank for Reconstruction and Development. But they could not meet all the needs of developing countries. In Asia, at least 800 billion dollars are needed every year to be invested in infrastructure. From 2010 to 2020, Asia still needs 8 trillion dollars to be funded in infrastructure. But the World Bank can only provide 60 billion in loans. Such a huge amount of funds is also beyond Asian Development Bank.

From Panda Bonds, Dim Sum Bonds to the establishment of offshore RMB centers, China's financial market is growing and will provide better protection for the Belt and Road. Capital in place, the blueprint will become reality step by step.

8.5.4 People-to-people bond

People-to-people bond provides the public support for implementing the Initiative. We should carry forward the spirit of friendly cooperation of the Silk Road by promoting extensive cultural and academic exchanges, personnel exchanges and cooperation, media cooperation, youth and women exchanges and volunteer services, so as to win public support for deepening bilateral and multilateral cooperation.

The Belt and Road cooperation features mutual respect and trust, mutual benefit and win-win cooperation, and mutual learning between civilizations. As long as all countries along the Belt and Road make concerted efforts to pursue our common goal, there will be bright prospects for the Silk Road Economic Belt and the 21st century Maritime Silk Road, and the people of countries along the Belt and Road can all benefit from this Initiative.

Special economic zones of China (SEZs) are special economic zones located in mainland China. The government of China gives SEZs special (more free market-oriented) economic policies and flexible governmental measures, compared to the more planned economy of most of China. This allows SEZs to utilize an economic management system that is more attractive for foreign and domestic firms to do business in than the rest of mainland China.

亚洲基础设施投资银行（Asian Infrastructure Investment Bank，简称亚投行，AIIB）是一个政府间性质的亚洲区域多边开发机构。重点支持基础设施建设，成立宗旨是为了促进亚洲区域的建设互联互通化和经济一体化的进程，并且加强中国及其他亚洲国家和地区的合作，是首个由中国倡议设立的多边金融机构，总部设在北京，法定资本1000亿美元。截至2018年12月19日，亚投行有93个正式成员。2013年10月2日，习近平主席提出筹建倡议，2014年10月24日，包括中国、印度、新加坡等在内21个首批意向创始成员国的财长和授权代表在北京签约，共同决定成立投行。2015年12月25日，亚洲基础设施投资银行正式成立。2016年1月16日至18日，亚投行开业仪式暨理事会和董事会成立大会在北京举行。

New Words

theme	n.	the subject matter of a conversation or discussion	主题；主旋律
mutual	adj.	common to or shared by two or more parties	共同的；相互的
recovery	n.	return to an original state	恢复，复原
complementary	adj.	of words or propositions so related that each is the negation of the other	补足的，补充的
potential	n.	the inherent capacity for coming into being	潜能；可能性
coordination	n.	the skillful and effective interaction of movements	协调，调和
facility	n.	a building or place that provides a particular service or is used for a particular industry	设施；设备
financial	adj.	involving financial matters	金融的；财政的
bond	n.	an electrical force linking atoms	债券；结合
vision	n.	a vivid mental image	视力；美景
apart	adj.	remote and separate physically or socially	分离的；与众不同的
logistics	n.	handling an operation that involves providing labor and materials be supplied as needed	后勤；后勤学
infrastructure	n.	the basic structure or features of a system or organization	基础设施；公共建设
grid	n.	a system of high tension cables by which electrical power is distributed throughout a region	栅格；输电网
industrialization	n.	the development of industry on an extensive scale	工业化
solid	adj.	of definite shape and volume; firm; neither liquid nor gaseous	固体的；可靠的
hydropower	n.	hydro-power or water power is power derived from the energy of falling water and running water	水力发电
excavate	vt.	lay bare through digging	挖掘；开凿
unleash	vt.	release or vent	发动；解开…的皮带

expand	vt.	extend in one or more directions	扩张；使膨胀
capital	n.	assets available for use in the production of further assets	省会；资金
bilateral	adj.	having identical parts on each side of an axis	双边的；有两边的

Exercises

I. Simple Selection

1. According to "the Belt and Road Forum for International Cooperation", The Silk Road Spirit is concluded as: peace and cooperation, openness and inclusiveness and _____.
   A. policy coordination   B. unimpeded trade
   C. mutual learning and mutual benefit D. peace and development

2. Wind power, hydropower thermal power, photovoltaic, the total amount of equipment China is exporting to countries along the Belt and Road equals the power installed in Beijing. At the same time, the hidden energy sources under the ancient Silk Road are being excavated. These achievements belongs to the field of _____.
   A. policy coordination   B. facilities connectivity
   C. unimpeded trade   D. financial integration

3. Cooperation zones between Xinjiang and Central Asia, between Yunnan and South Asia, between Guangxi and Southeast Asia, from port trade to pilot free trade zone, from inland to the sea, has gradually become reality. These achievements belongs to the field of _____.
   A. facilities connectivity   B. unimpeded trade
   C. financial integration   D. people-to-people bonds

4. Improving the transportation infrastructure will reduce logistics costs and giving back the profit to the trade partner. In order to increase economic growth, the countries along the Belt and Road are busy developing their infrastructure. These achievements belongs to the field of _____.
   A. facilities connectivity   B. unimpeded trade
   C. financial integration   D. people-to-people bonds

5. We should carry forward the spirit of friendly cooperation of the Silk Road by promoting extensive cultural and academic exchanges, personnel exchanges and cooperation, media cooperation, youth and women exchanges and volunteer services, so as to win public support for deepening bilateral and multilateral cooperation. These achievements belongs to the field of _____.
   A. facilities connectivity   B. unimpeded trade
   C. financial integration   D. people-to-people bonds

II. Translation

I proposed the Belt and Road Initiative in the hope that with a focus on connectivity, the free and convenient flow of all elements of production will be encouraged, multidimensional cooperation platforms developed and mutual gains and shared development achieved. The Belt and Road Initiative draws inspirations from the ancient Silk Road, and aims to help realize the shared dream of people worldwide for peace and development. Shining with wisdom from the East, it is a plan that China offers the world for seeking common property and development. The Belt and Road Initiative is based on the principle of extensive consultation, joint contribution and shared benefits. It's not exclusive but open and inclusive. The Initiative will not be solo for China, but a chorus of all countries along the routes.